## DATE DUE

# PEOPLE'S CHINA

# People's China

## A BRIEF HISTORY

### SECOND EDITION

# Craig Dietrich

*New York   Oxford*

OXFORD UNIVERSITY PRESS

1994

ss

to

Karachi

ng  Tokyo

Town

rid

n

Berlin    Ibadan

Copyright © 1986, 1994 by Oxford University Press, Inc.

Published by Oxford University Press, Inc.
200 Madison Avenue, New York, New York 10016

Oxford is a registered trademark of Oxford University Press

Library of Congress Cataloging-in-Publication Data
Dietrich, Craig.
People's China : a brief history / Craig Dietrich.—2nd ed.
p.    cm.    Includes bibliographical references and index.
ISBN 0-19-508185-4.—ISBN 0-19-508186-2 (pbk.)
1. China—History—1949–    I. Title. DS77.55.D52    1994
951.05—dc20    93-12489

1 3 5 7 9 8 6 4 2

Printed in the United States of America
on acid-free paper

*To the memory of*
*Helen and Harold*

# Acknowledgments

In the first edition, I thanked Ramon H. Myers, Nancy Lane, Benjamin Harrison, Kristen Sommer, Winston Barton, Lesley Jones-Holloway, Judith Manton, John Major, and Sherilyn Dietrich for their support and assistance. I also owe a debt of gratitude to all who commented on the book after publication, in particular Professor Dennis Grafflin of Bates College who graciously shared with me numerous criticisms and suggestions. For the second edition I would also like to thank Benjamin Harrison for additional portraits and Ronald Levere for graphs. Of course I must also once again thank my wife Sherilyn for her support.

# Contents

Xiaoping (1904–   ): Apparatchik Supreme.   Peng Dehuai (1898–
1974): General.  Jiang Qing (1914–1991): Rebel Actress.

## Was China Ripe for Revolution? 43
Marxism.   Other Views.

## 2   REVOLUTIONARIES SEIZE POWER: 1949–52, 50

### Establishing Sovereignty, 51
Military Victory.   Leaning to One Side.

### Installing the New Order, 55
Restoring Normalcy.   The Party.   Party Center and Party Cadres.
The State Bureaucracy.   The Military.

### The Korean War, 65

### Campaigns, 68
Land Reform.   Resist America, Aid Korea.   Marriage Law.
Oppose Counterrevolutionaries.   Thought Reform.
Oppose Bureaucracy.   Oppose Corruption.

### Disappointments, Ironies, and Contradictions, 79
The Sweet and the Bitter.   Institutional Development Versus
Revolutionary Transformation.

## 3   SOCIALIST TRANSFORMATION: 1953–57, 83

### The First Five-Year Plan, 85
Industrialization.   Agriculture.   Education.   Health.

### The High Tide of 1955, 91
Mao Counterattacks.   High Tide in Industry and
Commerce.   Implications of Socialist Transformation.   A New
Political Climate.   Retreat from the Reckless Advance.

### The Eighth Party Congress, September 1956, 102

### The Hundred Flowers Campaign, 105

# A Note on the Romanization of Chinese Words

No doubt every reader of this book will be at least dimly aware that Chinese writing is based on radically different principles from our own phonetically based alphabet. Already two millennia ago, the Chinese had developed a script composed of several thousand "characters," which either singly or in pairs constitute the words of the language. Essentially the same sytem is still in use today.

The difficulties of learning Chinese are evident enough, but readers may not have had occasion to realize the problems that such a system creates for Western scholars whose audience has no familiarity with these characters and yet must be introduced to various Chinese names. It is a problem that goes back to sixteenth-century Christian missionaries and even to Marco Polo in the fourteenth century.

Because these characters all have spoken pronunciations, the obvious answer to the difficulty is simply to adopt phonetic conventions, using Roman letters to represent the sounds. Such is the answer that has been pursued from the start. Inherently this is not a bad solution, even though the several "tones" that constitute part of the pronunciation are usually lost, and despite the fact that the many homonyms of Chinese make the phonetic spelling more ambiguous than the written characters.

The most annoying difficulty has been the fact that Western scholars, never satisifed with their predecessors' efforts, have seemed unable to stop contriving new systems. There have been literally hundreds. The result is, for example, that the family name of one of the paramount leaders of modern China, which sounds much like the English name *Joe,* can be rendered *Jou, Tchou, Chow,* and *Cheo*—to name but a few. Responding to the need for standarization, in English-speaking countries a system known as Wade-Giles has been widely used for many decades. By its dictates the name in question is spelled *Chou*. More recently—and it is hoped for the last time—one more new Romanization scheme has been introduced. Since 1979 the Chinese government has officially promoted a system known as "pinyin," under whose rules the name is *Zhou*. Pinyin is coming into worldwide use and is employed throughout this book.

Unfortunately, pinyin conventions are not ideally suited to give English speakers an immediate idea of certain pronunciations. For example, how does one read *zhi* or *qi* or *ze?* In this book names, when first introduced, are accompanied by a pronunciation based on the closest sounds in common American words and spellings and without reference to any Romanization system. More rigorously inclined readers may wish to know the equivalencies of the various letters and combinations of pinyin. Most vowels are pronounced fairly close to how they would sound in English. A few consonants have special values:

> *c* sounds like *ts*
> *q* sounds like *ch*
> *x* sounds like something between *s* and *sh*
> *z* sounds like *ds*
> *zh* sounds like *j*

These rules may be enough to permit tolerably close approximations of the originals. To learn the finer points, the reader should consult texts on the language or general texts on Chinese civilization, which always include a page or two on pronunciation.

Because pinyin has only recently replaced the Wade-Giles system, it will be useful here to provide a list of names used in this book together with their Wade-Giles equivalents.

## Personal Names

| *pinyin* | *Wade-Giles* |
|---|---|
| Chen Boda | Ch'en Po-ta |
| Chen Yun | Ch'en Yun |
| Chen Yi | Ch'en I |
| Chen Yonggui | Ch'en Yung-kuei |
| Deng Xiaoping | Teng Hsiao-p'ing |
| Deng Zihui | Teng Tzu-hui |
| Fu Yuehua | Fu Yueh-hua |
| Gao Gang | Kao Kang |

| | |
|---|---|
| Hu Yaobang | Hu Yao-pang |
| Hua Guofeng | Hua Kuo-feng |
| Jiang Qing | Chiang Ch'ing |
| Kang Sheng | K'ang Sheng |
| Lei Feng | Lei Feng |
| Lin Biao | Lin Piao |
| Liu Shaoqi | Liu Shao-ch'i |
| Luo Ruiqing | Lo Jui-ch'ing |
| Mao Zedong | Mao Tse-tung |
| Mao Yuanxin | Mao Yuan-hsin |
| Nie Yuanzi | Nieh Yuan-tzu |
| Peng Dehuai | P'eng Te-huai |
| Peng Zhen | P'eng Chen |
| Ren Wanding | Jen Wan-ting |
| Wang Guangmei | Wang Kuang-mei |
| Wang Hongwen | Wang Hung-wen |
| Wēi Jingsheng | Wei Ching-sheng |
| Wu Han | Wu Han |
| Yao Wenyuan | Yao Wen-yuan |
| Zhang Chunqiao | Chang Ch'un-ch'iao |
| Zhang Zhixin | Chang Chih-hsin |
| Zhao Ziyang | Chao Tzu-yang |
| Zhou Enlai | Chou En-lai |
| Zhu De | Chu Teh |

## Place Names

| *pinyin* | *Wade-Giles* |
|---|---|
| Beijing | Peking |
| Changsha | Changsha |
| Guangzhou | Canton |
| Nanjing | Nanking |
| Shanghai | Shanghai |
| Tianjin | Tientsin |
| Wuhan | Wuhan |
| Yanan | Yenan |

Finally, the following names have become so familiar in their own idiosyncratic or Wade-Giles spellings that they have been retained in this book: Chiang Kai-shek, Sun Yat-sen, and Hu Shih.

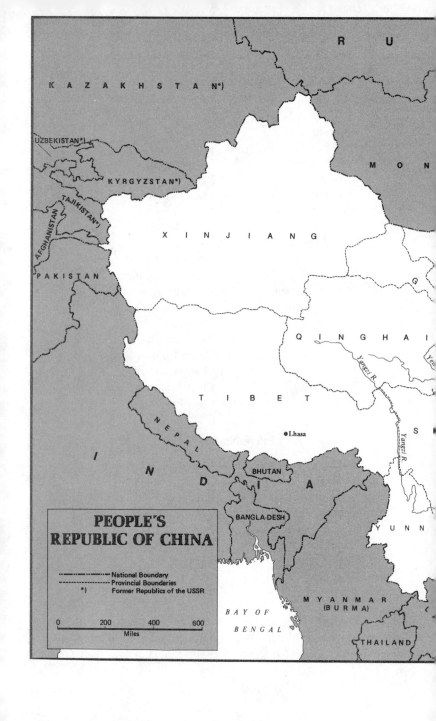

PEOPLE'S
REPUBLIC OF CHINA

—·—·— National Boundary
--------- Provincial Boundaries
*) Former Republics of the USSR

0      200      400      600
            Miles

# PEOPLE'S CHINA

# Introduction

*A long night stayed the dawn of China's crimson day.*
*Hundred-year hobgoblins galloped up and down.*
*But the people . . . oh the fragmented five hundred million . . .*

*Suddenly a crowing cock illuminates the world.*
*From far-off Yutian, from everywhere, musicians come.*
*What gathering of poets could equal this?*

Mao Zedong addressed these verses to a fellow poet in 1949 during the celebrations marking the Communist victory in China.[1] The poem seemed to point both forward and backward. In form and diction, it recalled a traditional scholar-gentleman's literary amusement. But the content was new. Mao Zedong scarcely resembled a robed scholar sipping tea with friends and sharing poems in his exquisite garden. He was the redoubtable commander of an insurgency, the Chinese Communist Party and the Red Army, that had seized control of the world's most populous country. He had just proclaimed the birth of the People's Republic of China. It was a moment that marked the victory over numerous hobgoblins—the rulers, warlords, and foreign aggressors who had presided over a century of national humiliation. The curtain was now rising on some extraordinary historical scenes as China, under communism, sought to achieve social change, economic development, and power. To sketch these scenes briefly is the objective of this book.

Chapter 1 describes the genesis of revolution. One important ingredient was poverty: Pre-1949 China was scarred by want and

3

suffering. It was not a temporary or incidental poverty but a fundamental condition in the sense that land, labor, and capital were not yet "developed" to a degree capable of producing modern abundance for the entire society. It was a condition that could be ameliorated only through a sustained process of nation building, requiring commitment of resources to massive investment, social orderliness and organization, foreign assistance, and wise policies. Just as material abundance was always crucial to Marxism, so economic development was a central objective of the Chinese revolution. Not surprisingly, economic issues figure prominently in the chapters that follow.

In the mid-1950s China adopted a Soviet central-planning approach, which was embodied in its First Five-Year Plan. This plan called for the largest possible program of investment, especially in "heavy" industry (iron, steel, machinery, and the like) at the expense of agriculture and consumer goods. But Mao soon soured on the plan for economic as well as other reasons, and he launched a radically different solution to the poverty problem, called the Great Leap Forward (1958–60). When that effort nearly wrecked the economy, Mao agreed to a tactical retreat back to Soviet-style arrangements. For the next fifteen years (from the early 1960s to the mid-1970s), these two approaches—the Soviet and the Maoist—jostled one another at policy-making tables. Not until after 1978, under Deng Xiaoping, did the country experience sustained programs capable of reaching the elusive economic goal that had always seemed to recede like the horizon. Even into the mid-1980s, China was still a poor country with formidable difficulties along the road to abundance.

Speaking again of the pre-1949 era, one must say that want and suffering by themselves cannot breed successful revolutions. If poverty were sufficient, the world would surely witness the daily success of social upheavals. In addition to grievances, revolutions require leaders and a cause. In China the cause was communism, and the leaders were the men who fought to the top of the Chinese Communist party. Chapter 1 discusses the principal tenets of Marxism-Leninism. It also provides information about Mao Zedong's early life and includes biographical sketches of a handful of other prominent personalities. Both at that time and later, the revolution was profoundly affected by the relationship between the supreme chief and the rest of the Party elite.

Few modern political figures can equal Mao Zedong. He was active in the Chinese Communist party for fifty-five years, of which forty were spent as the Party's undisputed leader. His influence compares in scope to the combined careers of Lenin, who like him led a victorious insurgency, and Stalin, who like him oversaw its subsequent development for a quarter century. Today the current official wisdom of the Chinese government, a view widely shared by outside observers, is that Mao's contribution up to 1949, the Leninlike phase of his career, was of a high and unique order. It is not too much to say that his audacious, decisive, and inspiring leadership was an absolutely crucial ingredient in the movement's success. However, after liberation he was responsible for some extremely costly and brutal mistakes (for which he has been compared to Stalin).

As subsequent chapters show, the relationship between Mao and his revolutionary colleagues began to change after 1949. His position became ambiguous. He enjoyed unrivaled prestige, but the others did not lack power to influence events. The People's Republic became a great congeries of bureaucratic machines in which some of the other leaders were rather more adept, and the interaction between Mao and his old comrades grew strained. Economic disagreements fed this estrangement as Mao's approach conflicted with the more systematic majority. Power struggles also contributed as Mao resisted being pastured out to honorific retirement and as a latent succession struggle developed. This split at the top first appeared during the Great Leap Forward in 1959 and in the recovery years after that campaign. It became acute in the Great Proletarian Cultural Revolution (1966–69), at which time Mao nearly destroyed the Party. It was known as a "two-line struggle": romantic revolution against organized development, mass campaigns versus bureaucracy, slogans as opposed to plans, zeal vying with structure, purity struggling with pragmatism. Only following Chairman Mao's death in 1976 were these polarities adequately resolved.

The struggles among the leaders corresponded to a vaster but less visible tension between the new regime's principles and the Chinese people. There can be little mistake about what the Chinese Communist party wished the people to accept as fundamental values: nationalism; rapid economic development; personal sacrifice for the nation; socialist ownership; central planning; class struggle against identified counterrevolutionaries; policies to promote equality between cities and villages, rich and poor, men and women, rulers and ruled. There can also be little doubt that these principles found some degree of acceptance throughout the society.

But exactly what was the official line, and how should it manifest itself in concrete policies? Was there not a contradiction between the push for economic development and the desire to promote equality through redistribution? Could the party that monopolized power also be responsive to the people in the absence of legally guaranteed rights and free public expression? Once, briefly under Mao's urging, the government encouraged public feedback only to retaliate harshly when the criticisms were deemed excessive. This was known as the Hundred Flowers movement (1957). The Anti-Rightist movement, which brought it to a close, resulted in the imprisonment of many thousands of intellectuals. There were other periods of excess, especially that of the Cultural Revolution (1966–69), in which mob violence was encouraged in the name of lofty Marxist principles. Later the Cultural Revolution would be officially condemned. These changes, contradictions, and excesses inhibited popular acceptance of the regime and its doctrines—although it would be equally unjustified to conclude that the people utterly repudiated the People's Republic.

The Chinese revolution was also the product of outside pressure that was usually referred to as *imperialism* and had economic, religious, cultural, and of course military aspects. Japan was the last great aggressor (1932–45). Britain was the first—in a conflict known as the Opium War (1839–42). At that time, Chinese generals and admirals at Canton in south China noticed a strange new warship. Her name was *Nemesis*. Double the tonnage of the typical Chinese war junk, her squat, flat-bottomed hull enabled her to ply the shallowest waters. Protruding halfway between her two masts was a smoke-belching funnel, and amidships on either side turned a huge paddle wheel. Chinese shot barely dented her iron-plated hull while fore and aft her own pair of thirty-two-pound swivel guns dealt mayhem to any unlucky junk within range. Western science, technology, and ideas: They were indeed a kind of nemesis that dogged the isolated Chinese nation. Even the Chinese Communist movement, with its ideological and organizational debt to Western Europe, was a product of European influence.

It is not surprising then to discover that after 1949 China continued to be affected by the outside world. The Korean War (1950–53), in which China fought against American-led United Nations forces, and a military and economic alliance with the Soviet Union produced the so-called "lean to one side" policy of close friendship with Moscow and bitter hostility toward Washington. In the early 1950s, China seemed well on the way to becoming a carbon copy of the USSR. Then with the Great Leap Forward Beijing (formerly Peking) began to chart its own course. The two Communist powers drifted rapidly apart, and by the early 1960s they were already deeply split.

China and the United States had nursed their mutual antagonism since the Korean conflict. Even though some sort of Sino-American strategic relationship might have seemed logical by the mid-1960s, when China and the USSR appeared to be on the verge of open warfare, cooperation between the champion of capitalism and the self-styled model for people's liberation movements seemed out of the question. It became all the more unlikely in the mid- to late 1960s, when China experienced the radicalism of the Cultural Revolution and the United States drifted into a large-scale war against Beijing's socialist ally Vietnam. Yet in the early 1970s, rather unexpectedly, China began to build relationships with America and the other developed nations. Since that time and especially since Mao's death in 1976, the People's Republic has abandoned its doctrinaire aloofness. Despite impediments and setbacks, relations with the United States, Japan, and all the other industrialized democracies have blossomed. Concurrently with this "open door," Marxism and especially Mao's version of it have been given fresh interpretations to permit pragmatic modernization policies, making the People's Republic a rather different society from what it was under the sterner hand of Mao Zedong.

These are the outlines of the narrative found in the following pages. It is a vast story for which there exists a correspondingly massive literature. An increasingly sophisticated phalanx of historians, sociologists, anthropologists, economists, political scientists, geographers, and humanists has, in the last quarter century, written articles, monographs, and books by the hundreds on every facet of contemporary Chinese life. This is not to suggest that there is not a great deal yet to be learned. But it is clear that for the interested learner, even one confined to materials in English, there exists a wealth of scholarship on China.

Why, then, a book such as this which attempts to compress in a few pages such a vast subject? From personal experience as a teacher of college undergraduates, experience confirmed by my colleagues, I am convinced of the need for an abbreviated account of the history of the People's Republic, a book that can be integrated into various courses (political, historical, comparative) and do a tolerably good job of representing the subject. In addressing this need, I have been under no illusion that a condensed version can fully replace fuller analyses of events. Because human affairs are complex and their causes and relationships elusive, the treatment possible in a few hundred pages necessarily oversimplifies, glosses over, and even ignores important points. Competing interpretations of events and different perspectives necessarily cannot all be represented. Thus, the reader is cautioned to treat this book as no more than an introduction to a subject so vast that its study could consume many lifetimes.

And yet, all that being said, it may still be possible for a brief account to give the reader a reasonably good idea of the general contours of historical events in China over the last several decades. That, at any rate, is my hope. The student who wishes to pursue certain questions further may begin by consulting the Suggested Readings at the end of this book.

# 1

# Old China and
# Young Revolutionaries

## Village China and Young Mao

*China: Vast Agrarian Empire*

On December 26, 1893, a first son, Mao Zedong, was born into a peasant family in Hunan Province. Neither background nor upbringing marked him as other than a typical son of the soil. The odds were that he would live out his life, as did so many others, in a single landscape of terraced hills that glistened brilliantly in the spring, grew richly green in summer, and, barring floods, droughts, and infestations, turned brown with ripe grain in the fall.

China then was a vast, feeble agrarian empire whose population was concentrated in the eastern half of the country in nine greater regions[1] (see Fig. 1). These regions were the economic building blocks of the empire. They differed from each other in size and wealth, but each contained a central, populous, fertile core located on an important river system. Each was largely self-sufficient in food and fiber although there was also a great deal of trade between the regions. Collectively, they were home to about 397 million people in the year of Mao's birth. This was perhaps one-quarter of the earth's population.

Mao was born in central China in the heart of the second most

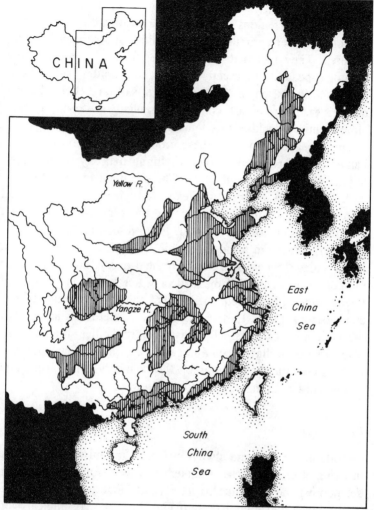

FIG. 1 Greater agricultural regions of China.

populous of these nine regions. Through it flowed China's longest river, the Yangzi. The rich soils and abundant rains of the three provinces that comprised this region produced a grain surplus for export to other parts of China. Mao's father was a rice farmer and broker. Besides rice, which was the staple crop in six of the nine regions, the products of China consisted almost entirely of other agricultural commodities and handicraft manufactures. They included wheat, millet, maize, potatoes, sweet potatoes, peanuts, rapeseed, tobacco, tea, opium, silk, cotton, processed foods, paper, furniture, rugs, salt, and coal. The economic system was a vast, complex, essentially self-contained one, almost entirely lacking in science and industrial technology.

The peasants who grew these crops and made most of these handicrafts constituted an overwhelming majority of the population. About 94 percent of all Chinese lived in the country's 800,000 villages.[2] These villages were typically clusters of mud or brick houses with thatched or tiled roofs and dirt floors. Each dwelling was enclosed by a wall. From fifteen to thirty of these small villages were arranged within walking distance around a larger village, where markets were held every few days. These markets were connected by road or water to still larger market towns, where more frequent, larger, and more specialized exchanges took place. Further up the scale, there was an ascending system of towns, small cities, and great cities. Mao's birthplace appears to have been a large market village. Thus he grew up in a community that was on the boundary between peasant China and the China of towns and cities.

## Poor China

Outside observers were always struck by the miserable standard of living of most Chinese. Although Mao was certainly not among the poorest, he remembered later in life that as a child he virtually never got animal protein with his rice. His father, who may have been excessively stingy, gave his hired laborers eggs just once a month and meat never. Most people spent almost all their income just to eat. This poverty reflects principally one central fact about China: population density. With one-quarter of the world's people, China possesses only six percent of the earth's arable land. For example, in a typical southern community in the year 1929 just over half of all farm families owned plots of land totaling between one and two acres. Another third owned between two and eight acres. Eight percent of farms contained less than two acres while only five percent contained more than eight acres.[3] With land scarce and valuable, the peasant lavished attention upon his scattered strips of soil and managed to achieve, especially in rice cultivation, a high yield per unit of land.

Unfortunately the peasant's capital (some hand tools and perhaps an animal) and other inputs were the kind that had been used for centuries. Night soil, animal manures, and green manures were used but no chemical fertilizers. Chemical pesticides and scientifically bred seeds were unknown. Human or animal labor pumped the water and pulled the plow without the assistance of motors and engines. As a result, high per-acre yields were lower than they could have been by using modern inputs. Achieved at the cost of unremitting, backbreaking toil, these yields were very low in terms of labor inputs.

For generations China's harvests had just kept pace with her huge and slowly expanding population. There was little surplus. In most places over the long run, things didn't get much better, and they didn't get much worse. In the short run in a given region, a good year could be followed by a year of flood, drought, or pests; and hunger or even famine could result. For example, not long after sixteen-year-old Mao had first moved away from his native village, Hunan Province suffered a famine. In one incident, revolting peasants seized a grain shipment being sent to the city market. It belonged to Mao's father.

## Haves and Have-nots

The career of Mao's father is an instructive example of the distribution of wealth and income among the peasantry. Before Mao's birth, his father had gone into debt and lost his land. The reason for his borrowing is not known, but it is known that peasants commonly pawned or mortgaged property to get working capital for farming or to pay for important occasions, particularly parents' funerals and children's weddings. Mao senior left his village, spent some years as a soldier, and later returned. Then he took up petty trading.

He prospered and saved enough to reclaim his land. At this point he owned about two and one-fourth acres, which raised his status from landless "poor peasant" to "middle peasant." Through hard work and watching every coin, his assets grew. When Mao Zedong was still a young boy, Mao senior bought an additional acre, thereby becoming a "rich peasant." He also began to use his savings to deal in grain. He bought up rice and shipped it to the city market. He also made loans to other peasants. He hired farm labor in order to free his own time for brokering and moneylending. He had every reason to consider himself a success. As a farmer he produced a profitable surplus of rice. His other enterprises also made money. As he came up in the world, he replaced his thatched roof with tile; but, according to his son's later testimony, he never relaxed his stinginess.

This case history exemplifies the distribution of wealth. Every village had its landless or nearly landless peasants who scratched out a living through day labor, tenant farming, handicrafts, or service occupations. Above them on the economic ladder were families who owned enough land to sustain themselves through agriculture, and those considered "rich" because they owned more land than they could personally cultivate and were able to rent some of it out. At the top of the scale were wealthy landlord families who avoided all manual labor and lived on their rents and other business income. The larger their holdings, the more likely they were to live in the towns or cities.

Figure 2 represents one analysis of the distribution of farm land. The poorest 60 percent of households, corresponding roughly to what the Communists came to refer to as "poor peasants" and "lower-middle peasants," owned only about 18 percent of the land. Those whom the Communists would call "middle peasants," constituted about one-third of the households and owned one-third of the land—a proportion that would seem fair.

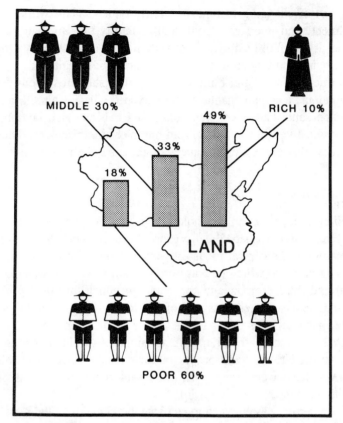

FIG. 2 Proportion of farmland held by poor, middle, and wealthy households (1936).

At the top of rural society, the ''rich peasants'' and landlords, who constituted 10 percent of all households, held title to nearly half of all the fields.[4] It is clear that a great economic gulf separated the mass of have-nots from the small minority of haves.

The case of Mao's father is also interesting because of its portrayal of economic mobility. From middle peasant to landless soldier to penny entrepreneur, then back up to middle peasant and ultimately to rich peasant, rice broker, and moneylender Mao senior had a career that covered a considerable range. Over time this sort of changing fortune was fairly typical. Hard work, investment, and good luck could pull a family up. But bad luck could drag a family down. The custom of equal inheritance by male heirs also tended to fragment accumulated wealth. Though it is true that some big families managed to stay prosperous for generations, a certain egalitarianism pervaded village China. Many poor peasants had once seen better times. Many rich peasants had risen, like Mao's father, from humbler circumstances. They all knew that these circumstances might easily be reversed.

## The Family

Economically, socially, psychologically, and in every other way, the family system shaped and organized life in China. Since time immemorial the central focus of every person's life was the nuclear family into which he was born (or into which she was married) and the larger lineage or "clan" to which that family belonged. Most villages consisted of just a few lineages, and there were many villages that had but one. Succor in childhood, inheritance of land and skills, the acquisition of a suitable spouse, security in old age, and proper burial with the fullest possible rituals—these were among the important functions carried on exclusively in the family setting.

Each person was enjoined to cultivate the virtue of "filial piety" or deference toward parents and elders. Everyone was expected to marry, families often betrothing their offspring while they were still children; and the principal objective of conjugal life was to produce sons to carry on the family name. It was acceptable for a husband with means to take secondary wives for this purpose or merely for his greater pleasure. It was expected that wives would be fertile, strictly segregated from contact with other men, and confined to the home. They were expected to subordinate themselves to their parents-in-law, their husbands, and, when parents and husbands died, to their sons. Thus, the family system was both protective and demanding. It was hierarchical and conservative. For centuries it had been the bedrock on which Chinese civilization was built.

## To the City

It was the intention of Mao's father that the boy remain at home. Having received a rudimentary education, he was supposed to help with the family accounts while also working the land. To this end, Mao was taken out of school at thirteen.

But the father had not counted on his son's rebelliousness. There had been some early signs of this. When Mao was only ten, he ran away for three days in protest against his teacher's harsh methods. Then, soon after being withdrawn from school, he got into a furious verbal exchange with his father in the presence of guests. Enraged by such filial disrespect, the father came after Mao. Mao ran off. The mother pursued them both, trying to calm the situation. When they got to the pond at the front of the house, the boy stopped and threatened to drown himself if his father came one step closer. With the mother mediating, negotiations resulted in a compromise: a limited apology from the son and no beating by the father.

Mao's father must have begun to realize that his hold on the boy was extremely weak. Mao continued his education through private reading. Before long he ran off to the nearby home of an unemployed law student and managed to find a teacher for further instruction in the classics. By fourteen or fifteen he was becoming aware of the wider world and was about to depart from Shaoshan. The succeeding stages of his career took him to the other arena of Chinese life, the towns and cities.

The first stage of that odyssey was a year (1910) at a "modern higher primary school" in the large town that served as the seat of the neighboring county. Mao was sixteen years old and still quite provincial. He was not even aware of the death, two years earlier, of the emperor of China. From then on his broadening and education accelerated. In 1911, Mao managed to enter another school in the city of Changsha. The county seat he had just come from was an important town, but it paled to insignificance beside Changsha, provincial capital and regional metropolis. He spent the next seven years, a very important period in his development, in that city.

A brief stint in a secondary school was interrupted by the dramatic events of the fall and winter of 1911. Revolutionary groups had been active for years, and one of their attempts to overthrow the Qing dynasty began on October 10 at Wuhan, the great tri-city metropolis to the north of Changsha. This uprising and the events that followed led to the abdication of the last Qing emperor in 1912. And while all this was still in progress, Mao decided to go up to Wuhan to serve in the revolutionary army. But the insurgency came to him in Changsha, where he served as a soldier for six months. Finally, the disturbances ceased, and he turned his attention to a future career. After considering police work, soapmaking, law, and commerce, he matriculated at the provincial normal school to train as a teacher.

In his five years at the First Provincial Normal School, Mao got not only an academic but also a political education. By the time he graduated in 1918, he had become a political writer and organizer with a growing reputation. Back in his army days, he had been introduced to newspapers and the steady diet of current affairs that they provided. He encountered socialist ideas. He also observed a great deal of social injustice. For example, in 1912 he came across the murdered bodies of the two populist leaders who had established the first revolutionary government at Changsha. They had been assassinated by conservative enemies.

The three years following graduation were still more eventful. In the summer of 1919, every city and town in China was convulsed with prolonged demonstrations and boycotts against the great powers. Workers and the middle classes joined students in protesting the Versailles treaties, which gave to Japan, as part of the settlement of World War I, Germany's former sphere of influence in Shandong Province. But as widespread and passionate as these demonstrations were, the ferment of these years went much deeper. In Russia the Bolshevik Revolution had occurred, and the optimism of this new regime infected some Chinese intellectual circles with a great interest in Marxism. Other currents of thought had a great vogue as well. For example, John Dewey and Bertrand Russell made extended speaking tours in China. Not even the Chinese language was immune to change; the difficult classical style was widely abandoned in favor of simpler colloquial writing. Chinese women took the first steps toward sexual equality.

The epicenter of this political and cultural disturbance was the national university at Beijing. Soon after graduating from normal school, Mao went to Beijing and briefly worked at the university as assistant librarian. Between that summer of 1919 and the summer of 1921, he spent two brief periods on the fringes of the university. He twice went to Shanghai, the greatest of China's commercial cities. Twice he returned to Changsha, first as a political organizer and later with the additional responsibility of directing a primary school.

By late 1919, Mao considered himself a Marxist and devoted his energies to writing and organizing for the new cause. The first great historic moment of his life occurred in the summer of 1921 although at the time it could not have seemed as significant as it later became. Having organized a small Communist group in Changsha, Mao journeyed once again to Shanghai. This time it was to participate in the First National Party Congress of the Chinese Communist party. This, in effect, brought the Party formally into existence.

## Urban China

The towns and cities of China contained only a small proportion of the country's total population, but their influence on national life was great. It had always been the case that governmental functions—the imperial court, provincial offices, and county magistracies—had their headquarters in the empire's 1200 walled towns and cities. Also, interregional trade and specialized handicrafts tended to locate in urban settings. Then in the nineteenth century, Chinese cities acquired a new aspect. Increasing numbers of the largest ones became "treaty ports."

The first treaty ports were established in 1842. In accordance with the provisions of the Opium War settlement between Britain and the defeated Qing dynasty, five cities were designated as locations where foreign trade could be carried on and where Westerners could establish "concessions," virtually self-governing communities. More treaties followed, and by the time Mao was born there were dozens of treaty ports, large and small, on the coast and on navigable rivers. Changsha was one. Wuhan was another, which also had a British "concession." At the capital, Beijing, the foreign diplomatic community acquired an enclave protected by their own troops.

Shanghai led all other cities in foreign influence. At the turn of the century, Shanghai was already China's great international port and was rapidly becoming the largest center for light industry as well. Companies run by the English, the Japanese, and other foreigners, as well as by Chinese businesspeople, were rapidly expanding in the period from 1895 to about 1920. Down in the villages, peasants were still mired in the timeless cycles of sowing and harvesting. But the cities were experiencing a vigorous industrial growth. Between 1912 and 1920 industrial production increased nationally at an average rate of over 14 percent per year. During this period the major trunk lines of north China's still limited but very important railroad system were built. Telegraph lines connected major cities.

Urban change was not limited to economics. The Western cultural impact was also very great. Until about the time of Mao's birth, China's educated elites had generally resisted foreign culture, which they considered barbarian. The few open to new ideas were vastly outnumbered by an uninterested majority. But in 1895, China suffered a humiliating defeat at the hands of modernizing Japan. The Sino-Japanese War settlement imposed a huge indemnity and required China to relinquish Taiwan. Three years later Germany, Russia, England, and France forced the Qing government to grant them special "spheres of influence" in selected regions of the empire. Then in 1900 the United States and Japan joined these same powers in retaliating against government-encouraged, anti-Christian mobs. This was the Boxer incident, and it cost the dynasty a huge indemnity and further humiliation. As a succession of catastrophes, these incidents were unprecedented since the collapse of the Ming dynasty three hundred years earlier. Only after this succession of blows to their self esteem did the intelligentsia begin to take an interest in Western ideas.

Thus, when Mao was growing up, a great upsurge in foreign influence was underway. It was then widely recognized that Japan had made herself powerful by emulating the West. Unless China did the same, she would grow progressively weaker until the great powers decided to dismember her at will. Although the sense of crisis was particularly strong in the cities, it even reached Mao's Shaoshan village. "Alas!" said one of the pamphlets that young Mao read, probably without appreciating its full significance, "China will be subjugated." [5] A new, Western-influenced intelligentsia emerged from about 1900 to 1920. In school Mao's generation studied a curriculum that included increasing amounts of modern subject matter. Western technology, science, social philosophy, economics, political thought, literature, art, architecture, music, military organization, strategy and tactics, dress, social mores, business methods, administrative techniques—and much more—flooded into China. The impact of all this was principally felt in the cities.

But the Chinese not only admired and copied foreigners. They also resented and even hated them. They fumed inwardly against the national loss of face that had accumulated for decades and against Western arrogance and opportunism. In 1917, Mao attended a soccer match between his school and one that had links to Yale University. He jumped up and shouted, "Beat those slaves of foreigners!" Later in Shanghai, to persuade an old friend to stop wearing Western clothes, Mao led him to the British park and showed him the sign barring entry to dogs and Chinese.

Thus, in this period a few rays of hopeful economic, social, and intellectual change faintly illuminated a generally gloomy landscape. The cities experienced rapid economic, social, and intellectual changes, but the countryside was different. Agriculture was still dominated by vast populations toiling in tiny plots with simple tools. Politically, China suffered from two massive problems. First, the government was weak. Until 1911 the declining Qing dynasty was struggling to survive and could not play a vigorous leadership role. When it collapsed, there ceased to be any effective administration at all. Second, foreign meddling continued. In 1914 it actually intensified as Japan exploited the war to pursue imperialistic expansion in China.

## Unification, Invasion, and Civil War

### Postwar China: 1920–36

After World War I the economy entered troubled times. Industrial growth slowed down, and agriculture began to experience a prolonged crisis. The world economy was partly responsible for all this. The disappearance of wartime demand for Chinese products was followed by harmful international currency manipulations in the 1920s and world depression in the 1930s. The absence of strong, stable central government made it doubly difficult for the country to cope with this economic adversity.

Politically, the early 1920s saw the emergence of two significant movements: the Nationalist party and the Communist party. The Nationalist Party has for decades been referred to in the literature as the KMT. This acronym stands for the party's Chinese name, transcribed according to an older system of spelling. Although this spelling departs from the system used throughout the present text, it will be retained because of long usage. The same applies to the names of the party's two major leaders, Sun Yat-sen and Chiang Kai-shek, which have long been thus spelled in Western writings.

The KMT, as it existed in the 1920s and beyond, was reorganized by Sun Yat-sen in 1923 and 1924 out of earlier parties. Sun had been a well-known revolutionary since the turn of the century. Although his new organization had Soviet advisers and funding, its members ranged from moderate to conservative. The party quickly became the largest and strongest in the country. When Sun Yat-sen died in 1925, the KMT came under the control of General Chiang Kai-shek. He soon began to tower over the political landscape and remained China's acknowledged leader from 1927 through the late 1940s. From 1927 until war with Japan broke out in 1937, Chiang presided over a new government called the Republic of China with his capital in Nanjing on the Yangtze River. He achieved a loose reunification of the country.

Chiang had to cope with three extremely serious political enemies. One of them was the warlords. Ever since the collapse of the Qing in 1912, the problem of local militarists had been growing until, in the late 1910s and early 1920s, hundreds of warlords, large and small, dominated the entire country. Although Chiang was able to bring some of them into his government and to subdue others, local warlords continued to plague most provinces and to frustrate administrative unification. A second problem was Japan. Of all the factors that shaped China's destiny in those years, Japanese aggression was perhaps the most damaging. In 1928, Japanese generals and diplomats tried to block Chiang's efforts at reunification. Then, in 1931, Japanese troops occupied Manchuria, China's rich northeastern region. In 1932 they established the puppet state of Manchukuo there, and during the next few years they pushed southward into the provinces around Beijing. Finally, in 1937, they mobilized a full-scale invasion, which resulted in Japanese occupation of all the major cities, from Beijing in the north to Wuhan and Shanghai in the center to Canton in the south. As a result of this, in 1938, Chiang's government was driven deep into the western province of Sichuan where he remained for the duration of World War II (1938–45).

Chiang's third major headache in the 1920s and 1930s was the Communist movement. As noted earlier, in 1921 a handful of young radicals, including Mao Zedong, held the first congress of the Chinese Communist party (CCP). Back then, the fledgling Party seemed unlikely ever to rule China. Its members were few and young. It depended heavily on Moscow for doctrinal and financial support as well as for strategic and tactical direction. In classic Marxist fashion, it was preoccupied with the industrial proletariat and gave top priority to organizing unions and fomenting strikes. But despite some temporary successes, these efforts did not constitute a formula for long term victory because the number of factory workers in an underdeveloped country like China was too small.

In 1924, when Sun Yat-sen was building the KMT with Russian assistance, Moscow prevailed on the Chinese Communists to enter into a cooperative relationship with Sun's much larger party. Chinese Communists joined the KMT as individual members and worked within the KMT. This collaboration continued during the first two years of Chiang Kai-shek's leadership and while Chiang's national reunification efforts got under way (1925–27). But Chiang and most of the KMT were essentially conservative whereas the CCP, which had begun to grow rapidly, pushed for socially radical policies such as land reform and labor unions. Conflict was inevitable. In the spring of 1927 these two forces had a violent falling out. Chiang took the initiative and attacked the radicals in a bloody purge that the Communists called the "White Terror." Thousands of CCP and union members were executed. Communist counterattacks failed. So the remnants of a shattered party either went underground in the cities or took to the hills.

But Chiang was mistaken if he thought he had cured his CCP headache. In their adversity and cut off from Russian assistance and interference, the surviving Communists began to fashion a homegrown strategy for success. Having earlier ignored military action for purely political action, a disadvantage that allowed Chiang nearly to wipe them out, they now began to nurture a Red Army under close Party control. Second, they began to abandon their urban preoccupations, realizing that the cities were precisely where Chiang's strength was greatest and that their opportunity lay in the vast, suffering countryside.

At the center of this rethinking was Mao Zedong. He was one

of those who had retreated to the hills in 1927. By 1930 his peasant-based guerrilla strategy began to take shape. Together with other Communist rebels, he established a rural base area in the southeastern province of Jiangxi, named the Jiangxi Soviet. They began to work out land policies, military tactics, and other doctrines for success among the peasantry. Before long they were ruling perhaps nine million people. To Chiang Kai-shek's horror, the CCP had risen from the ashes.

Chiang renewed his attack in a series of five encircling campaigns. The first four went badly for Chiang, requiring him to pull back his columns, which had been badly mauled by Communist guerrillas. But by 1934 under German advisers, Chiang adopted a methodical, massive encirclement approach that threatened to crush the Communist movement once again. In desperation the Reds decided to break out. In October 1934 about 100,000 began a famous trek known to history as the Long March. It was to last a year and cover 6,000 miles as the beleaguered Communists fought their way to the northwest. Perhaps 90 percent of those who started out never made it to the end. It happened that, prior to this serious setback, Mao had been demoted by Moscow-backed Chinese Communists who had migrated to the Jiangxi Soviet from Shanghai and other cities. He thus escaped responsibility for the debacle.

Although the Long March was a tactical defeat, it had very beneficial psychological and organizational effects and gave the Communists an important strategic advantage. Psychologically, the Long March was not unlike Valley Forge in the American Revolution. The suffering and heroism actually strengthened the movement and proved that it was indomitable. Organizationally, the Long March clarified the leadership of the Party. Mao began to emerge as the undisputed leader. (One biographer describes him as a latter-day Moses.) With the support of several talented military and political men, some of whom had opposed him in earlier times, he reclaimed his position at the top.

To understand the strategic benefits of the Long March, one must remember that Japan's aggressiveness had been increasing throughout the 1930s. On the Long March, the CCP trumpeted a new purpose and thereby transformed a retreat into a holy cause. The Communists proclaimed that they were marching to fight Japan. People all over China had grown increasingly disturbed by Japanese incursions in the north. In the public mind, Chiang Kai-shek's standing diminished each time he bowed to Tokyo's insatiable demands. Why should Chinese fight Chinese, it was asked, while Japan was overrunning the country? The Communists seized this issue of anti-Japanese nationalism and thereby preempted an extremely powerful emotional force.

## The Yanan Years, 1937–45

The Japanese invasion of 1937 ruined everything for Chiang. It drove him out of the big cities, which were his economic lifeline. His plan for consolidating Nationalist rule required large modern armies to crush the warlords and the Communists. Funding for these forces came from taxes and other impositions on commerce and manufacturing, especially in Shanghai. Without these urban revenues, where was he to get adequate support for this military consolidation? The invasion also crippled his rural strategy. Although agriculture was by far the largest sector of the economy, the government amazingly did not tax landowners. This was the price that a weak regime paid for their political support. Now, in addition to denying Chiang the cities, the invasion destroyed village stability in many places. Under Japanese occupation, many conservative local leaders fled, thereby removing their direct influence. Others collaborated with the invaders, thereby branding themselves with the traitor's mark. In either case, the old local hierarchy received a severe blow. A kind of political vacuum resulted, into which stepped the CCP.

In contrast to causing the Nationalists difficulties, World War II was a boon to the Communists, who were now able, in their northwest sanctuary under Mao's firm leadership, to practice guerrilla warfare. It was something they had become increasingly good at since they had taken to the hills in 1927. Japanese atrocities played into their hands by driving millions of peasants into active resistance. With the local notables frequently absent or weakened, as just described, the Communists were able to place themselves at the head of this movement. Thus, it was they—and not the government—who increasingly enjoyed the reputation of leading the nation's struggle against Japan.

But a full analysis of the CCP success must also take into account the political skills that they had sharpened in the preceding decade. The Party had schooled itself in promoting the interests of the ordinary people. It had learned how to give voice and muscle to popular demands for things like land, elemental fairness, and women's liberation. Its leaders did without offices, fine uniforms, and motorcars. Consequently, as Mao put it, the Party was like "fish" in the people's "water."

Mao had a theory covering this relationship. He called it "mass line," and it might be thought of as his answer to Western democracy (or "bourgeois democracy," as he called it). The goal was solidarity in the effort to achieve the goals of the people. Both disciplined leadership and responsiveness to the needs of the masses were indispensable. To do this, the Party must remain intimately involved with the masses, consult them about their problems, and work out appropriate courses of action. As the resulting policies were implemented, the Party would monitor their effects, consult with the people, and adjust them accordingly. Thus, instead of mere majority rule, Mao aimed at total solidarity between the CCP and the masses.[6]

Party organizational structures also adapted to the fragmented character of guerrilla warfare. The center at Yanan had to promote flexibility and decentralization while still maintaining control over general policy. Intense indoctrination was one tool for achieving this. Every member was required to participate in reading and discussions on such subjects as Marxist theory and guerrilla war. Strict party discipline was also vital. The leading group of every military and administrative unit contained its Party "fraction," and these people were expected to implement Party directives. As a result, broad strategy could be decided at the top and adapted tactically in the field.

The Party's popular image added to its organizational strength.

The superhuman feats of the Long March had already given the Communists a romantic glamour. Their cause was just. They could be battered but never beaten. The Yanan years only added luster to their reputation. Yanan was located in the poorest of China's eight agricultural regions. Even the Communist leaders lived in caves like ordinary peasants. Supplies were scarce; and luxuries, unknown. Everything seemed simple, wholesome, and honest. The troops were strictly taught to respect the people and pay for what they took. If one word could encompass their myth, the word would be "purity." [7] Consequently, the Communists built up a solid reputation as the one positive and effective political movement in China.

The cult of Mao was also forming. Certain other leaders won wide fame as well, but Mao was becoming preeminent. Already the messiah of the Long March, he was increasingly the personification of the Communist party. From his pen came a body of doctrines on guerrilla warfare and theoretical writings in which Marxism was applied to Chinese conditions. A rewritten Party history portrayed him as always central and always correct. In 1942 a move to consolidate Mao's position resulted in a "rectification" campaign. The entire Party was set to studying and discussing doctrine (mostly Mao's writings), criticizing comrades, accepting criticism of themselves, and rectifying their mistakes. At this same time, the propaganda apparatus came under Mao's control.

As a result of these favorable conditions, the CCP grew rapidly. Tables 1 and 2 show this dramatic expansion. The Party's original 1921 membership of fifty-seven had grown to about 58,000 by the spring of 1927. After the disastrous falling out with Chiang Kai-shek in that same year, the numbers went as low as 10,000 and only gradually recovered to 122,000 by 1930. In the early 1930s, the heyday of Mao's guerrilla base in the southeast, membership grew to about 300,000, but the Long March again reduced the ranks to 40,000 on the eve of the Japanese invasion. Then within three years of the onset of hostilities, the CCP boasted 800,000 members. Under severe military

**Table 1.** Growth of the CCP

| | |
|---|---|
| 1921 | 57 |
| 1922 | 123 |
| 1923 | 432 |
| 1925 | 950 |
| 1927 (April) | 57,967 |
| 1927 (end) | 10,000 |
| 1928 | 40,000 |
| 1930 | 122,000 |
| 1933 | 300,000 |
| 1937 | 40,000 |
| 1940 | 800,000 |
| 1945 | 1,200,000 |
| 1947 | 2,759,456 |
| 1948 | 3,065,533 |
| 1949 | 4,500,000 |
| 1956 | 10,730,000 |
| 1969 | 22,000,000 |
| 1973 | 28,000,000 |
| 1977 | 35,000,000 |
| 1982 | 39,000,000 |
| 1992 | 51,000,000 |

**Table 2.** Growth of
the Red Army

| | |
|---|---|
| 1937 | 92,000 |
| 1939 | 320,000 |
| 1940 | 500,000 |
| 1941 | 440,000 |
| 1943 | 464,000 |
| 1945 | 860,000 |
| 1947 | 1,950,000 |
| 1949 | 4,000,000 |

pressure from both the Japanese and the Nationalists, they saw their numbers contract slightly in 1941 and 1942, but by 1944 they were once again on the upswing: over 1 million by 1945, more than 2 million by 1947, and almost 5 million by 1949.[8]

The Red Army experienced a similar expansion. From slightly

over 90,000 troops in 1937, the Communist forces reached half a million in 1940. The numbers then leveled off for four years and began to grow rapidly again toward the end of the war. There were almost 900,000 troops in 1945, and that number swelled to 4 million by 1949.[9]

## Civil War, 1945–49

Still, Generalissimo Chiang Kai-shek and his KMT seemed to be in an enviable position at war's end. Recognized throughout the world as China's legitimate government, they had a large army and faced excellent prospects for returning to Nanjing in triumph. Two of the impediments to consolidation had now been eliminated: Japan lay in rubble under Allied occupation, and the remaining warlords were no match for Nationalist armies. United States aid could be counted on because a cornerstone of American foreign policy was a strong non-Communist government in China. When the United Nations was established, the United States insisted that China be considered a great power with a permanent seat on the Security Council.

Unfortunately for Chiang, the third of his three major stumbling blocks, the Communists, were stronger than ever. With their large party and army, they controlled the rural hinterland in most of north China and in many other regions as well. The populations under their control numbered perhaps 90 million. For Chiang to meet this serious challenge would require every material, organizational, and moral resource available to the government. His regime was simply not equal to the challenge. Although there were many decent and dedicated civil servants, the government as a whole was incompetent and corrupt. The generals, under the generalissimo's direction, pursued a losing strategy and proved tactically inept. "The world's worst leadership," one U.S. general called them.[10] They committed a massive error in attempting in 1946 to take and hold vast regions from the Communists. The result was well-equipped but overextended armies in Manchuria and elsewhere in the north. With such a strategic deficit and short on tactical brilliance, the Nationalist armies were a force that was doomed to defeat.

While the generals were thus engaged, the Nationalists' civil administration received inadequate resources. Above all, it could not solve the critical problem of hyperinflation. By late 1946 it took a million Chinese dollars to buy the equivalent of one 1937 Chinese dollar. And that was only the beginning. The wholesale price index topped 16 million in December, 1947, 21 billion a year later, and well over 2 trillion by the last report in March 1949. With this cancer eating at the morale of government and citizens alike, it was scarcely likely that the numerous other administrative problems would be solved. In fairness it should be noted that this same regime ruled Taiwan from 1950 on, providing stable administration and fostering economic development. What this might or might not prove about the causes for the Nationalist defeat is subject to debate. But it does perhaps suggest that the outcome of the civil war may be best accounted for by the momentum that the Communists had gained during the war. In smoother times, Chiang's regime might conceivably have proved adequate.

By 1945 the Communists were a completely rejuvenated movement. All the elements of a successful insurgency were present: leadership, organization, doctrine, and popular support. But their true strength was not then widely appreciated. When civil war erupted in 1946, few expected the Reds to achieve a rapid, sweeping victory. The CCP leaders themselves, although confident of the final outcome, overestimated the time they would need. Stalin, even after their decisive victory in November 1948, urged them to consolidate the north and leave south China to the Nationalists. But by that time the Communists could sense victory. They would not be denied.

Red armies were isolating and surrounding government forces. In the far northeast, entire government divisions surrendered in the fall of 1948, giving the Communists possession of Manchuria, China's greatest industrial prize. Then the Communists moved down into the north China plain. The government defenders of cities and strategic crossroads were defeated during the winter. In February 1949 the Communists occupied Beijing (Peking), China's capital until 1927 and soon to be restored to its former importance.

Would the government be able to hold south China? Militarily, it was possible. The Yangzi River, which cuts China into northern and southern halves, is a great natural bulwark. "The Nationalists could have defended the Yangzi River with broomsticks if they had the will to do so," said a senior American general.[11] But the crack armies of the KMT had already disintegrated, and the fighting spirit of what remained was spent. Demoralization was epidemic. Generals bungled. Troops surrendered or fled. By spring Communist armies had battled across the Yangzi. Waves of refugees washed across the landscape while officials shamelessly looked to their personal advantage and carried off what they could. In October 1949, China's southern metropolis, Guangzhou (Canton), was taken by the Reds. Appeals for more American aid fell on deaf ears. Finally, Chiang Kai-shek removed the remnants of his government and army to the island of Taiwan for a last stand.

Communist initiatives were moving forward in every sphere. In northern villages, land reform was under way. In national politics twenty-three non-Communist parties agreed to participate in a constitutional convention to be called, "The Chinese People's Political Consultative Conference." Conventions of labor confederations and women's and youth organizations convened. Then in Beijing on October 1, 1949, Mao Zedong, wearing a military tunic with a single decoration, proclaimed the establishment of the People's Republic of China (PRC).

## Personalities and Causes

Mao did not stand alone on that podium on October 1, 1949. Nor were the Communist movement and the People's Republic his personal creations. Beside him, literally and figuratively, stood many personalities whose heroic contributions gave them a claim to important roles in the new regime. It would not be possible to understand the history of the People's Republic without meeting at least some of these figures. In the brief biographies that follow, the first five are people who came to Beijing in the spring of 1949 to set up the new central government. They are Liu Shaoqi, Zhou Enlai, Zhu De, Chen Yun, and Chen Boda. Next come four who served temporarily as Party and army commanders in the military regions overseeing the transition to permanent provincial administrations. They are Lin Biao, Chen Yi, Deng Xiaoping, and Peng Dehuai. Finally, Mao's fourth wife must be introduced.

## *Liu Shaoqi (1898–1969): Organization Man*

Liu Shaoqi (pronounced something like "Liew Shao Chee") was born into a rich peasant family in Hunan Province not far from Mao's home village. As a young Marxist he organized labor unions. By the late 1920s his duties had expanded to include establishing underground Party cells, supervising political work in the army, overseeing Party administration, and writing theoretical articles. During the anti-Japanese resistance he was out in the field perhaps more than any other senior leader, getting to know many of the second-level cadres and laying the groundwork for his later position as top organization man. As Mao consolidated his leadership of the Party at this time, Liu became one of his principal supporters. Liu was one of the first to hail Mao's contributions to Marxism.

By 1949, Liu had become the second-ranking leader in China. He was the number two man in the Party. He was also a vice-chairperson of the People's Revolutionary Military Council, which oversaw the armed forces. He played a leading role in the Chinese People's Political Consultative Conference, a united front assembly that legally established the People's Republic of China and that continued to meet in later years. That conference named an interim legislature, the Central People's Government Council. Liu was one of its six vice-chairpersons. He was the head of China's labor federation and chaired the important Sino-Soviet Friendship Association. He took over temporarily as head of state when Mao went to Moscow in late 1949.

Tall, seldom smiling, and prematurely gray, Liu had little public personality compared to some of his colleagues. One foreigner described him as "dour, unemotional, and colorless in manner but an intelligent man who is practical, thorough, and assiduous in his work."[12] Until 1966 the betting was that Liu would be Mao's successor.

## Zhou Enlai (1898–1976): Premier

Zhou Enlai (pronounced something like "Joe Un-lie") was probably the most engaging public figure produced by China in this century. Although he came from a prosperous Tianjin family in north China, he became a leftist around 1920 like so many of his contemporaries. Zhou joined the wave of young Chinese who went to Europe in the 1920s and became a Communist there. Returning home in 1924, he immersed himself in radical politics both as a Communist and as a member Sun Yat-sen's Nationalist Party. His most notable exploit in these years was the 1927 workers' insurrection, which seized control of Shanghai. They delivered the city to Chiang Kai-shek's Nationalist troops, who were completing the first phase of reunification. Unfortunately, the bloody Nationalist-Communist split was in the offing. Within weeks Chiang turned on the workers. Zhou barely escaped with his life, and thousands of his comrades faced the KMT execution squads.

In the difficult years that followed, Zhou became increasingly prominent in the CCP. By the time of the Long March he joined Mao's faction. He became the Party's leading diplomat and negotiator. Because the Communist-Nationalist united front was reestablished to fight Japan, he spent much of the war as CCP liaison officer in Chiang's wartime capital. Beginning in 1949, Zhou began a long and distinguished career as premier, the head of China's government apparatus. He was particularly active in foreign affairs, concurrently holding the title of foreign minister for several years.

The handsome, charming Zhou was immensely liked by Chinese and foreigners alike. He was an inexhaustible worker, well suited to take on the administrative duties of premier. In addition he had a unique instinct for political survival. He remained influential and active through every swing to the left or right until the day he died.

## Zhu De (1886–1976): Commander in Chief

When the revolutionaries entered Beijing in 1949, one of its two best-known figures was Zhu De (pronounced "Joo Duh"). Sixty-three years old at the time, he had been the CCP's senior soldier since the late 1920s and, more than any other person, was responsible for the growth and success of the Red Army. He had come to the calling of revolutionary as a result of a sort of mid-life career change. Originally he was an officer in warlord armies, enjoying wealth and concubines and able to indulge an opium addiction. But around 1920 he was affected by the cultural changes that transformed so many young people, and in 1922 he renounced his comfortable position to work for China's salvation. He had to break his narcotic habit, pension off his wives, and subordinate himself to much younger men. For example, when he joined the CCP in 1922 at the age of thirty-six, his sponsor was twenty-four-year-old Zhou Enlai. But pride could not stand in the way of his determination. He was a most appealing character, plain—even slightly ugly—in appearance, modest and unassuming, affable, undogmatic, and devoted to his troops.

After 1928 it was he and Mao who built up the Red Army and the guerrilla bases that enabled the CCP to survive against Chiang's attacks. Zhu excelled as commander in chief, as a field general, and as an inspiration to his soldiers. His name became legendary; peasants claimed he had superhuman powers. Yet his relationship to Mao exemplified Mao's famous dictum that political power grows out of the barrel of a gun and that the Party controls the gun.[13] Without the Red Army, the Communists could not have won China, and Zhu was the architect of that army. Yet, despite some serious disagreements, Zhu worked closely with Mao and never challenged the supremacy of Party leadership. He supplied the perfect combination of great talent and restrained ambition.

Zhu's principal contributions to the revolution were made in the 1930s and 1940s. After 1949 he continued as commander in chief of the army, which was renamed the People's Liberation Army (PLA). He played various other roles as one of the great luminaries of the Party, always counted among the highest circle of leaders.

## Chen Yun (1905– ): Economic Expert

Of all the leaders discussed here, Chen Yun (pronounced "Chun Ywin") was the only one who had actually been an industrial worker. As a labor union organizer, he entered the Party in the mid-1920s and soon found himself embroiled in Zhou Enlai's 1927 Shanghai uprising. He joined Mao in his soviet, participated in the Long March, and worked in Yanan during the anti-Japanese war. As a member of Mao's faction, he became a leading theorist. After 1942 he found his vocation in economic affairs.

In the early years of the People's Republic, holding positions at the highest levels of the Party and government, Chen Yun operated principally as chairperson of the very important Finance and Economic Committee. He directed the rehabilitation of China's industry, transport, and infrastructure and led the successful battle against hyperinflation. In the mid-1950s he was one of the promoters of the Russian-style Five Year Plan. Chen was a genial person without overweening ambition. He had a good mind for practical details and a grasp of what was realistically possible. In this respect he differed from Mao and some others, who sometimes saw what they wanted to see. Yet Chen Yun remained on good terms with everyone. Consequently, although sometimes shoved to the background, he was never purged.

## *Chen Boda (1904–1989): Theoretician*

Chen Boda (pronounced "Chun Bwo Dah" and no relation to Chen Yun) came from poor peasant stock in southern coastal Fujian province. It is not entirely clear how he managed to get an education, but, according to most sources, he graduated from a normal school and then attended a university in Shanghai, where he became a leftist activist. Having joined the Party during the first Nationalist-Communist united front period, he escaped elimination at the time of the 1927 split only by signing a false confession. Soon afterward he went to Moscow, where he became one of the few Chinese deeply conversant with Marxist-Leninist theory.

He was a professor at China University in Beijing when, in 1937, Liu Shaoqi brought him to Yanan. His work in the Propaganda Department caught Mao's attention because he had a powerful writing style, a thorough command of Marxist texts, and a determination to Sinicize Communist theory. Soon Chen Boda found himself serving as Mao's political secretary. In the early 1940s, when Mao launched a drive for unchallenged supremacy within the Party, Chen Boda's pen led the attack against his enemies.

In 1949, Chen Boda became deputy director of the Party's Propaganda Department and vice president of the CCP's most important school. He actively participated in the formation of various mass societies and professional organizations, including those set up for philosophers, economists, artists, writers, social scientists, and natural scientists. Equally heavy was Chen Boda's responsibility as the chief promoter of Mao's thought and of the Chairman's claim to a high place in the pantheon of Marxist-Leninist thinkers. He participated in editing the first three volumes of Mao's selected works, which appeared in 1952.

The "short, stocky [Chen Boda] with thick glasses and a strong [southern] accent made all the more unintelligible by a pronounced stammer'' was probably not the most sought-after dinner guest, particularly as he was severe and puritanical and disdained idle conversation.[14] But he wielded an eloquent and prolific pen. He was, as it were, Mao's house intellectual, and under this powerful patron a steadily ascending career path opened up.

## Lin Biao (1908–71): Battlefield Genius and Radical

Lin Biao (pronounced ''Lin Beyow'') got his start back in the 1920s as a military prodigy. Only twenty years old when the 1927 split erupted, he served under other Communist commanders, including Chen Yi (see later), when they took to the hills. They all linked up with Mao in 1928. That is when, as Lin told an American reporter in 1937, ''I first made a name for myself.''[15] A name indeed. Within months he emerged as one of China's most brilliant battlefield commanders and an authority on guerrilla tactics. He led his troops in numerous battles, distinguished himself during the Long March, and in 1937 treated the invading Japanese to one of their rare defeats. He received a serious battlefield wound in 1938, which kept him out of the field during most of the anti-Japanese war. During part of that time he served as president of the academy at Yanan and wrote on military questions. The years from 1939 to 1942 he spent in Moscow.

During the civil war the Party put him in command of battles in Manchuria and north China, now considered two of the three decisive military campaigns of the civil war. He secured Manchuria in 1948 and entered Beijing on the last day of January 1949. In the spring his troops moved south and soon took the central metropolis of Wuhan as well as Mao's old city, Changsha. By late 1949 and early 1950 he had taken Guangzhou (Canton) and other major southern cities. Thereupon he installed himself in Wuhan as head of the ''Central-South'' Party bureau and military region and as chairperson of the committee governing the 175 million residents of six provinces. He remained active in this role for a couple of years. His precise activities until about 1956 are not always clear. He was probably seriously ill during part of this period. A slight, sallow, bespectacled man, Lin withdrew from the forefront of events until the 1960s, when he returned with explosive effect.

## Chen Yi (1901–72): Field Commander

Chen Yi (pronounced "Chun Yee" and no relation to the other Chens) came from a prosperous family in the western province of Sichuan. But he became a radical in the period following World War I. His career as a top Communist soldier began in the late 1920s, when he was part of Lin Biao's guerrilla band. They linked up with Mao in 1928. Later, having been left behind by the Long March as a rear guard, he excelled as the commander of the famous New Fourth Army. This force expanded vigorously during the anti-Japanese war and gave the Communists a strong presence in the southeast (although not so secure as their Yanan base). During these years Chen Yi worked closely with the army's political commissar, Liu Shaoqi. Then, rounding off his military career, he commanded the PLA forces that took the Shanghai region in May 1949. This was the third of the three decisive campaigns of the civil war.

Chen Yi stayed on in Shanghai, China's most important industrial city, to preside over the establishment of the regime in this key area. He was head of the East China Military Region and mayor of Shanghai. At this time he began to forge close links with Zhou Enlai, premier and foreign minister, and eventually replaced Zhou in the latter office. A U.S. diplomat described Chen Yi during the anti-Japanese war as "a man of commanding presence, evident vigor and determination." [16] Quite bald, he was outgoing, jovial, and blunt and also rather disdainful of strict ideological conformity.

## Deng Xiaoping (1904– ): Apparatchik Supreme

Deng Xiaoping (pronounced something like "Dung She-owping"), like Zhou Enlai and Chen Yi, began his revolutionary career when he was a work-study student in France in the early

1920s. Having joined the Communist party, he returned to China, via Moscow, in the late 1920s. He helped establish a short-lived guerrilla base in the southwest and then in 1930 made his way to Mao's Jiangxi Soviet. He was assigned military staff duties under Peng Dehuai (see later), the editorship of the Red Army's newspaper, and a lecturing post at the Red Army Academy. He soon became a member of Mao's faction. During the political infighting on the Long March, Deng rallied to Mao and thereafter climbed steadily higher in the Party hierarchy. He spent the anti-Japanese war as a political commissar in one of the three main armies in north China. During the civil war, these troops fought crucial campaigns against the Nationalists.

From late 1949 to mid-1952, Deng was one of the key officials in southwest China, headquartered in his home province of Sichuan. Not primarily a military man, he was the top Party secretary in the region. When he was recalled to Beijing in 1952, his career advanced still further. He was appointed one of five deputy premiers in 1952 and took charge of the Ministry of Finance in 1953. In 1954 he left the latter post to become the secretary general of the Party, a position of great importance. He went still higher in later years, emerging after Mao's death in 1976 as China's leader.

Although barely over five feet tall, Deng always made a powerful impression on people. Back in 1938 a U.S. military observer described him as "short, chunky and physically tough," mentally "as keen as mustard."[17] Colleagues commented on his encyclopedic knowledge, his decisiveness in making decisions, and a certain arrogance and argumentativeness. He was a fervent nationalist and convinced Marxist, but he retained a strong streak of pragmatism.

## Peng Dehuai (1898–1974): General

Peng Dehuai's story (his name is pronounced something like "Pung Duh Why") is particularly arresting. He came from the same county as Mao Zedong and from similar rural roots. He apparently exceeded Mao in childhood rebelliousness, being expelled from home at nine years of age for disrespectful conduct (he had kicked over his grandmother's opium pan). He wandered through a succession of jobs until joining the army at sixteen. Among his later adventures was a month of torture at the hands of warlord troops. "I was hung from the roof with a rope round my wrists. Then big stones were piled on my back, while the gaolers stood round kicking me and demanding that I confess."[18] He had found his calling and began to rise as a revolutionary leader.

In 1928, when Communists, hounded by Chiang Kai-shek, were taking to the hills, he linked up with Mao and his group. From that moment his life intertwined with theirs. He became, like Lin Biao, a brilliant battlefield general. He rose to occupy a military status inferior only to that of Zhu De, Mao's co-founder of the Red Army. He played a major role in the campaigns of the early 1930s and in the Long March. During the anti-Japanese war he became top field commander in the north. In the civil war he led an army that conquered the northwest and the far west. Then, like Lin Biao in the south, Chen Yi in the east, and Gao Gang in the northeast, he undertook the job of overseeing the establishment of regular administration in the Northwest Region. In 1950 the Korean War broke out. Peng commanded the Chinese "volunteers" sent to fight the United Nations troops. He remained engaged there until 1953. When he returned to Beijing, he became minister of defense and de facto chief of the PLA.

## Jiang Qing (1914–1991): Rebel Actress

It is necessary here to introduce a different sort of person. Jiang Qing (pronounced "Jeeang Ching") exemplifies the special problems facing ambitious women as well as the readiness of many intellectuals to join the Communist movement. She was born in modest circumstances to an urban family in Shandong Province and was orphaned as a child. Raised by a grandfather, she ended her formal education with junior high school. From there she entered a drama school. Like many young women at the time, she admired Nora, the character in Ibsen's *A Doll's House*, who represented the awakened woman. Later Jiang Qing was to play this role on stage and was herself a Nora, striking out independently in defiance of Chinese norms.

At about nineteen she lived with a young Party member who introduced her to communism. When he deserted her, she gravitated to Shanghai's moving picture community. There she may have married a film critic (some say to advance her career), acted in plays and in minor film roles, and got a divorce. Her ambitious, aggressive, independent, and rebellious character was judged as rather scandalous by traditional standards of feminine behavior. She was neither happy nor successful.

The anti-Japanese war ended this phase of her life, for she left Shanghai. In the summer of 1937 she came to Yanan, following the path taken then and later by many leftist intellectuals. But her fate there was special because she happened to meet Mao. At that time his third marriage was either in the process of breaking up or had already done so. His wife, who had been wounded on the Long March, seems to have been suffering from depression or some nervous disorder brought on by the rigors of a revolutionary life. In any event, Mao was lonely and had already had a brief flirtation with a beautiful actress and interpreter. (It should be noted here that Mao married his first wife through a traditional, arranged match and never lived with her. His second wife, who bore him three sons, was beheaded by a Nationalist warlord in 1930.)

According to some, Jiang Qing made a calculated effort to attract the Chairman's interest. Before long the two had struck up a relationship, and she announced to his disapproving colleagues, "I have good news to report to you. The Chairman and I have started living together." [19] She had other news as well; she was pregnant (with a baby girl, as it turned out). With the reluctant consent of his colleagues, Mao married the young actress and gave her the name by which she is known to history (she had been using her stage name, Lan Ping). Through the anti-Japanese war and the civil war years she may have served to some extent as a personal secretary to Mao, especially in regard to artistic and literary affairs, her chief area of interest. She worked in the film section of the Party's Propaganda Department and began a long-term interest in reforming traditional theater.

As will be seen, Jiang Qing has not fared well in the public's esteem. She has become a prototype of the domineering, vain woman. A fair assessment of her life suggests that her sometimes abrasive personality did alienate people, eventually even Mao himself. On the other hand, it must be noted that she was probably forced to be pushy—or at least to seem pushy—by a culture that, even among supposedly liberated revolutionaries, discouraged independence and leadership in women.

## Was China Ripe for Revolution?

As we look back at the events of the first half of the century, it all seems so inevitable: a fragmented, impoverished country buffeted by foreign exploitation and aggression; the collapse of the old dynasty followed by a succession of equally ineffectual regimes; the failure of a middle- and upper-class party (the KMT) to unite and reorganize the nation in the 1930s; the steady expansion of popular political participation, gradually even including the peasantry; the emergence of a radical, populist movement (the CCP); the triumph of the Communists based on mass peasant support. It is hard now to imagine another outcome.

### Marxism

Was it all so foreordained? In particular, did China's poverty and unequal distribution of income create such a tinderbox of social discontent that the fires of revolution were bound to be ignited? This is one of those questions that it is important to ask—

and impossible to answer fully. One place to start is to ask about the significance of peasant poverty during the time of Mao's youth. Was the rural community so riven with class tensions that revolution was the necessary and inevitable solution to China's agrarian problems? For their part, Marxists have a ready answer to this question, and it deserves our attention because Marxists ultimately won out in the struggle for leadership.

Marxism rests on certain views about the forces really at work as any society changes over time. Karl Marx, living in an age that prized scientific, materialistic explanations, developed the idea that the nature of a society is determined by its technological or economic base (he called it the "mode of production"). The mode of production gives rise to certain "relations of production," that is, to a certain division of labor and a certain class system, for some people will own or control the technology while others will possess only their own labor power. As Marx put it, "The windmill gives you society with the feudal lord; the steam-mill, society with the industrial capitalist."[20]

As the mode of production gives rise to the relations of production, the ruling class (the ones who own the windmills or the steam-mills) will create law, politics, religion, philosophy, and artistic culture. Marx called these intangible phenomena the "superstructure," by analogy with the upper part of a ship, and he insisted that the superstructure is created by the ruling class in order to bolster its social dominance. Just as a ship's hull, not its superstructure, is its base, so a society's material base, not its high culture, is the fundamental determinant of the social structure. (It must be noted, however, that Marx and Engels realized that this matter is complicated and that sometimes the superstructure—especially politics—can affect the base.)

With time, the material base changes, owing to technological improvements. Such change, when great enough, creates a new division of labor, and new classes come into being, again comprising those who own the new means of production and those who provide labor. Also a new "superstructure" begins to emerge. But the old superstructure and the old ruling classes do not simply slink away. In fact, the old establishment resists change. What then emerges is a tension or, as Marxists say, a "contradiction," between the old class system and its superstructure on the one hand and the new system and its supporting culture on the other.

Marx saw the complex adjustments between the changing mode of production, relations of production, and superstructure as the engines of history. History is essentially humankind's progress through successive stages as one mode of production is displaced by another. He further felt that the transition from one type of society into another cannot be a smooth evolutionary process. The old guard defends its position, the new elite struggles for dominance, and the resulting "contradiction" is resolved by revolutionary upheaval.

How would a Marxist, using these concepts, describe the rural China of Mao's youth? The mode of production being peasant agriculture, the relations of production are primarily those between "feudal" ruling landowning classes and those who possess only their own labor, the peasants. The superstructure consists of traditional "feudal" authoritarian government and culture. Here is a more detailed description.

> The mode of production of late feudal China was one of land relationships in which state officials and their assistants, landlords, merchants, and moneylenders controlled the means of production, namely land. . . . The mass of poor farmers, artisans, and laborers claimed [only small scattered plots] and depended on their labor to earn a living. The powerful, wealthy feudal class extracted chiefly rent and taxes from the masses. . . . The surplus squeezed out of this economy by the feudal classes was expended partially for luxury consumption, but chiefly for supporting inefficient state organizations, the bureaucracy, and the military.[21]

Some groups, especially middling and wealthier peasants, seem to be in-between classes. But to the extent that they own land or expect to get some, they tend to side with the "feudal" establishment. In this view, the ills of the countryside at the turn of the century grew out of inequality and exploitation. Only redistribution of land and a new ruling class could solve the problem.

To return to Marx, his central purpose was not to expound on feudalism, but to analyze capitalism and to point the way to communism, the final phase of history. He saw that in the eighteenth and and nineteenth centuries a new mode of production had come into existence with the Industrial Revolution. The owners of the new industrial technology were the urban commercial and manufacturing classes. In terms of the relations of production, these are known as the capitalists. Socially they are also referred to as the bourgeoisie. They had sponsored a revolution that overthrew feudalism.

Capitalism is a new kind of exploitation. The value of manufactured products is created by laborers using the capitalists' machines. Out of the owners' receipts from sales of the product, the workers, who are referred to as the "proletariat," are paid just enough to survive. Competition drives the capitalists to appropriate the rest as profits and to reinvest these profits in still more capital. The internal dynamics of the capitalist system necessarily lead to the emergence of a few great capitalists and a wretched class of proletarians.

As the capitalists get richer and fewer and as the workers increase in number, a new historical stage is about to be born. Conditions emerge that will generate a new class of owners, the workers themselves. One day the crisis will erupt. The moment will come when "twenty years will be concentrated into a single day." The workers, made conscious of their plight and its causes, will make a revolution, dispossess the capitalists, take over the factories, and usher in a new final phase of history—communism. In this phase, exploitation is impossible because the workers themselves communally own the means of production.

What did all this have to do with China? By the World War I era, China's briskly expanding factories, mines, and railroads still constituted only the merest beginnings of industrialization. There were barely 2 million industrial workers in the entire population of hundreds of millions of people. Marx's vision of a few great capitalists exploiting a vast proletariat simply didn't fit. This is why Marxism failed to penetrate China before the war.

Marxist theory, however, was further developed by Lenin's concept of "imperialism." As Lenin guided the Russian Bolsheviks during the first quarter of the century, his theory made Marxism more applicable to backward countries like China. The new idea was essentially this: In a world where countries industrialize at varying rates, there will be some advanced and some backward peoples. The advanced nations are precisely those where the swollen proletariat is preparing to expropriate the capitalists. Faced with revolution, the latter stumble on a means of postponing their ruination.

Rather than continue plowing back all their profits domestically, they invest in the backward countries. Profits from overseas can be brought home. Some of these moneys may then be distributed as higher wages to a portion of the domestic proletariat, who will thereby be "bribed" into complacency. As a result, the revolutionary fever at home subsides. To save their necks, the capitalists have learned to exploit other nations, thereby transforming entire peoples into their proletariat.

Imperialism may be the shield that saves the capitalists, but it is also their Achilles' heel. If their colonies can drive them out, they will be unable to bribe the proletariat at home. With only their own fellow citizens to exploit, revolution will engulf them. The implication of this view is that the advanced countries are no longer the center of world history. The exploited backward countries have moved into the limelight. By defeating imperialism, they will bring on world revolution.

In China a century of bitter experience taught that the country was in the grip of some new force that the old traditions could not combat. In the beginning it was trade and missionary work carried on in the treaty ports. Then, after 1895, came ever larger investments in mills, mines, and railroads centering again on the treaty ports. Always these intrusions were secured by Western guns and arrogance.

In Marxist terms, China was partly feudal, with its traditional agrarian system, and partly colonial, thanks to the imperialist intrusions. The "people" in this "semifeudal, semicolonial" society consisted primarily of two classes: workers and peasants. Their historical mission, in cooperation perhaps with other classes, was to eject the foreigners and overthrow the old despotism. The leading role must fall, of course, to the industrial proletariat.

If all this is so, then what should Chinese do who want to save their country? First the workers must be made conscious of their condition. They must be called to action, perhaps in cooperation with peasants. And who will raise the workers' consciousness and lead the charge against the warlords and feudal elites? Naturally, the party of the proletariat, the Communist party. To help save China, one must join the Party.

In addition to his theory of imperialism, Lenin also showed how to build a revolutionary party. He perfected the techniques of creating an organization fired with the proletarian cause and disciplined under a central leadership. Only such a powerful force would be equal to the task of battering down the walls of resistance that the exploiters had erected to defend their system.

Lenin's doctrine that the masses must be led by an elite of professional revolutionaries appealed to many young Chinese of Mao's generation. For many who burned inwardly because of foreign humiliation and Chinese retardation, for many who dreamed of becoming saviors of the nation, Marxism-Leninism provided not only an explanation but also a clearly defined role. Like a militant religion, it held out the prospect of salvation and summoned chosen soldiers to take up the bitter struggle. These true believers could be certain about the historical forces at work, the class struggle, and the final outcome.

## Others Views

The fact that the Communists won does not guarantee that their analysis of China's poverty and of their own success is correct.

Other explanations have been offered. China suffered from general destitution and needed economic growth as much or more than it needed social revolution. Reforms could have put the peasantry on the road to greater abundance. From this point of view, the problem was the KMT government's inability or unwillingness to undertake reforms, an undertaking that would have required fiscal health based on a moderate, fairly apportioned land tax collected by a legitimate authority. Land tenure practices needed to be changed to allow owners to profit from improvements. Technical assistance to provide better seeds, fertilizers, and pesticides, together with better transportation and communication and easier credit, would have greatly improved farmers' crops, costs, and markets. Of course, given the political disorder and foreign pressures, these measures are easier to prescribe than to carry out. But the thriving agriculture in Taiwan and southern Manchuria, both of which contemporaneously experienced such reforms under the Japanese, seems to support the view that economically that is what needed doing.[22]

Political revolution may not have been primarily a matter of class struggle. North China, for example, experienced some class antagonisms, but in the words of a recent study, "the relations between landlord and tenant did not constitute a major contradiction."[23] Rather, the Communists' success came from their ability to mobilize support for a range of local grievances such as taxation, political oppression, and local corruption. In addition, once the anti-Japanese struggle began, the Communists gained additional support through their leadership of partisan warfare against the foreign invaders and their collaborators.

# 2

# Revolutionaries Seize Power: 1949–52

By late 1949 the Communist movement was riding a wave of success. Chiang Kai-shek and other domestic enemies reeled backward in disarray, yielding up city after city, finding no refuge. Meanwhile, boatload after boatload of foreign businesspeople, missionaries, and the rest of the treaty port communities set sail from Shanghai and other ports. For the first time in more than half a century, China was about to be ruled by a single, legitimate authority unhampered by foreign domination. As Mao proudly proclaimed, China "will no longer be a nation subject to insult and humiliation. We have stood up."[1]

There was still an enormous agenda. Control over the entire nation, from Tibet to Taiwan, had to be consolidated, and China's position in the international community had to be defined. After years of upheaval it would be necessary to return life to normal, decide policies toward social groups such as landlords and capitalists, and begin to establish new institutions of government. A start would have to be made on economic development. As these daunting tasks got under way, there would be some unwelcome surprises and interruptions.

## Establishing Sovereignty

*Military Victory*

In terms of population distribution and ethnic composition, China consists of two parts: a heartland and a great arc of large, sparsely settled border regions to the west and north. The heartland is based on the nine regions discussed in Chapter 1, and contains well over 90 percent of the population. The inhabitants are virtually all "Han," that is, people who speak Chinese dialects. Completing the conquest of this heartland was relatively uncomplicated for the Communists.

The peripheral regions are sparsely inhabited by ethnic minorities, supported primarily by pastoral economies. Their political ties to China had resulted from Qing dynasty conquests and had weakened from the time that the old regime collapsed. Tibet, vast and mountainous, is a strategically important buffer between China and India, whose people speak their own tongue. For centuries they been ruled by a Tantric Buddhist theocracy. A second region, Xinjiang (pronounced "Sin-jeeyang"), lies in the northwest. Its inhabitants include Turkic- and Mongol-speaking minorities of Islamic religion. Bordering on the Soviet Union, Xinjiang, too, has strategic importance and also contains rich mineral resources. The third region is Inner Mongolia, a 1,500-mile-long sweep of desert, steppe, and hills lying north of the Great Wall. It, too, has strategic importance for Manchuria, China's industrial heartland to the northeast.

By late 1950, Chinese armies penetrated Tibet, Xinjiang, and Inner Mongolia. Once again Tibetans, Uighurs, Kirghiz, Kazakhs, and Mongols found themselves subjects of Beijing. It was an uneasy conquest, one that required the development of a complex carrot-and-stick policy of control. Even then, naked force was occasionally needed in the years that followed. On the other hand, Outer Mongolia, situated north of Inner Mongolia and now known as the Mongolian People's Republic, was not recoverable. Once a part of the Qing Empire, it had declared its autonomy in 1911 and since 1924 has been the Soviet Republic of Mongolia, a satellite of Moscow.

To the east lay Taiwan and small coastal islands, particularly Jinmen and Mazu (frequently referred to as Quemoy and Matsu). Here the impediment was Chiang Kai-shek, whose forces had yet to be dislodged. Taiwan's importance extended beyond the Communists' desire to claim the entire country. The hostile Nationalist regime challenged the CCP's legitimacy. It constantly proclaimed its intention to retake the mainland and supported various forms of penetration and harassment. Nationalist planes even bombed some cities in early 1950. Conquest of these islands promised to be difficult, but Beijing intended to attempt it. Hainan Island in the extreme south was liberated in the spring of 1950, raising hopes for an early liberation of the others.

## Leaning to One Side

A second important aspect of establishing the new regime's sovereignty was defining China's relationship to the rest of the world. Close ties with the Soviet Union were inevitable, given historical and ideological connections. Relations with the "imperialist" powers were more problematic and sparked debates. Economics was at the heart of the issue. After initial reconstruction, the People's Republic would need to expand its productive capacity. National power, popular support, and desired social policies all depended on this. Yet undeveloped countries like China require technological and financial aid to achieve rapid growth. Who would help?

The list of candidates was not long. The nation most capable of providing assistance was the world's economic colossus, the United States. The Marshall Plan in Europe and past American help for China suggested that this was a serious possibility. Zhou Enlai seems to have led a school of thought that wanted to explore it. In May 1949 he sent a startling communication to Colonel David Barrett, an American military attaché. He said that a split existed within the Communist leadership. His faction, which was opposed by Liu Shaoqi's group, wanted to mediate between the USSR and the United States and desired to talk about American economic assistance.[2] At almost the same time Chen Yi, whose troops had just taken Shanghai, was soliciting U.S. and British economic assistance.

Chinese-American relations had not gone completely sour, so there might be reason to suppose normalization possible. At the war's end both Mao and Zhou had offered to go to Washington to discuss relations. In 1946, General George Marshall had attempted to mediate between the Communists and the Nationalists. In Nanjing, as the 1949 victories unfolded, Ambassador John Leighton Stuart demonstrated a willingness to go up to Beijing to initiate a dialogue.

On the other side, Sino-Soviet relations were not as warm as many thought. There was some rancor against Stalin, who had not always acted generously or wisely toward the CCP. His early China strategy led the Chinese Communists to near annihilation at the hands of Chiang Kai-shek in 1927. More recently, Stalin had sometimes acted like an imperialist, as, for example, in the 1945 Yalta Agreement with Roosevelt and Churchill, at which he received privileges in China for entering the war against Japan. The Soviets then plundered factories in Manchuria as war booty. Then Stalin held back full support during the civil war, maintaining relations with the Nationalists until the very end (the Soviet ambassador, still wangling for concessions, was the last to abandon Chiang's government in 1949). He tried to stop Communist advances north of the Yangtze, apparently preferring to have a weak and divided China for a neighbor. There was also Stalin's condescension toward the Chinese Communists. "Cabbage communists," "radish communists," "margarine communists," he called them.[3] Later Mao said that

the Chinese revolution won victory by acting contrary to Stalin's will. . . . If we had followed . . . Stalin's methods the Chinese

Revolution couldn't have succeeded. When our revolution succeeded, Stalin said it was a fake . . .[4]

Mao further claimed that only China's entry into the Korean War,
by buffering Moscow against a direct U.S. confrontation, legit-
imized the PRC in Stalin's eyes.[5]

Still, China faced an American military threat and desired
protection in order to begin demobilizing her huge armies and
getting on with national development. This was probably the de-
termining factor in China's decisive swing into the Soviet camp.
As the Communists conquered China, Washington took steps to
build a ring of containment in the Pacific. The motivation was
the familiar domino theory, always much in favor on the banks
of the Potomac.

> The extension of communist authority in China represents a
> grievous political defeat for us. . . . If Southeast Asia is also swept
> by communism, we shall have suffered a major political rout the
> repercussions of which will be felt throughout the rest of the world,
> especially in the Middle East and in a then critically exposed
> Australia.[6]

American military assistance for South Korea, Japan, Okinawa,
Taiwan, the Philippines, and Vietnam completed a ring around
the People's Republic. Despite Mao's thesis that imperialistic
atomic weapons were "paper tigers" to be respected tactically
but despised strategically, China needed a powerful protector.

Events in 1948 and 1949 caused Mao to agree with Liu Shaoqi's hard-liners and align China strongly with the USSR. The
United States contributed to the mutual alienation in various ways.
For example, Washington refused to release the new Chinese
government from preexisting treaty obligations. There were a
series of incidents. American journalists in Beijing were smeared
in the official press and, in effect, prevented from reporting. The
U.S. consul-general in Manchuria and his staff were held hos-
tage for nearly a year on an allegation of spying, jailed for a

month, and then expelled from the country. There were other incidents as well. The Korean War only put the final touches on this well-developed mutual antagonism. Two months after proclaiming the establishment of the new government, Mao paid his first visit to Stalin.

## Installing the New Order

As the new leaders extended their domestic sway and defined their international position, many problems required immediate attention. The country suffered from chaos and a vast array of social ills. The new regime had to establish its governmental institutions: chains of command, specialized bureaucratic systems, rules, and routines. In all these endeavors the Communists registered great success.

### Restoring Normalcy

Inheriting a desperate situation, the new regime rapidly got things under control and put the country on an orderly footing for the first time in decades. Twelve years of war and civil war had produced hyperinflation, stagnation in agriculture and industry, a crippled transportation system, flight of capital and managerial talent, massive unemployment and underemployment, refugees and demobilized Nationalist soldiers, hunger and malnutrition, social dislocation and festering evils of every sort, including opium addiction, prostitution, gambling, criminality, and female infanticide.

The new rulers moved quickly. Many of their measures were attempts to improve economic conditions, and here both Zhou Enlai and Chen Yun played important roles. Chen got inflation under control by a combination of austerity measures, balanced budgets, currency reform, and price controls. By expropriating major industries and the banks, Beijing achieved control over the urban sector. Former capitalists and managers were induced to help get industry and commerce back into operation. Railways and roads were restored and expanded. Thousands of overseas Chinese returned to the motherland to help build the nation.

Virtually the entire remaining foreign community was summarily ejected; and its property, confiscated. For many Chinese this must have been a sweet revenge after a century of imperialism. An assault was launched on criminal gangs, opium use, and prostitution. The educational system was reorganized and expanded. Old, "feudal" social patterns and values came under attack, including the patriarchal clan, female subjugation, and infant marriages.

## The Party

Drawing on Soviet models and twenty years of revolutionary experience, the new leaders built their regime around the Party. What follows is a brief description of the CCP's organizational structure (see Fig. 3). Speaking formally, the entity that defines and determines all structures is the Party Congress. This is a gathering of delegates representing the entire membership. But it meets too irregularly to function as an active component of government. There was a Party Congress in 1945, the seventh since the founding congress of 1921. The next one after liberation did not occur until 1956. This one held a "second session" two years later. The ninth through the fourteenth congresses were held in 1969, 1973, 1977, 1982, 1987, and 1992.

The Party Congress elects a Central Committee, containing from 100 to 300 regular and alternate members. The Seventh Central Committee, named in 1945, had 77 members and alternates. The Eighth Central Committee, elected in 1956, grew to 170 members; the Ninth, in 1969, to 279. The Central Committee convenes much oftener than Party Congresses and consequently constitutes a more active participant in policy-making. Its meetings, which often include outside officials and experts,

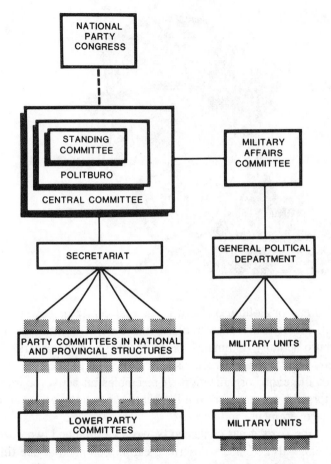

FIG. 3 Chinese Communist party structure (simplified).

are called "plenary sessions" or "plenums." Thus, the "Second Plenum of the Eighth Central Committee" refers to the second full meeting of the Central Committee elected by the Eighth Party Congress. Key turning points have frequently occurred as a result of decisions taken at these plenums.

The Central Committee is too large and meets too irregularly to direct day-to-day Party affairs. Consequently it elects a Polit-

MAO ZEDONG

ical Bureau or Politburo. Here is the real center of power. Although theoretically answerable to the Central Committee, the Politburo actually dominates the Party. It issues the orders, decisions, regulations, instructions, circulars, and notifications that govern the entire organization. It resembles an active board of directors whose members hold executive positions as heads of Party, government, and army.

Over the years it has contained between a dozen and two dozen members. All the leaders described earlier belonged at one time or another although some subsequently lost their positions. In 1949, besides Mao, there were eleven members, including Liu Shaoqi, Zhu De, Zhou Enlai, and Chen Yun. In the mid-1950s, Peng Dehuai, Lin Biao, Deng Xiaoping, and Chen Yi were added. Still later (in 1969), Chen Boda went on as Peng, Chen Yun, Liu, Deng, and Chen Yi were off. One constant was Chairman Mao. The Politburo was an extremely important vehicle for the exercise of power, and he insisted that all its documents cross his desk.

Even within the Politburo there are levels of authority. The highest possible power and prestige is vested in the Standing Committee of the Politburo (although this particular name did not come into use until 1956). This handful exercised a general oversight over central Party affairs whereas the other Politburo members had more limited, specialized responsibilities. The Standing Committee probably also had the power to act in place of the Politburo. In the 1950s it consisted of Mao, Liu, Zhu, Zhou, Chen Yun, and later Lin and Deng.

Because the Party controlled the state structure through its own hierarchy, certain other organs were very important, especially the Secretariat. This office communicated with and supervised all lower echelon Party committees. The director of the Secretariat was in a position to wield great influence and build up a constituency among lower Party leaders. In the early 1950s, Deng Xiaoping was appointed to this office.

There were other important bodies as well. Nearly as powerful as the Secretariat was the Control Committee. It exercised a police function within the Party, constantly monitoring the members and expelling those who failed to measure up. Repeatedly, the Party launched "rectification" movements to purify its membership and expel corrupt, lazy, or otherwise unsatisfactory cadres. There were also a handful of important Party departments, headquartered at Beijing, for rural work, propaganda, and other affairs. In addition, there were more than a dozen work departments and subordinate offices in charge of such activities as youth organizations, women's organizations, education, and health.

## Party Center and Party Cadres

The Party center in Beijing might be likened to the head, a relatively small nerve center that gathers information and issues signals for action. The vast body of the Party was to be found in the provinces, connected to the head through a hierarchical structure. This hierarchy ran down from the center, through six regional and twenty-nine provincial committees, to about 2,500 city and county committees that supervised the Party committees in individual units.

Most members were not on the Party payroll; they were primarily leaders in factories, stores, schools, military units, and agricultural units, government offices, and mass organizations. They constituted the "Party fraction" within the leadership group in all units. They carried the dual burden of their specific jobs and Party work. The term *cadre* is frequently used to refer to persons in positions of authority whether or not they belong to the Party. Through this dovetailing of Party and other social institutions, the CCP achieved unprecedented control over China's political, economic, and cultural life. Every citizen belonged to at least one unit, if only to a street committee, and usually to several, most importantly the work unit. As each unit required a Party fraction, it was necessary to recruit millions of members. Party rolls grew from around 4.5 million in 1949 to about 10 million in 1955. China's population at that time was approaching 600 million, so that the Party made up between 2 and 3 percent of the people.

The Party member was part of China's new ruling elite. Despite the Yanan traditions of frugality and mass line, he or she enjoyed many privileges. These included career mobility, material benefits, access to education, and protection against police power. As the system jealously guarded and controlled information, the Party member also had access to privileged material, depending on his or her level in the hierarchy. But there was a price. The person who joined the CCP (which he or she could be invited to do only after demonstrating activism, as in the Communist Youth League) was expected to work tirelessly for the Party. Political study, meetings, criticism, and self-criticism were permanent features of Party life. Important campaigns frequently required extra effort. If a campaign should fail, the rank and file usually took much of the blame for having failed to carry out directives well.

The historian James Harrison characterizes this massive organization with its "techniques of self-criticism and endless meetings and discussions. Until the disruptions of the Cultural Revolution [in the late 1960s and early 1970s], China was among the most internally secure states in history. Police in the usual sense were hardly necessary, as all activists were policemen, monitoring themselves, their neighbors, and even their thoughts."[7]

Clearly, this party-dominated system departed radically from the principles of Western liberal democracy. Where was the separation of powers? What corresponded to the executive branch? The legislative branch? The judicial branch? What justification could there be for a polity in which every act of government comes under the Party's authority? The answer to these questions must be drawn from Marxist theory. The class destined to lead the way toward a classless utopia is the proletariat. The CCP is the party of this proletariat. However the present era is transitional in that the vestiges of feudalism and imperialism still survive, particularly in the form of certain classes. As Mao put it, the revolution was not in a "proletarian-socialist" phase, but rather in a "bourgeois-democratic" phase. But by "democratic," he did not mean the "old" democracy. This was a "new democratic revolution" in which the proletariat and its party, the CCP, joined with other classes (the peasantry, the petty bourgeoisie, and the "national" bourgeoisie) to shepherd the country through the transition. With the proletariat in control, this "new democratic" coalition justly exercised a dictatorship over reactionary classes and other bad elements.

## The State Bureaucracy

As one writer says, "All government organizations in Communist China . . . function under very close Party direction; in fact they operate essentially as administrative agencies performing assigned tasks on behalf of the Communist Party."[8] The Party hierarchy was distinguished from the government organs through which it worked its will. It required ministries, agencies, and organizations to manage and tax agriculture, manufacture goods, transport, communicate, educate, entertain, and carry out all the other activities necessary to a national system. In the relationship between the two, the Party always asserted overriding authority.

In 1949 the new rulers discovered a diverse collection of leftover bureaus and organizations that they needed in the short run to keep the system functioning. Despite the authoritarian and centralized character of the CCP, it was very important for the new rulers to build their state through willing cooperation rather than coercion. They knew that much of the country's expertise belonged to non-Communists. Consequently, they took pains to pay at least verbal allegiance to "new democratic," cooperative methods. Of course, in the long run, they intended to create their own government institutions staffed by their own personnel.

In September 1949 the Chinese People's Political Consultative Conference (CPPCC) was convened. This assembly contained members from many non-Communist parties and groups although its deliberations were dominated by the Communists. The CPPCC proclaimed the establishment of the People's Republic. It elected a National Committee to function continuously and named Mao Zedong formal head of state. The CPPCC also selected a Central People's Government Council as a kind of legislature for the development of government decisions. This temporary body actively deliberated on and issued all the major legislation of the early 1950s.

Under the Central People's Government Council in a formal sense, but even more powerful in reality, was the State Council, a sort of cabinet that presided directly over the central government ministries. At the head of the State Council stood the premier, Zhou Enlai. He was concurrently head of the Foreign Ministry. At the same time he was a member of the Party's Politburo and of its Standing Committee. Other leaders we have met held major posts in the government. Peng Dehuai became minister of defense until 1959, when Lin Biao succeeded him; Chen Yun was named chairperson of the Finance and Economics Committee, which oversaw several economics ministries; and

Chen Yi took over the Foreign Ministry from Zhou in 1958. Like Zhou, they all held top posts in the Party hierarchy as well.

In 1954 a permanent government was established through the promulgation of a constitution. Elections were held to choose the 1,141 deputies to the First National People's Congress (NPC), which gathered in Beijing in September. They had been chosen through a multitiered process that began with 200,000 basic-level assemblies elected by some 275 million voters. These assemblies elected delegates to county assemblies, which, in turn, sent delegates to provincial and municipal assemblies, which elected the National People's Congress or NPC. The NPC and its Standing Committee then became the formal source of state authority and selected the head of state (Mao) as well as the premier and vice-premiers of the State Council.

Interestingly, the new system provided for other deliberative bodies in addition to the NPC. The National People's Congress itself was supposed to meet every year and be represented when not in session by its Standing Committee. It was the NPC that elected Mao president of the People's Republic, who in turn appointed Zhou premier of the State Council. Then the Chinese People's Political Consultative Conference continued to exist, no doubt because the presence of many non-Communist members made it a kind of united front organization, useful for co-opting prestigious individuals who were not members of the Party. Many CPPCC delegates were also NPC deputies, and the two bodies typically convened at the same time. Finally, the new constitution defined a Supreme State Conference, made up of eminent persons, which the president of the Republic could convene to consider issues and and make recommendations.

Despite this proliferation of assemblies, none exercised any real authority. As Mao put it, "Our constitution is of a new socialist type, different from any of the bourgeois type . . ."[9] This meant that the Party, rather than the electorate, was the ultimate authority for the "people's democratic dictatorship led by the proletariat and based on the worker-peasant alliance."[10] These bodies basically served to formalize, announce, and promote

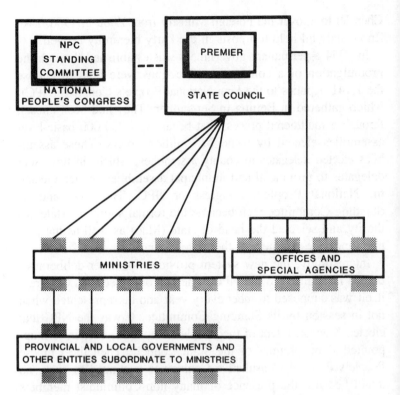

FIG. 4 Government of the People's Republic of China (simplified).

policies decided on by the Politburo or, in some cases, by Mao himself. Subordinate to the ministries and bureaus in Beijing were the provincial governments. The provinces supervised municipal and county governments. These provincial and local governments, together with other bureaus reporting to the capital, administered the farms, factories, and other parts of the economic system (see Fig. 4).

## The Military

The People's Liberation Army was established as the third major hierarchy. In its general structure it resembled the armed forces of other countries, with a ministry of defense, a general staff, and separate service arms. The Chinese followed their established practice of adding to this a strong element of Party control. To assure this control, the CCP had always maintained a Party-army linkage. Every military unit had its Party committee. The commander in chief, the chief of staff, the minister of defense, and all leading officers also occupied high Party positions. Subordinate to the Politburo was the important Military Affairs Committee, which set general defense policies and, through its General Political Department, supervised Party committees in all army units.

## The Korean War

In a speech to the Central Committee, on June 6, 1950, Mao declared, "The present international situation is favorable to us." He enumerated some of the tasks ahead: land reform, centralization of the economy, demobilization of troops, educational reform, unemployment relief, cooperation with non-Communist groups, weeding out counterrevolutionaries, and expanding and consolidating the Party.[11] Although the Communist leaders probably knew that a North Korean initiative against the south was coming, more war was the last thing they wanted or expected.

On June 25 conflict did break out between North Korea and South Korea when troops from the north poured across the 38th parallel. Just who was responsible for starting it has been much debated. The Russians may have encouraged North Korea. Secretary of State Acheson's earlier statement that Washington did not consider Korea and Taiwan to lie within the U.S. "defensive perimeter" may have invited adventurism, and South Korean provocations may have played a role. Clearly, however, the Chinese were merely bystanders.

When the conflict started, Beijing gave vocal encouragement to North Korea but seemed to have no plans for direct involvement. Pyongyang's forces were doing well enough by themselves, having pushed the South Koreans and Americans back to Pusan in the southeast corner of the peninsula. In any case, China's concern was Taiwan. Two days after the invasion, President Truman ordered the Seventh Fleet to prevent attacks in either direction across the straits separating Taiwan from the mainland. This frustrated Communist plans to recover the island. Beijing also noted other signs of U.S.-Nationalist cooperation, in particular a visit to Taiwan by General Douglas MacArthur, commander of the UN forces.

The situation changed in the fall as MacArthur's counterattacks drove the North Koreans back to Seoul, then Pyongyang, and finally pell-mell toward the Manchurian border. The Chinese leaders had to decide whether to intervene. Some, like Chen Yun, urged caution. He called attention to the impact on economic modernization, pointing out that initial calculations for a five-year plan would have to be scrapped. Some generals worried that involvement would absorb energies required for the liberation of Taiwan. Stalin was against Chinese entry at that time. Probably a majority of the leadership favored restraint, and it was Mao, Zhu De, and Peng Dehuai who forced the decision to commit troops.

The Chinese did not enter the war before making repeated attempts to convince Washington that they could not tolerate a Korea dominated by the United States because that would threaten Manchuria. On September 30, Zhou Enlai warned

> The Chinese people absolutely will not tolerate foreign aggression, nor will they supinely tolerate seeing their neighbors invaded by imperialists.[12]

Numerous other appeals, the massing of Chinese troops north of the Yalu River separating Manchuria from Korea, and even some firefights between Chinese and UN units failed to impress the more hawkish American leaders, especially General MacArthur, that Beijing would enter the war. Finally on October 8, in the teeth of Acheson's ominous warning that China would be risking a "tragedy of the most colossal nature"[13] and after pacing three sleepless days and nights, Mao issued the secret order. Chinese "volunteers" crossed the Yalu, as he put it, "to resist the attacks of U.S. imperialism and its running dogs."[14]

The intervention opened with a sensational Chinese success as 200,000 troops smashed the center of the UN line. MacArthur, who had engineered the brilliant Inchon landing just months earlier, now found himself in headlong retreat, complaining that China had committed "one of the most offensive acts of international lawlessness of historic record."[15] By January 1951, the front had swept back south of the 38th parallel. UN forces regrouped and counterattacked, restoring the front to approximately the 38th parallel. A cease-fire was agreed on in July 1951, but two years and 575 acrimonious meetings at Panmunjom would pass before an armistice was signed.

The war cost China dearly. According to American figures, the relatively lightly armed Chinese sustained a total of 900,000 killed, wounded, or missing. Economic reconstruction was set back. Hopes for the early recovery of Taiwan were ruined. A U.S-Taiwan alliance was forged that endured into the 1970s and beyond. The United States blocked Chinese admission to the United Nations until 1971. An American embargo further added to Beijing's isolation from the non-Communist world and its dependence on the USSR.

The war brought benefits, too, not the least of which was a boost to the country's self-esteem. The world had witnessed that Chinese soldiers with mortars could match, blow for blow, American heavy artillery. China had truly "stood up," and in the eyes of many citizens this further enhanced the Party's legitimacy. The war also seems finally to have won Stalin's respect. There were other gains as well. Aroused nationalism became an instrument for rooting out or silencing opponents of the regime. Land reform and other movements that had been proceeding with moderation suddenly intensified as the anticounterrevolutionary campaign was launched. Ironically, this hysteria was mirrored in America, although without the bloodshed, as

McCarthyism sought to hunt down the alleged traitors who had "lost" China.

## Campaigns

### Land Reform

Although the new rulers had to establish formal bureaucracies, as revolutionaries they favored mass upheavals where the people would come together in one voice to overthrow injustice. As Zhou Enlai expressed it in 1960

> The Party has always paid attention to combining its leadership with broad mass movements, guiding the masses to raise the level of their revolutionary consciousness constantly, and to organize their own strength to emancipate themselves step by step, instead of imposing revolution on the masses or bestowing victory on the masses as a favor.[16]

The techniques of organizing mass campaigns had been under development for many years and would continue to be used. At the time of liberation, the most important campaign was land reform. Moving from north to south between 1948 and 1952, it was one of the largest social upheavals in history. China's landlords were stripped of their wealth, and over one-third of the farmland changed hands.

To spearhead the movement, thousands of young volunteers trained to go to the villages as land reform teams. A team's first objective, on arrival in a given village, was to organize an Association of Poor and Middle Peasants. This would serve as the organizational base for the drama about to happen. The young activists explained the program to the peasants and learned which landlords or local toughs had been particularly oppressive. Mass meetings would be organized, featuring public denunciations of these bad elements. Peasants would gradually gather the courage to blurt out the humiliations and injustices they had suffered. The landlords' records would be examined for irregularities. All this would lead to the seizure and redistribution of their property and sometimes to their death. Although the land reform team generally orchestrated the events, the peasants' accumulated bitterness could not always be controlled.

Still, the number of executions is not thought to have been high through the middle of 1950, by which time about one-third of the peasantry, mostly in the north, had redistributed the land. Suddenly in late 1950 and in 1951, with the onset of the Korean War, the movement grew much bloodier. At this same time a fierce campaign against counterrevolutionaries was launched (see later). The toll of lives mounted as China began to taste true revolutionary terror. The total number of executions between 1949 and 1953 has been estimated at wildly different levels by various students of the subject. Many Western scholars have now accepted a range of between 2 and 5 million victims of all campaigns taken together.

Land reform changed the patterns of ownership and eliminated the landlords and rich peasant classes. In other respects, the villages remained little changed. The relationship between land and labor had not been fundamentally altered. Millions of households still worked their tiny scattered plots with hand tools. Although inequalities had been reduced, they had not been eliminated. Some peasant families remained richer than others, and some provinces and regions were relatively prosperous whereas others experienced endemic poverty. Even aspects of the old system reappeared as functions formerly performed by landlords, such as moneylending, were now done by rich peasants and even local cadres. This represented an incomplete solution to the problem. The leaders accepted it temporarily for the sake of production. But in the long run they intended to socialize agriculture like all other sectors. Mao said, ''Without socialization of agriculture, there can be no complete consolidated socialism.''[17]

## Resist America, Aid Korea

Once the decision to fight America had been made in October 1950, China's leaders lost no time in organizing the people behind the war effort. They launched a series of campaigns collectively referred to as "Resist America, Aid Korea." These campaigns continued from late 1950 until Mao declared "a great victory in the war to resist U.S. aggression and aid Korea" in September 1953.[18]

The goals of these campaigns were to explain the nature of the conflict, to suppress any lingering pro-American feelings, and to collect funds to support the "volunteers" at the front. This last objective was particularly important because Soviet assistance did not become significant until around 1951. The propaganda system generated indictments against the United States, particularly charges of "germ warfare." There were campaigns to "comfort the Korean People's Army and Chinese Volunteers," to gather peace signatures, to collect donations, to sell Victory Bonds, to sign "patriotic pacts" for increased production, to pay taxes, and even to sever the links between Chinese Christian churches and their Western counterparts. There were many local variants. For example, Beijing college students were organized to trek to surrounding villages to explain the campaigns to the peasants.

## Marriage Law

Women's liberation had long been promoted by the Communist movement and was particularly dear to Mao. So in May 1950 the new government enacted one of its first major pieces of legislation, the Marriage Law. It was decreed that henceforth a "New Democratic" form of marriage would prevail. Evil customs of the past, such as family marriage contracts against the individuals' consent, buying brides, polygamy, and child marriages were declared illegal. There were also important provisions relating to divorce. The principle of sexual equality was applied so that women could now apply for divorce under the same rules as men. They were no longer considered essentially chattels of the husband's family.

The Marriage Law did not automatically transform the status of women. Because traditional customs were deeply ingrained, it was necessary to publicize and promote the new regulations. Between 1950 and 1953 a series of national and local campaigns was launched for this purpose although in terms of intensity and expenditure these drives could not compare with the others discussed here. Traditional attitudes and practices survived, especially in the countryside. Indeed, the government proved to be unenthusiastic about free marriage and divorce. Some observers have felt that the primary intent was to weaken family and clan authority over the individual in order to facilitate totalitarian political control of every citizen. Nevertheless, after the new law was passed, the country witnessed a rash of divorces sought mainly by women. Gradually, new marriages and egalitarian values became more the norm, especially in the cities. As one writer recently put it, women in China have *risen* to second-class status.

## Oppose Counterrevolutionaries

When China entered Korea, fear of external enemies and internal subversion intensified.[19] This brought about a change in the relatively restrained social policies. Mao must have felt considerable urgency about this because the fifth volume of his Selected Works contains several directives admonishing cadres and the people to "strike surely, accurately and relentlessly" against internal enemies.[20] Starting in February 1951, the Suppression of Counterrevolutionaries campaign got under way. It was purely political in its objectives and explicitly sanctioned violence although who all the targets were is not entirely clear. Generally speaking, the campaign aimed at bad elements who could be shown to be criminals or actively hostile to the regime.

A wave of arrests and mass trials swept the country. Millions of people were required to attend tens of thousands of accusation meetings. In Shanghai over 2,000 committees for the suppression of state enemies were organized and within a single two-day period 10,000 people were arrested. Altogether 3,000 accusation meetings disposed of 40,000 cases. In Guangdong Province during a ten-month period nearly 90,000 were arrested, of which over 28,000 were executed. In the end, between a half million and a million executions took place throughout the country, prompting observers to describe 1951 as a reign of terror.

## Thought Reform

In December 1950 a privately produced film called *The Life of Wu Xun* (pronounced something like "Woo Shwun") premiered to favorable reviews. It told the story of a nineteenth-century philanthropist who rose from beggar to wealthy landlord. Wu Xun used his fortune to establish schools for the poor; he persuaded the imperial government to assist as well. His purpose was to give poor children a chance to rise through education. Suddenly, in the spring of 1951, this seemingly inoffensive and perhaps even touching film became the target of criticism from high places. The source of the criticism may well have been Jiang Qing, who had recently taken a position on the Film Steering Committee of the Ministry of Culture. She apparently converted Mao to her viewpoint. Before long newspapers were devoting as much as one quarter of their pages to denouncing the film. Wu Xun was unmasked as a wrongheaded, idealistic reformer who imagined that education and reform could save China. Marxism taught that only revolutionary class struggle could truly change society. Thus, the film violated proletarian thinking. There could be no defense of it as being apolitical. Filmmakers had no right to indulge in private expression. A person "is either progressive or reactionary--there is no third way."[21]

Soon many of the best-known writers were publishing confessions and self-criticisms, owning up to bourgeois thoughts, and thanking the Party for setting them straight. The filmmaker published his own confession in *People's Daily*. What was the meaning and purpose of this sudden campaign? The answer lies in the ambivalent attitudes of Mao and the Party toward intellectuals, a paradoxical mixture of hostility and support.

The hostility grew from the belief that the intelligentsia had sold out to the West. Many professors, writers, doctors, and scientists had studied abroad, assimilating foreign culture. The most famous one was Hu Shih (pronounced something like "Who Should" without the *d*). A philosopher and humanist, student of John Dewey, he believed in evolutionary social reform. The Communists saw this Western influence as "imperialist cultural aggression." Mao's feelings on this matter were unchanged since 1923, when he complained that "when one of our foreign masters farts, it's a lovely perfume." [22]

Another strike against the intellectuals was Mao's contempt for theoretical, ivory tower scholarship detached from the practice of revolution. For him "truth" meant applied truth.

We do not study Marxism-Leninism because it is pleasing to the eye, or because it has mystical value, like the doctrines of the Taoist priests. . . . Marxism has no beauty, nor has it any mystical value. It is only extremely useful. . . . Dogma is less useful than excrement . . . [23]

Like everyone else, intellectuals should roll up their sleeves and work for the revolution. They must not only work in their respective fields but also respond to the needs of the people and the Party. Mao wanted them to cultivate both "spontaneity" and "discipline." [24] Nothing irritated him more than intellectuals who carped from the sidelines. In one outburst against a well-known "democratic personage" in 1953, he sneered, "What service did you do . . . ? In all your life what service have you ever done to the people? Not the slightest, not the least bit." [25]

Third, many intellectuals had straddled the political fence. Although critical of the Nationalists, they also rejected communism. They longed for a middle path of liberal reform. The Communists, Mao in particular, derided such timidity. As he put it, where are you going to "set your buttocks"?[26] Finally, the Party disliked intellectuals because of their traditional prestige in Chinese culture. Like the landlords and the business leaders, they were potential rivals for social leadership. The CCP could tolerate no rival. To the degree that intellectuals were not thoroughly Chinese and obediently "proletarian," Mao and the Party found them wanting.

On the other hand, many of the top Communist leaders were themselves intellectuals. Mao had received a higher education and wrote poetry as well as revolutionary theory. The same was true of Peng Dehuai and others. Chen Boda had been a professor. Moreover, in the preliberation years, many intellectuals did, in fact, rally to the left. Novelists exposed social injustices, supporting the Marxist critique of feudal society. And although many upper-class people left for Hong Kong and Taiwan in 1949 and 1950, many others stayed or returned from overseas to join in the building of a new China.

The talents of the educated were critically important for modernization, particularly because there were so few of them. Some appreciation for this can be gained by noting that in the countryside about half the cadres were illiterate or had less than two years of schooling. The situation was nearly as bad in the cities. In the short run, the country had no choice but to depend on the Western-educated intelligentsia for educators, engineers, geologists, and doctors despite their political shortcomings. Therefore, they had to be won over to the revolution—if not as true believers, at least as fellow travelers.

By 1949 the CCP already had a history of transforming intellectuals. At the famous "Forum on Art and Culture" held at Yanan in 1942, Mao lectured the participants on their duty toward the revolution. Individual expression must serve collective liberation. Literature and art must contribute to the cause, criticize the old, and inspire the audience through portrayals of the new socialist person. Writers and artists must drop Western styles. They must speak to the masses—through native folk idiom where possible. Above all, they must follow the Party line. "The science of Marxism-Leninism is a required course for all revolutionaries, not excepting artists and writers." [27]

In 1949 efforts to remold intellectuals got under way. "Revolutionary universities" were established in many cities. They were institutions to provide crash courses in Marxism-Leninism and Mao Zedong Thought. The students were mostly new cadres, either in the Party or government administration. In the second half of 1950, there was also a campaign to reform all intellectuals.

Then in the spring of 1951, with the Korean War, thought control intensified. The Party launched the campaign to criticize the Wu Xun film. Newspapers began to carry a series of quotations from Mao's *Selected Works*, the first volume of which appeared in October. In late 1951 the press began attacks on Hu Shih, who had moved to Taiwan. Soon the entire educational system was subjected to an intensive thought control campaign that lasted through 1952.

Thought control was a sophisticated program. Intellectuals were summoned to take part in mass meetings. Then they were assigned to small groups that met day after day. They discussed Marxist readings and engaged in criticism of others and in self-criticism. Everyone wrote his or her autobiography and repeatedly reworked it as the sordidness of his or her former bourgeois existence revealed itself. One feature of the program was the denunciation of one's father and family. As one writer puts it, "He had to write and rewrite until he satisfied the thought reformers with the thoroughness and sincerity of his confession." [28] When this grueling and often traumatic process was complete, the students could post their confessions. Large accusation meetings would then be organized. It all resembled a giant, coerced program of religious conversion.

Not only academics in universities, but also teachers and educated people of all sorts were put through the program. In the end it tamed this group just as land reform had crushed the landlords. Unlike the campaigns against landlords and counterrevolutionaries, this movement was not an effort to eliminate a class. Imprisonment and execution were not part of it. The object was to achieve conformity and, if possible, conversion. Just as with intra-Party purges and class struggle in general, the Party conceived of thought reform as an ongoing and recurrent process. Indeed, there were further campaigns in 1953. But there were also periods of relaxation when those leaders prevailed who worried about the numbing effects of brainwashing. In any case, the goals of thought reform remained unrealized as the dramatic events of the "Hundred Flowers" episode in 1957 were to demonstrate.

## Oppose Bureaucracy

As the new rulers contrived to get the upper hand over landlords, counterrevolutionaries, and intellectuals, they scheduled two other groups for taming: deviant Party cadres and the business community. A pair of closely linked campaigns unfolded in the first half of 1952 to deal with these groups. The first one was called the "Oppose Bureaucracy" campaign. It was followed by a campaign to "Oppose Corruption" (see later).

A key ingredient in the Party's ability to mobilize people was the responsiveness of the the rank and file to the center. To ensure such responsiveness required monitoring of cadre performance and thought. In addition to routine measures such as regular study groups, personnel files, and yearly assessments, the Party launched recurring campaigns to weed out bad elements. The first major "rectification campaign" took place in the early 1940s. There was another in the years 1947–48 and yet another in 1950. In 1951 the leaders concluded that still a new rectification was needed. As one leader explained, there were three particular deficiencies that wanted correcting. Some cadres seemed to think that the revolution was over. They intended to relax rather than strive still harder for modernization, and they soft-pedaled "class struggle" now that the easy targets, the Japanese, landlords, and counterrevolutionaries, were eliminated. A second failing was "bourgeois individualism," which caused many cadres to concern themselves primarily with their personal careers. Third was the involvement of some cadres in business activities, both in the countryside and in the cities.

A major source of these problems was the rapid expansion of Party membership. Between 1945 and 1952, the rolls had doubled and redoubled to around 6 million. Some had joined less from idealism than to advance their personal fortunes and began to exploit their power and prestige. When rural cadres transferred from their villages to the cities, the temptations of urban life tended to corrupt them. There were also the cadres who ignored the approved leadership techniques. They committed "commandism" (ordering the people around) and "tailism" (doing what the people wanted), as well as "bureaucratism."

Consequently a "Three-Anti" campaign (anticorruption, antiwaste, and antibureaucratism) was launched. Party members studied prescribed documents, criticized their comrades, criticized themselves, and, in serious cases, went before mass "struggle" meetings where their failings were publicly exposed. Some severe punishments were meted out, especially for corruption, although most cases resulted in censure, demotion, or expulsion from the Party. By the summer of 1952 the campaign was terminated. About 10 percent of the membership had been expelled, resulting presumably in a tighter and more responsive organization.

## Oppose Corruption

Businesspeople were the urban counterparts of landlords. But unlike the landlords, they were not to be immediately expropriated. For the time being, their skills were necessary to maintain production, and they were encouraged to continue operations. This conformed to Mao's theory of the New Democracy. Liu

Shaoqi, for example, spoke to the businesspeople of Tianjin (Tientsin) in the spring of 1949. He encouraged them to cooperate with the Party, increase output, and struggle against imperialists and backward classes. He reassured them that the transition to socialism and the elimination of private enterprise would take a long time.

Nevertheless, after little more than a year the Party abruptly changed its policy. In many cases, it seems that business community in the cities was "corrupting" the political system by influencing the cadres. The Party leaders may have believed that the bourgeoisie was blocking their efforts to control the cities. Labor union organizing was hampered by the close ties between small employers and their workers, who were often relatives or from the same native place. There were also financial considerations. The 1951 national budget was out of balance, and the government wanted to reduce the deficit to avoid reigniting inflation. In a situation where every bit of revenue was important, the tax evasion that businesses practiced was a serious concern. A campaign against this group could generate large amounts of back taxes and fines for the treasury.

Consequently, in the first half of 1952, a campaign to "Oppose Corruption" was set in motion. (Specifically, it was called the "Five-Anti" campaign, in reference to its five targets: bribery, tax evasion, stealing state property, cheating on government contracts, and stealing government economic data.) Just as poor peasants had been organized against the landlords, the workers were mobilized in the name of class struggle and soon found themselves confronting their capitalist masters. Everything was organized and coordinated by a high Party committee in each city. Even squads of repentant businesspeople and their relatives were used to pressure other capitalists to cooperate. Inspection brigades combed over each firm's books. There were letters of denunciation, confrontation meetings between businessmen and their workers, and public confessions. The press, public blackboards, posters, loudspeakers, newspaper reading teams, demonstrations with banners and kettledrums all played their part in informing the public and increasing the level of excitement.

It was a trying half year for businesspeople. Some committed suicide. Most made confessions and payed fines, reparations, and back taxes. In the end, the private sector was transformed. The financial penalties weakened businesses to the point where they became dependent on the government for loans and other assistance. A huge windfall, amounting to as much as 1.7 billion U.S. dollars from 450,000 disciplined businesses, poured into the national treasury. The once confident and influential bourgeoisie, the "tigers" as they were called during the campaign, had lost their teeth and claws. They remained thereafter a grateful and compliant class. As one writer put it:

> The combination of economic hardship and psychological demoralization so weakened the bourgeoisie that the Party leadership was able to set up, or reinforce, a variety of economic, political, social, and ideological control mechanisms and prevent any resurgence of bourgeois power.[29]


## Disappointments, Ironies, and Contradictions

### The Sweet and the Bitter

It may be that these initial three years of its existence were the regime's most successful period. They brought order to a disintegrated nation, consolidated political control, realigned foreign relations, and fought a formidable foe to stalemate. For a rustic band of insurgents, these were no small accomplishments. Still, the new rulers tasted some bitter disappointments.

The Korean conflict introduced an enemy that could not be defeated by Yanan-type warfare. The People's Liberation Army had built its early success on small units that equipped themselves with captured weapons, used primitive communications, and prevailed despite little coordination between armies. In Korea the PLA confronted an enemy that enjoyed a great advantage in firepower. Against such a foe, the lightly equipped Chinese won victories only at a dreadful cost in terms of casualties. Initial hopes of clearing the Americans out of the peninsula were completely frustrated.

Moreover, this experience presented the PLA with a fundamental choice: It could nourish its hallowed guerrilla traditions, or it could try to become a technologically advanced, professional army. But it couldn't very well do both. The roles that Peng Dehuai and Lin Biao played in Korea seem to have determined their stand on this dilemma. Peng commanded the Chinese "volunteers." Having experienced advanced warfare firsthand, he undertook to build a modern army when he became defense minister after the war. Lin Biao, on the other hand, took no part in the action, probably because of ill health. He remained strongly committed to the Yanan style. And the day eventually came when he displaced Peng at the head of the PLA.

Taiwan too was deeply disappointing. Not only did the Communists fall short of recovering all national territory. But they also saw the Nationalist regime revive and lead a successful program of economic modernization, even including a successful land reform. The Nationalists loudly proclaimed their right to rule the mainland and occupied China's seat at the United Nations. Taiwan became Beijing's most constantly annoying foreign policy problem.

A third disappointment also came in an area where greater success had been anticipated. Early in 1950, Mao went to Moscow to meet Stalin and seek Soviet assistance. Stalin did not throw out a warm welcome mat, and he proved to be a tough negotiator. The Chinese did come away with a Treaty of Friendship, Alliance and Mutual Assistance. And they received long-term credits for economic development and other concessions. But the amounts were disappointing, and there were strings attached, such as Soviet participation in joint stock companies to exploit Chinese mineral wealth and continued Russian occupation of the naval base at Port Arthur. Although for the moment it looked as though the Sino-Soviet alliance would be strong and permanent, there were already indications, whose significance would only become apparent later, that the Chinese expected far more out of the relationship than the Russians were prepared to provide.

## Institutional Development Versus Revolutionary Transformation

Even as the new rulers successfully developed both political institutions and mass campaign techniques, they were creating a deep contradiction. It is simply this: Bureaucracy conflicts with mass mobilization. Regular, predictable hierarchies cannot easily coexist with irregular, unpredictable initiatives. A great modernized nation cannot at the same time continue to be a Yanan insurgency. It was a conflict between the head and the heart, between the rational requirements of national development and the emotional power of a revolutionary vision. Unfortunately, neither could be easily given over: institutionalization because there was no other way to run a country; revolutionary romanticism because that was the soul of the Chinese Communist movement and especially of its leader Mao Zedong.

In the early 1950s, however, this contradiction was not acute. Everything was in flux. So many urgent problems demanded attention that there was little time to consider whether important principles were being violated. The new regime was also understandably extremely optimistic. As Mao exclaimed in response to the possibility of an American economic blockade, "Let them blockade us! Let them blockade us for eight or ten years! By that time all of China's problems will have been solved."[30] So many insuperable difficulties had been overcome that there was no reason to suppose that institutional issues could not be ultimately worked out as well. Even in the mid-1950s, enthusiasm for building a mighty, Soviet-style socialist state obscured the contradiction lurking underneath.

In 1948 and 1949, the Communists organized victory parades in every city they captured. Possibly the largest took place in

Beijing in early February 1949. Thousands of students and workers, shouting slogans and dancing the popular peasant *yang ge* step, led a massive, hour-long parade of troops brandishing American and Japanese weapons. ''Enormously impressive,'' thought one American observer.[31] This parade suggested something about the future. On that day Beijing's first big dust storm of the year blew in. Banners and posters were buffeted by the wind until they hung in tatters. At times it was difficult to see across the street. The elements seemed to be reminding that victory celebrations would soon give way to coping with great storms and blinding difficulties.

# 3

# Socialist Transformation: 1953–57

The five years after initial consolidation were a period of successful institution building. It appeared that the new regime, however harsh toward its domestic enemies, had mapped out a clear direction, which it was following with determination and remarkable results. The 1954 state constitution defined a centralized administrative hierarchy. Industrialization, education, and public health all experienced dramatic improvements. But the clarity of direction was less sharp than it seemed. Achievements were offset by serious shortcomings. Debate flared on fundamental questions of policy. The struggle between the necessity of institution building and the cause of revolutionary transformation was not yet settled, particularly because the most formidable revolutionary of them all was determined to keep the flame burning.

Soviet influence dominated this period. In almost every sphere from governmental institutions to school curricula, from central economic planning to industrial management, from military uniforms to "wedding cake" architecture, the Chinese patterned their system on Russia's. Thousands of Russian advisers came to China, and thousands of Chinese went to study in the Soviet Union. Russian became the most popular foreign language as millions joined Sino-Soviet friendship associations. Little wonder, then, that the outside world perceived the People's Republic as another of Moscow's subservient satellites.

After Stalin died in 1953 and Nikita Khrushchev finally emerged as his successor, Sino-Soviet relations grew still closer. Khrushchev relinquished various concessions that Stalin had demanded. He negotiated more economic assistance. The new Soviet leader visited Beijing for talks with Mao on the occasion of the PRC's fifth anniversary in 1954. There were various other meetings where Chinese leaders flew to Moscow: Zhou in 1953, Liu in 1956, and both Zhou and Mao himself in 1957. Both sides frequently hailed their fraternal and indestructible relationship.

## The First Five-Year Plan

With inflation tamed and key components of the economic system either owned or controlled by the state, specialists in the State Council, under the leadership of Chen Yun, worked out China's first Five-Year Plan for 1953 through 1957. Even though the plan was still very sketchy at the time (it was not even published until 1955), true to its Soviet inspiration, it laid out ambitious goals: to double industrial production and raise agricultural production by one-fourth.

Such goals required funneling about 20 percent of the nation's income to investment, a large share for a poor country. The necessary revenues would come from taxes and profits from state-owned enterprises. In the allocation of investment funds, "heavy industry" (steel, machine tools, and other producer goods) got the largest share, which reflected the determination to industrialize along Soviet lines. Lower priority went to industries making "light" or consumer goods. Finally, a very small portion of state investment was to go to agriculture. In fact, the agricultural sector was to be the main source of investment funds, meaning essentially that the farmers would "pay" for industrialization through taxes, low state prices for their crops, and high prices for the manufactured goods they bought.

## Industrialization

Developing industries was not simply a matter of placing money into a magic box called "investment." The Chinese frequently lacked the expertise and equipment to design, build, and operate modern manufacturing plants. Consequently, they needed foreign experts, blueprints, machines, and materials. They needed credits in order to finance these purchases. The major source of both technology and aid was of course the Soviet Union. Agreements were negotiated in 1950 and again in 1953 and in the following years.

Soviet aid must be considered rather modest in view of China's great needs. The repayment terms were rather stringent. By 1955, China was already paying back to Moscow more than it was receiving in new credits. But China did benefit greatly from Russian technology. Moscow supplied the expertise to build 130 separate industrial projects by 1960. These enterprises constituted a very important contribution to China's modernization.

The result of these ambitious industrialization measures was a very rapid growth in heavy industry during the First Five-Year Plan. Consumer goods manufacturing also increased, but at a less rapid rate—a reflection of its lower priority.

## Agriculture

In farming, Beijing had less to learn from Moscow. Stalin's brutal method of socializing agriculture had had catastrophic results and stood out as a negative model. China's Marxists shared the goal of eliminating private ownership of land and other vestiges of capitalism. But they knew that this transformation would be protracted and would have to be managed carefully. During the land reform, from 1948 through 1952, Mao urged moderation in the name of production. Landlords and rich peasants could be expropriated, but not middle peasants.

With land reform complete, the new regime was prepared to begin the gradual introduction of peasant socialism. As Liu Shaoqi put it,

For three solid years . . . we applied ourselves to awakening the class consciousness of the peasants. . . . [Consequently] the peasant masses stood up on their own feet, got themselves organized, closely followed the lead of the Communist Party and the People's Government, and took the reins of government and the armed forces in the villages firmly into their hands. . . . Conditions were thus created which were favorable to the subsequent socialist transformation of agriculture . . .[1]

The plan was a gradual one. First the peasants would be organized into mutual aid teams, four to ten families sharing production tasks. As mutual aid teams spread, the grass-roots Party apparatus would be expanding and preparing the way for the next step toward socialism: "lower" Agricultural Producers' Cooperatives (APCs). The "lower" or "semisocialist" APCs would encompass a small village or section of a village (twenty to forty households). Its members would derive income both from their their work in the fields and according to the land and tools they had contributed. Gradually, the lower APCs were supposed to develop into "higher" APCs (one hundred to three hundred households). The members would pool all their resources and allocate the collective income solely on the basis of labor contributions.

This social transformation was expected to succeed because it would make the peasants better off. As Mao said,

Output must not remain at the individual peasant or mutual-aid team level, for that would mean failure; what point, then, in having co-operatives at all? Still less can yields be allowed to fall.[2]

The reason that output was expected to rise, despite the the Five Year Plan's modest allocation of investment to this sector, was that socialism would be inherently superior to individual farms. The innumerable tiny plots would be joined into more efficient fields. Labor, including that of women, would be pooled and organized more rationally. Work gangs could be mobilized to dig irrigation canals, plant trees, reclaim land, and accomplish other capital formation projects without state investment funds. Also, social services could be better performed by the larger co-operatives.

Unfortunately, events did not follow this scenario. The transition from mutual aid teams to lower APCs, which began in 1952, did not always go smoothly. Peasant resistance, particularly from better-off households, was one problem. Cadre ineptitude was another (it must be remembered that many rural cadres were barely literate). Harvests did not increase as expected. The crops of 1953 and 1954 were disappointing. Grain output grew at between 1 percent and 2 percent. There were even smaller increases and even some declines in important industrial crops like soybeans, oilseeds, and cotton.

This sluggish growth was a serious problem because the growing population had to be fed and clothed. In addition, China had to export farm products to pay for the imports of Soviet technology. Light industry, which included the very important cotton textile industry, required increasing quantities of raw materials if it were going to grow according to plan. The fate of the entire program of economic development was being adversely affected.

> It is no exaggeration to say that by mid-1955 agriculture's performance was beginning to undermine the credibility of all the industrial targets of the First Plan.[3]

This put the Party in the classic dilemma of rulers whose policies fail to produce expected results. Did they prescribe the wrong medicine, or was the dose too small? Should they go backward or forward? Just this sort of dispute arose in 1953 and intensified in 1954 and 1955.

Gradualists of more pragmatic leanings held that the disappointing results could be attributed to basic flaws in the program. APCs were being pushed too soon and too hard, which resulted in inefficiencies, dissatisfaction, and mismanagement. Furthermore, almost sole reliance on brute labor to create agricultural capital was unrealistic. Socialism in the countryside could be truly realized only when the economy could provide the farm sector with mechanized tools, chemical fertilizers, and other industrial inputs and support.

One of these gradualists was Deng Zihui (pronounced something like "Dung Dsuh-hway"; he was not related to Deng Xiaoping). He held important positions as director of the Party's Rural Work Department and director of the State Council's office in charge of agriculture. Although he had strong connections with Mao, the practical job of increasing farm output pushed him into agreement with Liu Shaoqi, Zhou Enlai, Chen Yun, and Chen Yi—all of whom advocated a slow socialization process in the interests of production. As Deng Zihui said in 1954,

> We [lack] the necessary conditions [for collectivization]. . . .
> Moreover, the Chinese peasants' conception of private ownership
> is relatively deep, while our rural task is heavy and we have not
> enough cadres.[4]

In 1953 and again in 1955 he presided over the dissolution of large numbers of APCs that were deemed premature. He favored the retention of private plots and some free markets to stimulate output.

There was another school of opinion that was led by Mao himself. To the handwringers who worried that the APC policy was too much, they answered that it was not enough. The Party should certainly not "get off the horse quickly." It should "get on the horse quickly."[5] Mao spoke these words at a 1953 conference on mutual aid and cooperation. Calling these efforts "a matter of vital importance," he declared that "if socialism does not occupy the rural positions, capitalism inevitably will."[6] Mao's kindred spirit in these views was Chen Boda, his longtime theoretical collaborator. They grew increasingly frustrated by the gradualists' inclination to moderate the APC program when difficulties surfaced. "We must guide the movement boldly and must not fear dragons ahead and tigers behind," urged Chairman Mao in 1955.[7] And further:

We must have faith, first, that the peasant masses are willing to take the road of socialism step by step under the leadership of the Party and, second, that the Party is capable of leading the peasants onto this road.[8]

During the first two years of the Five Year Plan, tugging and pulling between these two positions resulted in a seesaw APC policy. It began in the spring of 1953, when a decision was taken to push cooperatives. Late in the year Chen Yi (now the major Party leader in the Shanghai region) and others in east China felt that some APCs had been organized too hastily. They dissolved 15,000 of them. Mao disapproved strongly, and Chen Yi was obliged to criticize himself for his action. In the fall of 1954 and the spring of 1955, the call went out to push APCs. Because of disappointing harvests there was widespread reluctance to comply. In May, Liu Shaoqi chaired meetings in which Deng Zihui, with the support of Chen Yun, moved to dissolve 20,000 co-ops.

The like-minded minister of finance delivered the economic report to the National People's Congress soon thereafter. He stated that collectivization should proceed slowly, building up a solid core of well-organized and effective voluntary APCs. He anticipated that only one-third of the peasants would be in co-ops by 1957, and those would mostly be lower APCs. In the spring of 1955, the "get off" advocates seemed to have neutralized the "get on" enthusiasts even though they could not prevent repeated attempts to hasten rural socialism.

## Education

In the First Five-Year Plan period, great strides were made in education. The system was brought under the control of central government ministries. New schools were established at all levels. Literacy increased. Primary school attendance shot up from 24 million in 1949 to 64 million in 1957. The numbers of those graduating from middle schools quadrupled, from technical middle schools doubled, and from universities more than doubled.

Still, problems lingered. As one scholar has said, "Revolutionary China's educational system presents a picture of tragedy and glory."[9] One major difficulty was that the country's needs were enormous and her resources meager. It was important to increase general literacy and education. It was also critical to produce large numbers of scientists, engineers, and other experts. Both of these needs could not be fully satisfied at once. Another source of difficulties was that the system aped the Soviet Union's to the disregard of China's special characteristics. There was too much stultifying central control. High standards, heavy demands on students, restrictive entrance policies, and elitism all conflicted with revolutionary ideals and with the need to spread education as widely as possible. The bureaucrats in charge of assigning graduates did a poor job of matching educational skills to China's manpower needs.

Toward the end of the Five-Year Plan, almost everyone had complaints. The Maoists criticized too much centralization and elitism and too little indoctrination. The more pragmatically minded were alarmed about poor manpower utilization. In early 1956, Zhou Enlai complained that many experts had been assigned to posts unrelated to their qualifications. Students themselves were dismayed by the narrow, difficult ladder of upward mobility. In 1957 two-thirds of primary school children completed that level of education. Only about 7 percent of the twelve–to–fourteen-year-olds graduated from junior middle schools. Less than 2 percent of fifteen–to–seventeen-year-olds completed senior middle schools. As for higher education, less than 1 percent of that age group received diplomas.

The graduates frequently received disappointing assignments. The system remained discriminatory against women. Males outnumbered females in primary schools by two to one and by progressively larger ratios at higher levels (in the universities, it was three to one). There was massive disadvantage for rural residents because the good middle schools and all the higher institutions were in cities.

## Health

The general picture of public health improvement was highly positive during this period. Social order, an equalitarian distribution system, and improved medical care contributed to the results. Epidemic diseases were eliminated or brought under control. The mortality rate dropped. Here as well, however, difficulties persisted. One was the disparity between the relatively better health care and diets available in the cities and the more stringent health care and diets available in the rural villages. Another was the fact that as death rates dropped, birth rates declined more slowly. The result was an annual net population increase of around 2 percent. Given the huge population base, this pace of expansion put a severe burden on the economy. China had to run fast just to keep even.

## The High Tide of 1955

### Mao Counterattacks

By 1955 the dissolution of APCs and the cautious agricultural policies endorsed by the majority of Party leaders dismayed Mao and Chen Boda. The Chairman took steps to counter what he later derided as "the sad and dismal flatness and pessimism of the bourgeoisie."[10] Finding himself unable to prevail in the Politburo on this issue, he disregarded the normal procedures and mobilized his own support. He began with an extensive early summer tour of the provinces during which he no doubt pushed his views on the cadres who entertained him. In late July, when the National People's Congress met, he worked on the provincial Party leaders who came to Beijing.

With this base of support, he made his move. One day after the NPC had approved the cautious agricultural program of Deng Zihui, Chen Yun, and their colleagues, Mao summoned an ad hoc gathering of provincial and subprovincial Party secretaries.

His speech advocated policies utterly opposed to those just approved by China's supposed legislative body. "A new upsurge in the socialist mass movement is imminent throughout the countryside," he said. "But some of our comrades are tottering along like a woman with bound feet, and constantly complaining, 'you're going too fast' "[11] In measured and reasonable tones he warned against capitalist tendencies. He called for a "High Tide" of socialist transformation in the countryside, a careful and well-planned, but vigorous campaign to complete collectivization.

In a stroke Mao had regained the initiative. With Chen Boda he called upon each provincial Party apparatus to take the lead in forming APCs. The response was startling. Provincial officials, so sensitive to signals from Beijing that some of them kept restaurants in the capital as listening posts, decided that they did not want to be labeled rightists on this issue. Better to err in the leftward direction. Within weeks the stalled APC program took off. Across the country headlines like the following heralded the High Tide:[12]

STARTING A TIDAL WAVE CAMPAIGN FOR NATIONAL PROGRAM OF
AGRICULTURAL DEVELOPMENT

MARCH BOLDLY ON THE GREAT DEVELOPMENT OF AGRICULTURAL
PRODUCTION

Anxious to show not only that APCs should be formed but also that they could work well, Mao took great pains to strengthen his case. He solicited the cooperation of individual soldiers in his bodyguard detachment known as PLA Unit 8341. As most of them had been peasants, he sent them to their home villages to study local attitudes and views. Their reports, which they began to convey to him toward the end of the year, convinced him that he had a good feel for the situation in the countryside.

At this time Mao was assembling a collection of accounts of successful collectivization throughout the country, to be used as a guide for local cadres. He wrote enthusiastic editorial notes for the book, which was published late in the year. Typical of his commentaries was the following.

> This is an excellent article. . . . The party organization in this place never wavered on the question of cooperation. It stood four-square behind the destitute peasants in their demand for a coop and in their victorious competition with the well-to-do middle peasants; it firmly supported them as they grew from a small coop to a large one, increasing their output year by year, till by the third year the whole village was in cooperatives. The well-to-do middle peasants had jeered: "They've less money than an egg has hair, yet they think they can run a coop. Can a chicken feather fly up to heaven?" But that is just what this chicken feather did.[13]

During August and September thousands of APCs were formed. By the end of the year, two-thirds of all peasant households had been socialized. There were already thousands of higher APCs. The number of completely socialist cooperatives continued to increase until, by the end of 1956, 88 percent of peasant households were in them, with another 8 percent still in lower APCs.

Such an unexpected response was due in part to the fact that the Party had recruited large numbers of rural cadres. CCP membership had leveled off at around 6 million shortly after 1949. It began to grow rapidly again in 1954. By the end of that year, it reached 7.86 million. During the next year and a half, it burgeoned to 10.73 million. By mid-1957 there were over 12.5 million members, double the 1954 figure. These Party cadres were particularly responsive to the center at this time because of recent rectification campaigns. In the spring of 1955 the Party launched an internal purge and a tough campaign against non-Party intellectual dissidents and counterrevolutionaries. In the words of one historian

> The Party [carried out] a general campaign to liquidate all unorthodox thinking, hunt out counterrevolutionaries, and, most important, to purify political consciousness in accordance with the needs of the First Five Year Plan.[14]

With the Party thus enlarged, established in the villages, and disciplined, the center possessed a powerful instrument with which to mobilize the peasants.

Success also depended on the willingness of hundreds of millions of peasants to go along. Mao claimed that most farmers favored collectivization, especially poor peasants. Although he probably exaggerated, the formerly landless villagers were indeed a base on which cadres could build the APC movement. They remained a comparatively deprived group. Their attachment to the limited fields they had received through land reform may still have been weak. The tools, animals, and skills they possessed were often inferior to those of the middle peasants.

Starting with this core, the cadres used their repertory of pressures and blandishments to promote collectives. They painted a bountiful future. They said that the APC would assume all the risks of farming. Some promised free food. They mobilized group moral pressures against holdouts and even threatened to withhold community help, fertilizer, and other necessary things. The possibility also existed of labeling recalcitrant people as landlords, rich peasants, or even counterrevolutionaries.

The weather also aided the collectivization effort by contributing to good harvests. Mao said:

> In 1955 there was a bumper crop. Thus an increase in production coincided with a decrease in [government] purchasing, so that the peasants had 20,000 million extra catties of grain on their hands. All those peasants who had criticized us in the past now no longer criticized us. They all said, "The Communist Party is fine." [15]

The High Tide received what might be called its formal charter late in January 1956. For several weeks Mao's group had been developing a long term plan for agriculture, which they had circulated among the Party elite. It called for vigorous collectivization, use of off-season peasant labor for capital construction, and very rapid increases in output. Depending on the region, grain and cotton yields were to double or triple in twelve years. Mao presented this Twelve Year Program to the Supreme State Conference that he had convened for the purpose of enlisting both Party and non-Party support behind his bold vision.

The year 1955 ended, and 1956 began on a very positive note for Mao Zedong. In February a renewed burst of APC formation began. He had coined a slogan that in its defiant juxtaposition of seemingly contradictory objectives, captured the optimism of the moment. The slogan urged one and all to produce "*duo* [more], *kuai* [faster], *hao* [better quality], *sheng* [and more cheaply]." Mao also spoke about a "leap forward" in output.

## High Tide in Industry and Commerce

From the beginning, the Communists planned to socialize the entire nation and eliminate capitalism. But such a goal could not be reached overnight. The scarcity of cadres competent to manage industrial and commercial enterprises, not to mention the difficulty of organizing thousands of small-scale peddlers and services into cooperatives, had persuaded the policymakers against pushing socialism too fast. Even after the High Tide in agriculture began in July 1955, Guangzhou (Canton) businesspeople were assured that they would continue to own their firms for years.

Then, in October, Mao turned his bold approach to the cities, calling for wider collectivization. A former Shanghai businessperson told of being summoned to a meeting of manufacturers and merchants. To the group's astonishment, none other than the shuffling, slow-speaking, chain-smoking Mao Zedong had called them together. With true Chinese indirection, he asked them for their advice concerning the nationalization of private enterprises. Did they agree with those who wanted to hasten this process "lest the national bourgeoisie lag behind in the progress toward socialism?" Taking their cue, they all urged haste. But Mao's idea of haste was to leave them breathless. A few weeks later they received word that the transition to state ownership would be accomplished within six days.[16]

As a result of the tremendous political pressures generated by these drives, the socialization of industry and commerce was complete by the end of 1956. Virtually the entire private sector had been taken over or reorganized into cooperatives. The capitalists now worked as salaried managers and received bonds for their expropriated properties (although they were not entirely free to spend the interest payments). Huge celebrations were staged in which businesspeople joyously greeted the transition to socialism.

## Implications of Socialist Transformation

By the spring of 1956 the High Tide had introduced socialism to virtually every village, shop, and factory. Once again the Chairman's boldness seized victory where his more prudent colleagues had seen insuperable difficulties. It was hard to disagree when he said

> Provided [the workers, peasants, and working intellectuals] take their destination into their own hands, provided they have a Marxist-Leninist line and energetically tackle problems instead of evading them, they can overcome any difficulty on earth.[17]

Because of the High Tide's success, the People's Republic was entering a new era. The state had gained unprecedented (although far from absolute) control over the economy. Responsibility for the system's performance now rested squarely on the shoulders of those who controlled it. Central decisions, enforced by the Party apparatus, now had increased potential for huge successes—and massive blunders.

By early 1956, the leadership was already feeling out directions and strategies to fit this new situation. Mao's Twelve-Year Plan constituted a distinctive approach to agriculture. An analogous document for industry was under preparation. In March and April 1956, Mao presided over work reports and discussions involving thirty-four central departments and ministries. His summation of the principal findings were set out in a speech called "On the Ten Major Relationships." This address, which was intended for Party leaders only and remained unpublished for years, emphasized the complex relationships between the various parts of the economy. It suggested pragmatic, flexible modifications in the prevailing Soviet-style, heavy-industry-first approach to development.

## A New Political Climate

Actually only the first half of the "Ten Major Relationships" speech dealt with the economy. The last five "relationships" discussed all had a political dimension, reflecting the fact that this period was marked by a search for new political approaches as well. The need to reexamine these relationships came from several sources. From the Soviet Union came an early and especially unsettling stimulus.

In 1955, Nikita Khrushchev had established himself as first secretary of the Soviet Union's Communist Party. His leadership marked a transition from Stalin's tyranny to more liberalized rule. Perhaps the most electrifying moment came at his secret speech to the Party's Twentieth Congress in February 1956. To party stalwarts who for many years had both adored and feared the departed leader, Khrushchev read a bone-chilling litany of Stalin's transgressions, which included self-glorification, paranoia, capricious despotism, mass arrests, torture, extracted confessions, punishments without trial, deportations, mass murder of military officers, and inaction against the Nazi invasion. Stalin's central flaw, said Khrushchev, was his cult of personality.

Khrushchev's sensational speech was communicated to other Communist parties. In China, as elsewhere, it had a stunning effect. Five weeks passed before the *People's Daily* took up the subject. When it did, it emphasized Stalin's achievements as well as his shortcomings. The main reason for this reaction was that Mao was the obvious center of a personality cult. Criticism of Stalin struck uncomfortably close to home. Yet it was hard to deny Stalin's excesses and the evil effects of deifying the leader.

There were other stimuli for rethinking the relationships between rulers and ruled. As the People's Republic matured, regular and predictable patterns emerged. What form would "mass line" now take in order to remain vital? This was extremely important to Mao, believing as he did that popular participation, through mass line, was the key to the success of the system. According to the Yanan ideal, Party cadres were supposed to be selfless, humble, and committed to mobilizing the workers and peasants against their class enemies. Other classes were supposed to transform themselves and join "the people." Unfortunately, bureaucratic behavior, excessive centralism, and bourgeois vestiges clouded this scenario.

The Party had developed a whole lexicon of terms to define undesirable cadre behavior. In addition to ordinary bureaucratism, there were also "commandism" (ordering the masses around rather than using persuasion), "sectarianism" (caring only about one own office or locality), and "subjectivism" (substituting wishful thinking for facts), in addition to corruption, and wastefulness. Many cadres acted increasingly like imperial mandarins: arrogant, arbitrary, slow to serve yet quick to pursue their own self-interests. How could such people lead the social and moral transformation of society? It was, of course, not a new problem, as evidenced by the repeated rectification campaigns since the 1940s.

Centralization was a more recent concern. As the Soviet model took hold, the ministries in Beijing increased their jurisdiction and functions, thereby creating an inefficient, unresponsive monolith. Mao complained thus in his "Ten Major Relationships" speech.

At present there are dozens of hands meddling in regional affairs, making them difficult to manage. Every day various ministries issue orders to the offices of provincial and municipal governments. These orders are supposed to come from the [Party] Centre, even though the Centre knows nothing about them and neither does the State Council. They put a great strain on the regions. Statistics and reports come rushing in like a torrent. This must change. We must discuss ways of correcting it.[18]

Fujian provincial leaders complained that construction of a much-needed paper factory dawdled along for six years while the ministry prepared plans and changed them. Because the most desirable posts were those at the top of the pyramid at Beijing, the ministries tended to become overstaffed. A consensus was growing that somehow this sluggish pyramid must be made more flexible and responsive. In his "Ten Major Relationships" speech, Mao went so far as to suggest that "the Party and government organs should be streamlined and that two thirds of their numbers should be axed." [19]

The fact that this newly socialized society must now intensify its development efforts also had implications for urban policy, especially in relation to the educated classes. Up to now, efforts had been directed mainly at transforming these people's consciousness, rooting out counterrevolutionaries, and suppressing dissent. The Party had perfected techniques of mobilization, education, propaganda, and brainwashing. Coercion was there as a last resort, but police power alone simply alienated people and cost a lot of money. Everything hinged on how well the people took Marxist values to heart.

Now it was time for more relaxed policies because the educated elite would play a key role in modernizing industry, technology, science, and education. As Mao acknowledged in May of 1957

In China, the bourgeois elements and the intellectuals who served the old society number several million, and we need them to work for us; we must further improve our relations with them so that we can enable them to give better service to the cause of socialism and so that we can further remould them and help them gradually become part of the working class . . .[20]

By 1956 some were becoming convinced that the thought reform efforts since liberation had brought the intelligentsia around (although it was well understood that many mouthed tenets of Marxism-Leninism and Mao Zedong Thought without much conviction). It was now time to introduce a more predictable legal system and liberalization in art, literature, the press, and other cultural areas. Mao joined Zhou and others in calling for such changes. In the spring he raised two slogans. One was "Let a Hundred Flowers Bloom, Let a Hundred Schools of Thought Contend," meaning that diversity in culture and science should be encouraged. The second slogan was "Long-Term Coexistence and Mutual Supervision." This referred to the coexistence of Communist and non-Communist elements and to the need to have the latter "supervise," that is, criticize, the Party in order to keep it responsive.

Khrushchev's February speech and his recent actions contained other unsettling things for the Chinese to deal with. The Soviet leader had proposed things that Beijing received coolly. He said that in the nuclear era world war was not inevitable. Peaceful coexistence was possible. He argued further that socialism could win out through parliamentary means as well as through violent revolution. He took steps to reconcile the USSR with Yugoslavia's Tito, the arch "revisionist" whom the Chinese (and the Russians) had mercilessly criticized. And Khrushchev began moving away from Stalinist-style development of industry with its emphasis on steel, machinery, and other heavy manufacturing. He began to shift resources toward consumer goods and agriculture in order to improve living standards.

## Retreat from the Reckless Advance

One other major disequilibrating force was the disruptions caused by the High Tide itself. Serious problems began to arise by late spring. This was especially true in agriculture. The expansion of APCs had gone so fast that troubling symptoms were appearing. It became clear that rural cadres were better at corralling the peasants into APCs than at managing the resulting organizations. The list of typical excesses included planting too much grain and cotton at the expense of other crops, mobilizing too much labor to the detriment of income-producing sideline handicrafts, distributing collective income improperly or unfairly, allowing livestock to sicken or perish through poor management, indulging extravagance and wastefulness, and setting overly ambitious targets. The cadres' difficulties were compounded by pressures from higher cadres to achieve spectacular results. For example, although the center had specified that Fujian Province should increase its grain production by 9 percent, the provincial authorities increased the goal to 16 percent, and the local leaders upped it to an impossible 40 percent.

The center, too, made mistakes and on a grand scale. Mao and his supporters became very enthusiastic about a Soviet double-wheeled, double-bladed plow, which they believed to be a technological breakthrough. On their approval and with little field testing, the implement was manufactured in huge quantities and sold to thousands of co-ops. Unfortunately, in most places it did not work at all well. Peasants dubbed it the ''hanging plow'' because the only thing it did was hang on the wall. In the end, 700,000 of these plows remained unsold, a massive waste of scarce steel.

Also, state revenues began to lag seriously behind expenditures, creating renewed inflationary pressures. Exacerbating these failures, nature took a bad turn. In August, Typhoon Wanda, the worst in fifty years, brought terrific winds and rain to many provinces. In the fall the harvest fell short of the expected bumper crop. Indeed, it only moderately surpassed the previous year. The peasants grew discontented. There were food shortages in some places. Many households clamored to get out of the APCs. Households slaughtered livestock rather than turn the animals over to the cooperative. In the cities, there were factory strikes and disturbances at the universities. Mao's High Tide seemed to have produced some very unfavorable results.

By the fall, Zhou Enlai, Chen Yun, Deng Zihui, and others were leading the retreat back to gradualism reminiscent of early 1955. An editorial appeared in the June 20, 1955, issue of *People's Daily* entitled, ''Oppose Both Conservatism and Hastiness.'' Ostensibly an admonition against excess in either direction, this document was in actuality an attack on "reckless advance," that is, on Mao's brand of economic mobilization. The author advised "seeking truth from facts," that is, pragmatism over dogma in deciding on effective policies. When shown the draft of this document before its publication, Mao angrily scribbled, "Bu kan le" ["I won't read this"] in the margin.[21] Mao's ambitious Twelve-Year Program dropped quietly from discussion.

## The Eighth Party Congress, September 1956

All these things were in the air at the September 15, 1956, Eighth Party Congress. Slightly over 1,000 delegates and 140 foreign guests representing 56 Communist parties assembled in Beijing for the first CCP congress since 1945. For 12 days the gathering heard well over 100 speakers and took action on a new Party constitution, the election of a new Central Committee, and various resolutions and proposals.

In terms of economic policy, the Congress heard provincial Party secretaries, one after another, complain about the High Tide and the Twelve Year Program. One of them added that rapid socialization had disrupted rural exchange patterns, thereby damaging production even more. Zhou Enlai's speech dealt with the economy. He, too, warned against impetuosity and criticized the Twelve-Year Program. His speech reflected retrenchment policies that had been put in effect a few days before the Congress opened.

Mao was not happy with these displays of vacillation. Even as the moderates were having their way prior to the Congress, he pleaded for speedy development:

you are said to be building socialism, which is supposed to be superior; if after working at it for fifty or sixty years you are still unable to overtake the United States, what a sorry figure you will cut! . . .[22]

As the go-slow approach continued to prevail into 1957, he remained convinced that socialism was both necessary and workable. Hundreds of collectives had succeeded. If the Party would just remain bold and systematic and quickly rectify its errors, then success could be achieved in every county and province. His speeches and writings of the time contain many statements like the following:

> If [achieving big harvests in APCs] could be done here [in Zunhua County, Hebei Province], why can't it be done elsewhere? . . . I can see only one reason—unwillingness to take the trouble, or to put it more bluntly, Right-Opportunism.
> Why can't 600 million "paupers" create a prosperous and strong socialist country in several decades by their own efforts?[23]

Organizationally, the Party emerged from the Congress significantly altered. Collective leadership was the new watchword, thanks to Khrushchev's de-Stalinization speech and the recent problems with the High Tide. Consequently, the drafters of the new constitution did what would have seemed unthinkable a year earlier. They dropped references to Mao Zedong Thought as the Party's guiding doctrine. Mao himself decided to reduce his participation in day-to-day affairs. The "first line," as he called it, he left to Liu Shaoqi and Deng Xiaoping. He intended to occupy the "second line," considering broad policy directions. Time was to show that Mao did not find these new arrangements entirely congenial. The Congress also addressed the problem of overcentralization and bureaucratism and passed a resolution calling for more administrative efficiency.

Some significant power shifts occurred. At this time there was as yet no deep division between Maoists and moderates. Liu, for example, who differed with Mao on organizational questions, took his side on economic issues. Still, personal loyalties and the relative standing of various leaders were important matters. Deng Xiaoping was a supporter and spokesperson for Mao. That fact was not unconnected to his appointment to be Party

LIU SHAOQI

general secretary, in charge of the reorganized Secretariat, the Central Committee's powerful administrative arm. Lin Biao, another Mao loyalist, emerged with a higher relative standing within the Politburo, as did another former general, Chen Yi. Liu Shaoqi, widely considered Mao's successor, saw his standing slip slightly when Deng rose to more nearly Liu's level.

The most significant loser in the power game was the minister of defense, Peng Dehuai, now inferior to both Lin Biao and Chen Yi in the Politburo rankings. The reasons for this are not entirely clear. It is known that Peng was the person who moved to omit Mao Zedong Thought from the constitution. This would seem like a slim reason to demote him because others agreed to Peng's move. Perhaps a more substantive cause was the blunt general's resistance to military budget cuts, an important item in Mao's "Ten Major Relationships" speech. It is also said that Mao was unhappy with Peng's generalship in Korea, a grievance made personal by the battlefield death of Mao's eldest son in 1950. Finally, although there is no evidence for it, one wonders if Peng was not already grumbling about Mao's mobilizational strategies, as he was to do with disastrous consequences three years later (see further on).

## The Hundred Flowers Campaign

The subject of Party-mass relationships had been vexing the entire Communist bloc ever since Khrushchev had denounced Stalin. It continued to be a live issue in China, especially for Mao, as his High Tide economic plans were being abandoned. As indicated earlier, his thinking on the relationship between intellectuals and the Party was encapsulated in two slogans: ''Let a Hundred Flowers Bloom, Let a Hundred Schools of Thought Contend'' and ''Long-Term Coexistence and Mutual Supervision.'' The issue of Party-mass relationships became more insistent after October 23, 1956, when the people of Budapest revolted against their Communist government.

The Hungarian uprising was another symptom of de-Stalinization, but it presented agonizing questions to Marxist leaders. What did the insurgency mean? Who was to blame? Mao's initial answer was that overly repressive policies toward the intellectuals had alienated them. Although it was imperative that Moscow crush the revolt, all socialist countries should learn a lesson from it. In the last part of 1956, Mao turned his full energies to promoting Party rectification, involving ''big democracy,'' that is, open criticism from non-Communists.

This open door to outside censure did not sit well with much of the Party establishment. There was every reason that cadres from the local levels up to the top should resist it. Although Zhou Enlai supported Mao, Liu Shaoqi and Peng Zhen led the opposition. Throughout the closing months of 1956 and the spring of 1957, the Chairman continued to press for his special brand of rectification while Liu and the others worked to dilute his efforts. The most striking episode in this contest occurred in late

February. As head of state, Mao had convened a meeting of the Supreme State Conference, which included many non-Communists. His audience was a very large one as he delivered one of his most famous speeches, ''On the Correct Handling of Contradictions Among the People.''

''Contradictions among the people'' was a special term in Mao's thought. It referred to social conflicts that could be reconciled without the violent suppression of one class by another. Its opposite was ''contradictions between ourselves and the enemy.'' In his speech Mao argued that even in socialist societies conflicts (contradictions) continue to exist, as for example between poorer and better-off peasants, between the peasants and the cities, and between the government and the citizens. But these ''conflicts of interest,'' as a capitalist might call them, were all ''contradictions among the people'' and could be handled peacefully. (Incidentally the thesis of contradictions continuing in socialist society was always strongly rejected by the Soviet Union.)

One particularly important contradiction was the one between the Party and the intellectuals. China needs the intellectuals, and bureaucratic tendencies in the Party need exposure to the light of day. Once again Mao was promoting his program for allowing untrammeled criticism of the CCP. In presenting his case, Mao argued that the Party historically had been less harsh toward dissidents and opponents than was commonly believed. He claimed that the thought-control campaign of the early 1950s, far from claiming millions of victims, as had been charged, involved the execution of only 700,000 or so. In November 1956, Mao had made a similar apologia, pointing out that, although the campaign against counterrevolutionaries had involved investigation into 4 million cases, only 38,000 were convicted. It is to be wondered whether his audiences were reassured or terrified by these statistics.

Even at this Supreme State Conference, opposition to the proposal was evident. Several top leaders, including Liu Shaoqi, were conspicuous by their absence. Some accounts even speak of Politburo members leaving the hall while Mao was speaking. Nevertheless, by April 1957, Mao achieved grudging acquiescence from his colleagues on the understanding that the rectification campaign would not be a harsh one. There would be criticisms but no sweeping purge. It would be like "gentle breeze and fine rain." With the approval of the Politburo, Mao issued a directive on April 30 that was finally to bring his long-sought rectification to reality. But it was rather more than he bargained for.

There had actually been some scattered response to Mao's call for outside criticism as early as 1956. One case in particular was a short story by a young author named Wang Meng. Entitled "A New Young Man Arrives at the Organization Department," it depicted the disillusionment of an idealistic young Party cadre as he confronted bureaucratism and incompetence in his new unit. (The hero's faith was rekindled in the end, however.) But only in May after Mao's directive went out, did criticism pick up momentum. Then it threatened to spin out of control.

In various publications, in public meetings, and on posters put up at universities, the Hundred Flowers criticism came in startling profusion. The pro-Soviet "leaning to one side" was derided in view of Russia's lack of generosity toward China. Some argued that under socialist democracy officials ought to have limited terms of office, as in capitalist democracies. There were demands for the release of persecuted intellectuals, because they had done no more than express themselves freely as was now being promoted. Communism itself was questioned, and Mao Zedong was criticized for being "very confident about the false reports and dogmatic analysis presented him by his cadres." He was called "impetuous in making decisions without first making a careful study of the facts." [24] Students in Beijing went on a spree of pasting up thousands of posters expressing every conceivable view, often in provocative language. Near Wuhan a mob of peasants demonstrated violently and were suppressed with some loss of life. In Wuhan itself students rioted.

By mid-May, Mao was in a most embarrassing position. From

Party officials in all the provinces telegrams poured in complaining about the campaign. Liu Shaoqi and Peng Zhen could say, "I told you so." Toward the end of the month the Chairman had to backpedal. He began to signal that criticism that exceeded the proper boundaries was unacceptable. Because the Party was "the core of leadership of the whole Chinese people . . . any word or deed at variance with socialism is completely wrong." [25]

The beginning of the end came on June 8. *People's Daily* carried an editorial entitled "What Is This For?" It signaled that criticisms of the Party would no longer be tolerated. Ten days later Mao's speech on the "Correct Handling of Contradictions Among the People" was published for the first time. But there were "certain additions." A section was added distinguishing "poisonous weeds" from "fragrant flowers." Poisonous weeds included any statements against unity, socialism, people's democratic dictatorship, democratic centralism, the Party, and international socialism.

Although not formally disowned, the Hundred Flowers campaign was over. Henceforth those who put forth "poisonous weeds" would be subject to punishment, not to mention those who had already unwisely done so. One of the last anguished student posters at Beijing University said

Intelligent friends! Everybody has been cheated! . . . Even after the Emperor has ordered the Party to mend its ways, the mandarins of all degrees are nevertheless still in place, everything remains just as before. [26]

Mao's "mutual supervision" suddenly became a repressive anti-Rightist compaign during which hundreds of thousands of intellectuals were arrested. Some 300,000 to 400,000 were "sent down" to the countryside, where most spent the next twenty years. In the countryside the Party launched a "Socialist Education Campaign" to reinforce socialist thinking at the grass roots. From the atmosphere of heady freedom that had prevailed for a few spring weeks in May, the country was plunged back into the fog of ideological conformity.

Meanwhile, Mao was defending himself to the public and to various Party audiences around the country. It had all turned out just as planned. "The purpose," he said, "was to let demons and devils, ghosts and monsters 'air views freely' and let poisonous weeds sprout and grow in profusion so that the people, now shocked to find these ugly things still existing in the world, would take action to wipe them out. . . . The Communist Party foresaw this inevitable class struggle . . ."[27] Mao called for more frank airing of views in the future.

# 4

# The Great Leap
# Forward: 1958–60

In the last half of 1957 the leaders of China confronted some intractable problems. Could they sustain the high industrial growth rate, simultaneously spur agricultural output, and still move ahead with the social revolution? Or must they moderate some of these goals? The attempt to solve these problems led to a massive explosion of events that included the reorganization of the entire farm sector in a matter of weeks, the downward transfer of up to 2.5 million cadres, the mobilization of 90 million people to learn small-scale steel making, and the migration of as many as 20 million peasants to the cities. As revolutionary drama, this so-called Great Leap Forward was brilliant and exciting. The Chinese themselves and many outside commentators have credited the movement with shaking up old habits and attitudes. Nor did it entirely lack good sense. But on balance it failed badly as a modernizing effort. It caused calamitous economic setbacks, damaged foreign relations, and opened serious political wounds that did not heal for years.

## Initial Stages of the Great Leap

*The Summer of 1957*

In June 1957, Premier Zhou Enlai addressed the fourth session of the National People's Congress. His long speech covered the whole spectrum of government, society, and culture. Acknowledging numerous criticisms, he minimized shortcomings and painted a picture of solid achievement and optimism. There was indeed cause to be pleased with the progress in the eight years since liberation. National consolidation (except for Taiwan) was complete, the Korean War had been successfully weathered, and China had become an important member of the socialist bloc. Domestic modernization efforts had created the constitution of 1954, an expanded educational system, and improved public health.

The first five-year plan, based on Soviet-style planning and Russian assistance, was concluding. Despite serious concerns, the overall results were very good. Especially impressive was heavy industry, where priority investment had produced an 18 percent annual growth rate. The overall economy had grown at a very respectable 10 percent per year. Figure 5, which graphs estimates of national income, adjusted for price changes, illustrates the relatively rapid growth in the economy as a whole.[1] Massive structural changes (the establishment of agricultural cooperatives and the nationalization of industry) had been smoothly accomplished by comparison with the historical experience of the Soviet Union. Even though statistics, pricing, and resource allocation were still inadequate to manage China's size and backwardness, central planning capabilities had greatly increased. Premier Zhou concluded his speech with the following words:

Fellow deputies! The international situation is favorable for our socialist construction. Basing ourselves on the brilliant directives of Chairman Mao Tse-tung on the correct handling of contradictions among the people, we Chinese people are forging an even

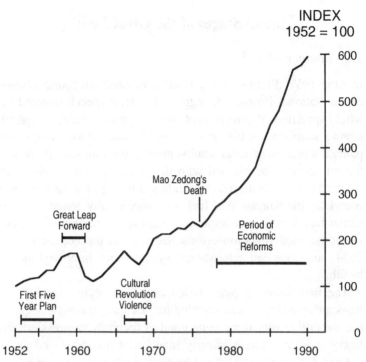

INDEX
1952 = 100

Mao Zedong's
Death

Great Leap
Forward

Period of
Economic
Reforms

First Five
Year Plan

Cultural
Revolution
Violence

1952    1960    1970    1980    1990

FIG. 5 Chinese national income estimates: 1950–83 (in 1952 prices).

stronger unity. . . . So long as we continue to exert efforts to strengthen national and international unity and carry through the policy of increasing production and practicing economy and building our country by hard work and thrift, no force on earth can block the victorious advance of our great socialist cause.[2]

On the other hand, as Zhou's acknowledgment of shortcomings attested, the overall picture in 1957 was not completely rosy. Politically, the Hundred Flowers Campaign had ended badly in a fierce persecution of rightists. Communists had been stung by the outside disapprobation. Mao resented the intellectuals' reluctance to give their hearts to the new regime. For their part, the frightened intellectuals could react only with cynicism and resignation at having been lured into criticizing the Party only to be sternly punished for what they said. This did not bode well for future cooperation.

The Hundred Flowers campaign had also created a rift among the CCP leadership. Mao's Yanan idealism was opposed by Liu Shaoqi and by Peng Zhen. Peng was a tall, bald, vigorous man whose genial countenance belied the fact that he was a tough, ambitious revolutionary veteran, capable of presiding over mass trials and executions in 1950. Born to a northern peasant family, he got involved in leftist labor organizing as a young man. The Nationalists imprisoned him for six years in the early 1930s, after which he joined the Party and began a long-standing connection with Liu Shaoqi.

Although not a Long March veteran, Peng rose rapidly in the CCP hierarchy in the anti-Japanese struggle and the civil war years. Soon after liberation, he was appointed mayor of Beijing, and here he built his political base. At the peak of his career in the 1960s, he was, among other things, head of the Beijing Municipal Party Committee, a member of the Politburo, and deputy director of the Party Secretariat, responsible for political and legal affairs. Having been a member of several delegations overseas, he had an international standing and was widely regarded as one of three or four possible successors to Mao. Even in June, when cultivating "flowers" gave way to rooting out "poisonous weeds," Liu and Peng remained at arm's length with Mao. The Beijing press, which Liu and Peng controlled, evidenced this divisiveness. It permitted veiled but bitter criticisms of Mao to be published under the guise of rightist confessions. One rightist even admitted to having said, "The peasants are cursing Chairman Mao." [3]

In foreign relations there were problems, not only with imperialists but also with other socialist powers. Taiwan continued to elude China's grasp. In early 1957, Beijing was trying to coax the Nationalists toward reunification. Suddenly anti-American riots erupted in Taipei. This welcome development seemed to promise a more favorable turn. But the Chiang Kai-shek regime quickly suppressed the disorders and proclaimed itself more fiercely anti-Communist and pro-American than ever. Worse yet, a U.S.-Taiwan accord was signed to install Matador missiles on the island, missiles that could hit many parts of the People's Republic. In the other diplomatic direction, relations within the socialist block showed strains. Although Sino-Soviet friendship apparently continued to flourish and the Chinese press admired everything Russian, an undercurrent of deep displeasure was growing over Khrushchev's de-Stalinization efforts, his thesis on the peaceful transition to socialism, and what the Chinese saw as his responsibility for unrest in Eastern Europe. The Hungarian uprising strengthened Mao's conviction that Communist parties in socialist countries must exert the utmost effort to keep in touch with the masses.

Among the many concerns of the day, perhaps the thorniest problem was agriculture. Despite Mao's glowing expectations, bad weather and the High Tide produced a disappointing 1956 harvest, and the government had to dip into its grain reserves. This also threw the national budget out of balance, causing inflationary pressures. Alarmed moderates, particularly Zhou Enlai and Chen Yun, spoke out against "reckless advance," and by the summer of 1956 Mao had to suspend his High Tide.

Unfortunately, forswearing radicalism did not achieve quick results. On the contrary, the 1957 harvest was even worse than the one of 1956. Grain production increased only 1 percent, just half the rate of population growth. In the demoralized co-ops, many cadres underreported the crops to evade taxes and forced sales to the state. They looked the other way as peasants produced vegetables, livestock, and handicrafts for sale on the free market. Inadequate staffing below the county level made it difficult to monitor these cadres. If this kind of slack leadership continued, socialized agriculture would be in serious trouble. In the cities, food rationing had to be tightened up. But it was more than merely a question of food because, as noted earlier, the agricultural sector produced exports, government revenues, and raw materials for light industry. If output did not improve, China's whole economic modernization effort, even its industrialization program, would be in jeopardy. Ironically, Zhou Enlai and Chen Yun, who had put the brakes on the High Tide, collected some of the blame for this crisis.

There were problems in overall management of the economy as well. Heavy industry had gobbled up so much investment that consumer goods and housing supply lagged far behind demand. The central planning bureaucracy was inefficient and cumbersome, especially in providing consumer goods. Many advocated decentralizing the management of factories and other enterprises, turning them over to the provinces. Uncertainty about Soviet aid arose. By 1957 the Chinese had exhausted all their credits and needed more. But Soviet willingness to satisfy their needs did not keep pace. One reason for this was the unexpected expenses incurred by Moscow in connection with with the uprisings in Hungary and Poland, which forced the Kremlin to scale down its own five-year plan. Thus starved for funds, Beijing's planners found it difficult to resist creative initiatives in both agriculture and industry.

Truly, the Chinese faced difficult economic choices. Skewed investment had created lopsided growth to the detriment of agriculture. To rectify this, some suggested more investment in the farm sector and less in industry. Others retorted that that would slow down industrial growth, a view that Liu Shaoqi aptly represented in his 1956 speech to the Party Congress.

> In order to develop our national economy according to plan, we must carry through the policy of giving priority to the development of heavy industry. Some comrades want to lower the rate of development of heavy industry. This line of thinking is wrong. . . . If we do not very quickly establish our own . . . heavy industry, how are we going to equip our light industry, transport, building industry and agriculture?[4]

Added to this was the question of the agricultural cooperatives: Should they be tightened up or relaxed? And how would harvests be affected?

## Revival of the Radical Agricultural Program

The conditions just described opened the door for Mao to revive his agricultural plan and Party rectification as well. During July and August 1957, even as thousands of intellectuals were experiencing persecution under the anti-Rightist campaign, Mao was inching toward a reconciliation with Liu Shaoqi and Peng Zhen. Their eventual understanding had both a political and an economic aspect. They agreed that ideological strengthening of rural cadres was a prerequisite for a prosperous socialist agriculture.

The first signs of reconciliation appeared in July, when Mao spoke to a conference of provincial officials. The surviving fragments of this speech reveal his concern for both politics and production.

> Our objective is to create a political climate in which there is both centralism and democracy, discipline and freedom, unity of purpose and personal ease of mind and liveliness, in order to benefit the socialist revolution and socialist construction, make it easier to overcome difficulties and to construct a modern industry and agriculture for our nation more quickly, and in order to consolidate further the party and the country to enable us better to weather the storms.[5]

In short, one for all and all for one, under the guidance of the Party, can solve all the problems at the same time. The solution of economic problems through political mobilization had always been the central strength of the CCP, especially in the glorious Yanan days. If it worked then, why not now?

During August, Mao and Liu came together still more in promoting ideological conformity. The Central Committee issued a directive launching a Socialist Education Campaign among the rural population. In particular, this prescribed a rectification movement to bring the rural cadres into line. About a week later, to facilitate economic control over the peasantry, the State Council ordered rural free markets closed. In early September the Party announced that the anti-Rightist movement would change into an "all-people's" rectification movement. That they were quite serious about conformity was clear from the announcement that the leaders of the Wuhan student demonstration had been executed.

But at the same time, other policymakers were promoting contradictory policies. In June word had come down to the rural cadres that private plots could be expanded from 5 percent to 10 percent of the land. In September a Politburo meeting that Mao did not attend promulgated a moderate agricultural policy of dissolving some APCs and administratively strengthening the rest. At this time, rural cadres were reassured that, once these adjustments were complete, they could expect no more changes for ten years.

Which of these two approaches would prevail was decided in September and October at the Third Plenum of the Eighth Central Committee. The Central Committee appeared to favor the central planners' second five year plan proposal. But then (shades of July 1955) late in the session, Mao, Liu, and Deng turned the meeting completely around toward their all-out agricultural mobilization. How they accomplished this is not clear. Perhaps they took advantage of the euphoria over Moscow's announcement of the launching of Sputnik, humankind's first artificial earth satellite. No doubt, Mao exercised his unmatched political wiles. When the meeting adjourned, the planners had been shoved aside again. "The Third Plenum gave . . . a clearer direction," Mao later said. "After[wards] we had the Great Leap Forward."[6]

Having prevailed at the Plenum, the Mao group now began to push their program. To give it more legitimacy, Mao convened the Supreme State Conference and the standing committees of the National People's Congress and the Chinese People's Political Consultative Conference. These bodies "basically" approved the Twelve-Year Program. Although such formal declarations were important, the Maoists needed more than that. Who would dare openly oppose the Chairman's policy? On the other hand, would everyone carry it out? The Maoists had to blunt silent opposition at Beijing and in the provinces. They had to persuade as many as possible and silence the skeptics. Consequently the anti-Rightist campaign was extended to the Party to combat pessimistic and retrograde views. Party leaders came under pressure, causing some of whom, even Zhou Enlai, to criticize themselves for having opposed the High Tide. The Party was expanded while cadres were transferred downward to lead the mobilization efforts. Mao promoted the decentralization of industry in order to weaken the central bureaucracies. These initiatives were increasingly successful. They were punctuated—and probably aided—by Mao's trip to Moscow in November 1957.

## Mao's Trip to Moscow

The fortieth anniversary of the Russian Revolution drew Communist leaders from all over the world. It was Mao's second trip to Moscow. This time, however, he came not as a fresh revolutionary waiting in Stalin's antechamber but as the canny old Marxist whose country commanded increasing influence and prestige. His performance in Moscow was uninhibited and bold. The Chinese were very excited about Soviet military progress. Russia's successful test of an intercontinental ballistic missile in August 1957 and Sputnik I in October had cheered the Maoists. The day after Mao arrived in Moscow, a second Sputnik rocketed into space, this one carrying a dog. Mao bubbled with optimism. Coining one of his more memorable slogans, he urged the Communist bloc to determined action.

> The wind has changed direction in the world. The struggle between the socialist camp and the capitalist camp is marked either by the West wind prevailing over the East wind or the East wind prevailing over the West wind. . . . At present it is not the West wind prevailing over the East wind, but the East wind prevailing over the West wind.[7]

He even went so far as to make light of nuclear war, arguing that the surviving populations of the socialist countries would soon be stronger than ever, relative to the rest of the world. This shocked most of the other participants.

Mao brought his own agenda. In the present situation, the triumph of socialism and China's needs could be simultaneously achieved. Soviet strength, the worldwide people's struggles, and the weaknesses inherent in the imperialist camp justified great optimism. Beijing argued that the principal "contradiction" in the world was now the struggle between imperialism and national liberation movements. To promote the collapse of the imperialists, the socialist bloc must foster revolutionary movements and exploit Soviet strength. In the process China could achieve the liberation of Taiwan.

But others, particularly the Russians, did not share Mao's easy optimism. Moscow emphasized the horrors of thermonuclear war and argued that peaceful transition to socialism was possible. To the Chinese, these views smacked of "revisionism." There was another doctrinal disagreement. As Mao said in his "On the Correct Handling of Contradictions Among the People," even a socialist society can have "contradictions," including conflicts of interest between the Party and the people. Bureaucratism and elitism do not vanish with capitalism and feudalism; they can persist within the Party itself. These contradictions were mostly nonviolent or "nonantagonistic contradictions among the people." Rectification could cleanse the Party. The Russians, however, disagreed. Perish the thought that contradictions, antagonistic or nonantagonistic, could exist between the Communist party of the Soviet Union and the Soviet people!

There were other irritants as well, one of them being economic aid. In Moscow, Mao began to realize that Soviet help would not come up to Beijing's expectations. There was also Chinese disenchantment with Russian influence. Mao even complained that his doctors wouldn't let him eat chicken soup for three years because they had read that the Russians considered it unhealthy. In literature and art, the leaders in Beijing began to worry about Russia's corrupting influence on Chinese writers. Mao returned from Moscow buoyed by Sputnik and his East wind theory and yet dissatisfied with the Soviet Union. More determined than ever to strike out in a new, revolutionary, Chinese direction, he immediately threw himself into the struggle already in progress.

## The Great Leap in the Ascendant

### The First Phase: December 1957–May 1958

In the next six months, Mao and his supporters mobilized the country for a frontal assault on economic backwardness. For them to succeed, it was important to convert or silence balky cadres and intellectuals at all levels so that the entire nation could pull together. Many provincial leaders harbored bitter memories of 1955 and 1956. In the winter, Mao and some of his lieutenants visited various provinces to help put friendly supporters in charge. Henan Province was the first to have a purge of moderates. The Chairman himself was in Zhejiang Province where the first secretary succeeded in ousting the governor on grounds of corruption, immorality, anti-Party activities, and provincial and sectarian views. Within months similar confrontations affected every province. The political casualties included "four Central Committee alternates, a provincial first secretary, five other provincial secretaries, eighteen members of provincial committee standing committees, four governors, ten vice-governors, and about twenty-five other provincial leaders . . ."[8]

The Socialist Education Campaign in the villages put similar pressures for conformity on the local levels. Basic level elections during the spring were used to eliminate "Rightists." Propaganda campaigns featured exemplars such as Liu Jiemei, whose life was the subject of a pictorial exhibition. A poor peasant, he had joined the Communists in 1949 and acquired some fields during land reform. By 1953 capitalistic ideas got into his head, and he lost interest in the collective. Demoralized after the High Tide retreat, he began hoarding grain. But his comrades "struggled" against him in 1957, causing him to see his selfishness. As a result he rededicated himself to the collective.[9]

In January, February, and March 1958, Mao convened three conferences of central and provincial Party leaders as well as a Supreme State Conference and the National People's Congress. His rambling speeches make interesting reading.[10] One of his themes was dislike for bureaucratic planners and managers. He disapproved of unquestioning mimicry of Russia. The Soviets taught us many things, he admitted, but we must learn from them creatively and avoid "dogmatism." He recalled the days when artists used to paint him shorter than Stalin. Mao also urged that the time was right for China to launch an all-out effort.

> Our nation is like an atom. . . . When this atom's nucleus is smashed the thermal energy released will have really tremendous power. We should be able to do things which we could not do before.

Rejecting the charge that he craved excessively for greatness and success, he retorted, "Well then, should we seek pettiness and failure?"

> There are two lines for building socialism: is it better to go about it coldly and deliberately, or boldly and joyfully? . . . If, in eighteen years, we can equal what [the Soviet Union has] done in the past forty years . . . we should do precisely that. For there are more of us and the political conditions are different, too: we are livelier, and there is more Leninism here. They, on the other hand, have let part of Leninism go by the boards, they are lifeless and without vitality.

He did recognize that movements can build up too much steam and run off the track. He cautioned against rashly publishing reports of the achievements in one province that would challenge others rashly to match or surpass them. But although the leaders must not nourish false illusions among themselves, the masses should not be publicly discouraged from forging ahead. "Pessimism is wrong."

> Right now there is a gust of wind amounting to a force 10 typhoon. We must not impede this publicly, but within our own ranks we must speak clearly, and damp down the atmosphere a little. We must get rid of the empty reports and foolish boasting, we must not compete for reputation, but serve reality.

Mao even admitted that only a minority of leaders were enthusiastic and that the others, although they were going along, would have to be shown concrete results. Again and again he reverted to airy optimism. He extolled creativity and youth against book learning and stale institutions. He said, "If you are too realistic you can't write poetry." As the poet of revolution, he had no intention of bogging down in reality.

In these meetings and dozens of others at the provincial level, the new strategy for development emerged. China must "walk on two legs," which meant building a capital-intensive modern sector while relying on less sophisticated technology in agriculture and small-scale manufacturing. At the same time, the social revolution must continue: The economic and social gap between village and city, between mental and manual labor, between bosses and workers, and between school and production must be closed. Slogans from the High Tide period reemerged. Everyone was urged to produce "more, faster, better, and more economically." China was carrying out a Great Leap Forward. The Party asked Chen Boda to set up a new theoretical journal, *Red Flag*. It became the clarion for the new developments.

These conferences heard reports of dramatic increases in output. Starting in December 1957, the upward adjustment of both agricultural and industrial targets began. It soon escalated to the claim that the goals of Mao's ambitious plan for agricultural development would be reached far ahead of schedule and that in industry China would surpass Great Britain in fifteen years. (But these claims were still modest compared with later ones.)

Rural mobilization took the form of off-season water control projects. As many as 60 million peasants were involved, being fed in communal mess halls. A movement was launched to spur technological innovations, such as the effort to "cartize" the south, that is, to replace carrying poles with wheeled carts. (This initiative failed to recognize that adequate roads and paths did not yet exist.) There was a campaign to eliminate the "four pests": flies, mosquitoes, rats, and sparrows. (When it was recognized that sparrows actually controlled other pests, they were replaced on the list of four by bedbugs.) There were mass mobilizations to gather fertilizer, reclaim land, and improve soil.

The modern sector was not neglected. In December the propaganda apparatus began to promote a Great Leap Forward in industry: not merely increased output but also the thorough decentralization of this sector. Starting in December 1957 and with further pushes in January and March 1958, ministries in charge of consumer goods were ordered to hand over their enterprises to provincial, municipal, or county governments. In addition, it was decided that every locality should establish small-scale industries by using its own financial resources and local labor power. This use of both large-scale and small-scale technologies was called "walking on two legs." Concurrently, there was a movement to revolutionize industrial relations and management. Reviving one of Mao's favorite themes, the Party began to attack the worship of technicians and experts and the social gulf between managers and workers. Cadres were expected to join in production work, and laborers were supposed to participate in management.

Because decentralization and mobilization required large numbers of supervisory personnel, the Party began a massive downward assignment of cadres: from the central government to the provinces, from the provinces to the counties, from the counties to the production line in agriculture or industry. In all, well over 8 million cadres were transferred down. They were joined by a million students sent to do manual labor and by large numbers of People's Liberation Army soldiers. Many demobilized soldiers were assigned as local cadres on their release from the army. At the same time, large numbers of male peasants were transferred to industrial work, which created, of all things, a labor shortage in the countryside.

By spring, results appeared to be excellent. Many water control projects had been completed and may have contributed to the abundant summer harvest of 1958. There was great hope for the flexibility and creativity of the decentralized and local industries. During April, Mao and his supporters traveled the provinces to inspect progress and to make sure of political support in the important upcoming Party meeting.

## Exerting Our Utmost Efforts: June 1958–November 1958

From summer to early winter, the Maoist program of revolutionary modernization reached its climax, punctuated by announcements of ever higher targets and achievements. Agricultural collectivization culminated in the formation of the Rural People's Communes. In virtually every other field there were vigorous initiatives inspired by the new line. Military confrontation added extra tension and excitement, particularly during the brief bombardment of the Nationalist-held island of Jinmen (Quemoy).

The stage was set by the meeting of the Eighth Party Congress (second session) in early May 1958. Mao and his allies had been pushing the radical program for six months, and, as early as February 1958, the National People's Congress had endorsed the Great Leap Forward. The May Party Congress was convened in an urgent and secret session to consolidate the Party behind the new movement. Mao and Liu were the dominant figures at this meeting, and they gained the support of a number of hitherto cautious leaders. Zhou Enlai receded into the background while Chen Yun, the chief spokesperson for a gradualist economic program, was not even in attendance. He had been on assignment to Moscow.

Liu Shaoqi delivered the major address at the Party Congress. Many have discerned a certain reserve underneath his enthusi-

asm, but Liu left no doubt about his commitment to the Great
Leap. Hurling a challenge at the remaining doubters, he said

> But some [comrades] have not yet learnt anything. They say:
> "We'll settle accounts with you after the autumn harvest." Well
> let them wait to settle accounts. They will lose out in the end! [11]

He announced that the Party had adopted a new "General Line,"
one of those statements of overall goals that the Party issues at
important transitions and that govern all policies. Back in 1952,
with consolidation completed, the General Line became

> to bring about, step by step, socialist industrialization and to ac-
> complish, step by step, the socialist transformation of agriculture,
> handicrafts and capitalist industry and commerce over a fairly long
> period. [12]

This emphasis on "step by step" and "a fairly long period,"
was briefly abandoned in the High Tide of 1955 with the introduction of "more, faster, better, and more economically," then
reinstated in 1956 as the country backed away from the High
Tide. Now the new General Line revived the urgent overtones

> to build socialism by exerting our utmost efforts, and pressing ahead
> consistently to achieve greater, faster, better, and more econom-
> ical results. [13]

Liu also spoke of a "leap forward on every front in our socialist
construction," [14] another revival of a High Tide slogan. Although Liu did not call it a "Great Leap Forward," the man
who delivered the important agricultural report did use these
words, and the Party Congress officially approved the movement under this heroic designation.

The Party Congress and the Central Committee Plenum that
followed effected some significant political reshuffling at the top
of the pyramid. Zhou Enlai and Chen Yun lost influence. Lin
Biao, moving up the ladder, was elected to the powerful Stand-

ing Committee of the Politburo. This promotion weakened the minister of defense, Peng Dehuai, whose position had already begun so slip in 1956.

Then Mao called an important meeting of the Military Affairs Committee. More than a thousand officers were in attendance from late May to July 22, 1958, and heard speeches by the highest Party luminaries, including Lin Biao, Deng Xiaoping, Peng Dehuai, and Mao himself. This meeting abandoned Peng Dehuai's approach. Rather than continue building a Soviet-style army dependent on Russian aid, the Military Affairs Committee mapped a course of complete independence, including the development of China's own nuclear weapons. This new policy spelled fewer advanced conventional weapons and a greater reliance on guerrilla strategy.

Another outcome of this military conference was renewed belligerency toward Taiwan. The Chinese leaders seemed to be acting on their view that the "East wind" could overcome the "West wind" and to be putting their Soviet support as well as American resolve to the test. Beijing may have acted to forestall anticipated action against the mainland from Taiwan. An additional motive (possibly the main one) was the emotional charge that a national military crisis would add to the Great Leap Forward.

At the end of July, Nationalist and Communist Chinese aircraft clashed in the Taiwan straits. This made the Russians extremely nervous, and on July 31, Khrushchev came secretly to Beijing with his minister of defense. He may well have tried to persuade the Chinese to dampen the Taiwan crisis. As inducements he offered several deals, including construction in China of a radio station for the Russian fleet, a joint Sino-Russian naval command in the Far East, joint air defenses, and perhaps even Soviet missiles in China. But what Khrushchev considered inducements the Chinese viewed suspiciously. They had no illusions about who would dominate joint ventures. Consequently, the first secretary returned to Moscow empty-handed. The Chinese began a campaign to increase steel production for a possible war over Taiwan. On August 24 the People's Liberation Army began heavy bombardment of the offshore island of Jinmen (Quemoy).

The Party launched a stepped-up and harsher rectification campaign in which all cadres examined their thoughts in small-group meetings. Although CCP membership was expanding rapidly at this time, as many as a million cadres were rebuked, put on probation, or expelled during the year. This further dampened potential dissent and predisposed Party members to embrace directives from the center with utmost enthusiasm.

The most spectacular of all the Great Leap Forward developments was the Rural People's Communes. Already in the winter of 1957–58 the massive water control projects demonstrated the need for a large organizational unit. This need converged with two notions dear to Mao and other Chinese Marxists. One was the memory of Yanan when distinctions of rank and status were at a minimum. Everyone did everything: Peasants fought, soldiers spun cotton, and Mao even grew his own tobacco. The second was the ever-present inspiration of the 1871 Paris Commune, when the lower classes briefly established an egalitarian dictatorship.

In the early summer of 1958 supercooperatives appeared, especially in Henan Province, which had become a hotbed of Maoism. The first and most famous was the "Sputnik Commune" established in July. Also in July, Chen Boda wrote major articles in the new Party journal *Red Flag*, outlining the theory of the commune. It was to be an all-purpose organization.

Our direction is to combine, step by step and in an orderly manner, workers (industry), peasants (agriculture), businessmen (exchange), students (culture and education), and soldiers (military) into a large commune, which is to constitute our nation's basic social unit. In this kind of commune, industry, agriculture and exchange are the people's material life; culture and education are the people's spiritual life which reflects their material life. The total arming of the people is to protect this material and spiritual life.[15]

As Chen Boda was known to be Mao's ideological collaborator, this article was bound to have great influence.

Soon the Chairman himself got into the act by touring some of the new communes. On August 12, the *People's Daily* carried a headline story entitled "Chairman Mao Inspects Henan Farm Villages," in which he praised their productivity and said, "If there is this kind of commune [here] then there can be many communes [everywhere]." [16] In September he called for extending the movement to the entire country. Coming just when the fulminations against American imperialism and its Taiwan lackeys were at their fiercest, this gave the commune movement a mighty push. Communes formed at an incredible pace. By the end of August, when the Party formally announced its approval, already 30 percent of peasant families were in communes. In all, it took only two months to reorganize virtually the entire peasantry of China in approximately 24,000 communes.

These new units attempted to mobilize the rural labor force to achieve many things at once. Bumper harvests were expected while at the same time a variety of other enterprises went rapidly forward. Most prominent was the movement to build "backyard furnaces" to make iron and steel in the belief that production of these basic industrial materials could be increased by adding thousands of simpler local operations to China's modern mills and foundries. Here again was the "walking on two legs" strategy in operation. Mao later said that 90 million were mobilized to construct and operate furnaces. An eyewitness described them as follows.

Furnace fields are everywhere in Lushan county, southern Henan province—plots of hundreds of small earthen furnaces were "growing," in late autumn when I was there, alongside fields of sweet potatoes and tobacco. From a distance the leaping flames and columns of smoke look like some new construction site accidentally ablaze. On the scene the atmosphere is like a fairground, with scores of people bustling in and out of the rows of furnaces.

Small red flags fly overhead indicating the sections belonging to the various companies and squads of farmer-steelworkers, who are organized like militia units. The air is filled with the high-pitched melodies of local operas pouring through an amplifier above the site and accompanied by the hum of blowers, the panting of gasoline engines, the honking of heavily-laden lorries, and the bellowing of oxen hauling ore and coal.

At one of the ten-foot-high furnaces, a man climbs a wooden ladder to dump coke and firewood through the top. After a few minutes beside the 1,000-degree heat, he descends and another worker goes up to tamp the fuel down with his rake. A third man follows to pull the hot rake away from the blast of the fire. Beside the furnace another crew is pushing the handle of the huge home-made wooden bellows. With all his might one of them pulls the handle, half as tall as himself, and pushes it back with the weight of his body. Three other men standing by to take their turns jokingly cheer him on.[17]


One striking feature of the Great Leap Forward was the massive entry of women into the work force. Millions of female peasants entered the fields as all those backyard furnaces and expanded operations in established plants drained men from the farm. One estimate suggests that between 1957 and 1958 the numbers of clerical and industrial workers increased by over 20 million. Demographic statistics show a sharp increase in urban population between 1957 and 1960 and a corresponding slight decline in rural population. To replace this labor, the communes had to mobilize women and free them from their household tasks. This required mess halls and nurseries to take over cooking and child care. Estimates differ, but by early 1959 there were possibly as many as 3 million of these commune canteens feeding perhaps 90 percent of the rural population.

Observers and participants have reacted variously to this massive infusion of women into the production front. Lamenting the disruptive effects of the changes, Peng Dehuai, the key critic of the Great Leap Forward, wrote the following verses.

Grain scattered on the ground, potato leaves withered;
Strong young people have left to smelt iron, only children and
old women reaped the crops;
How can they pass the coming year?
Allow me to appeal for the people.[18]

On the other hand, many saw these changes as a further step in the liberation and equalization of women.

Another striking feature of the Great Leap was its effect on education. Mao had ambivalent feelings about book learning. He had been trained as a teacher and in his last years claimed that he wanted to be remembered only as the Great Teacher. On the other hand, he had been bitterly disappointed by the criticisms of intellectuals during the Hundred Flowers campaign and hoped to create a new intelligentsia out of the peasants and workers. He was suspicious of stuffy, uncreative academics and convinced that true education must combine both theory and practice, study and labor. Nothing pleased him more than reports of ordinary people making important discoveries and innovations.

It was not surprising that the Great Leap included an assault on the existing school system and bold strides toward revolutionary, egalitarian education. Mao was adamant that China scrap foreign models, especially the Soviet Union, and chart its own course. She should revive the Yanan tradition, where study and propaganda had been an integral part of social revolt and guerrilla war. In January 1958, he instituted a work-and-study curriculum, combining labor and education. This approach de-emphasized classroom academics, memorization, and teacher authority. In the name of equity, Mao preferred to increase peasants' and workers' access to basic schooling rather than to extend expensive advanced training to the educationally advantaged in the name of economic development. Even in the elite track, he pushed for worker-peasant quotas, remedial classes, and decentralized admissions.

The administrative decentralization of the Great Leap Forward also hit the Ministry of Higher Education. The Beijing bureaucrats who had controlled over fifty institutions of higher education were absorbed by the Ministry of Education, and the new combined ministry lost control of all but fourteen of these schools. Mao also promoted local preparation of educational materials and committees of Party members, teachers, and students to determine curriculum and methods. Prior to 1958, educational opportunities had been contracting, but the Great Leap created thousands of new work-and-study schools and many new places in the ordinary secondary schools and universities. For a euphoric moment it seemed that "more, faster, better, and more economically" was a slogan for education, too, and that China could have it both ways: universal mass education and expanding secondary schools and colleges.

In the summer and fall of 1958 the "Three Red Banners" (the General Line, the Great Leap Forward, and the People's Communes) were being carried by the masses toward a great victory. In the cities there were boom conditions. The sense of a great people's crusade pervaded everywhere. Martial music and exhortations pouring from millions of loudspeakers were matched by slogans painted on every wall: "PUSH OUT THE WITHERED, TAKE IN THE NEW. . . . WALK ON TWO LEGS. . . . TURN OVER YOUR LIFE. . . . DON'T CRAWL BEHIND OTHERS AT A SNAIL'S PACE. . . . DOWN WITH ALL FOREIGN FRAMEWORKS. . . . SELF-RELIANCE. . . . STRIKE THE IRON WHILE HOT. . . . BETTER GET IT DONE IN ONE STROKE THAN DRAG ON." [19] Reports coming in from factories and communes indicated heroic increases in production. In late October the 1958 harvest was announced as virtually double the output of 1957. Steel output reportedly doubled as did the production of other commodities. Similar increases were anticipated for 1959.

Not only was there euphoria over quantitative leaps. The belief began to spread that the Great Leap Forward was leading to an early establishment of true communism. In factories, the new management-worker relations and the abandonment of the piece-rate payment fostered egalitarianism. The communes seemed to be even more advanced. Many of them had socialized virtually all property under communal ownership. Some inaugurated a free supply system for food and other commodities and services, thereby approaching the Marxist ideal of "from each according to his abilities, to each according to his needs." As an enthusiastic editorial in the *People's Daily* for September 3, 1958, said

> the people's commune is the most appropriate organizational form in China for accelerating socialist construction and the transition to communism. It will become the basic social unit in the future communist society as thinkers—from many outstanding utopian socialists to Marx, Engels, and Lenin—had predicted on many occasions.[20]

However, underneath the glittering surface all was not well. No doubt, the soundness of the Great Leap principles will continue to be debated, but clearly in 1958 they were pushed too far, too fast. The massive reallocation of labor and resources during this period ranks as one of the largest peacetime disturbances ever and caused massive disruptions in the economic system. Many of the initiatives were ill-conceived, the most blatant example being the backyard steel furnaces, which Mao himself later declared to be a great mistake. Other examples include deep plowing, close planting, and other inappropriate innovations. The tendency of commune managers to force socialized ownership and equal compensation and the disruptions in family life caused by mess halls, labor gangs, and long working days lowered worker incentives. By the winter of 1958, China's buoyant leaders began to realize that something had gone seriously amiss.

## The Great Leap in Decline

### *Readjustment: November 1958–June 1959*

In the winter and spring, signs of trouble multiplied. The summer harvest had been excellent, and the fall crop was hailed as no less outstanding according to glowing government statistics. How could it be then that grain rations in the cities were actually reduced? Later in 1959, Peng Dehuai claimed to have learned that average rice consumption fell below levels of the 1930s and 1940s. Even Mao himself later acknowledged that state procurement of grain from the peasants declined.

Other sectors experienced equally serious problems. During their brief heyday, the backyard furnaces produced 3 million tons of nearly useless steel while draining off resources that could have been used productively elsewhere. Forests had been chopped down to fuel the furnaces, causing long-term environmental degradation. Efforts to expand manufacturing output at all costs led to serious deterioration of quality and to the neglect of plant maintenance. With economic consequences beginning to affect the already pinched circumstances of most people, both in the city and the countryside, rumblings of restiveness and dissatisfaction began to surface (although it must be observed that probably nowhere in peacetime have the lives of so many people been so deeply altered with so little overt protest).

Foreign relations also deteriorated during the period of the Great Leap. Tension with the United States increased over the shelling of Jinmen. Moscow strongly disapproved of China's audacity both in foreign and in domestic affairs. And in March a new crisis arose in Tibet when Khambu rebels revolted and briefly threatened Lhasa, the capital city. The Tibet troubles, together with deep disagreement over the Sino-Indian border, began to put serious strain on relations with New Delhi.

Mao and the other leaders were not slow to notice these difficulties. High-level meetings, culminating in a Central Committee Plenum, punctuate this period and tell the story of how the leaders attempted to define and cope with the problems. They tended to explain the difficulties by blaming lower cadres for improperly carrying out central intentions. The Great Leap Forward, the Rural People's Communes, and the General Line remained correct, but implementation was too hasty and extreme. Therefore, the Party readjusted the inflated production claims and passed resolutions to dampen the excesses. Some have interpreted these meetings as the beginning of a retreat from the Great Leap. But this view may be too simple. Mao and his supporters shared with millions of regional and local cadres a heavy personal investment in the Great Leap. To repudiate it was out of the question. This was equally true of the Party organization. Having committed so much authority and prestige to radical modernization, the Party could not reverse itself without calling its vaunted judgment into question. In these circumstances, the proper course of action was, not to retreat, but to save the Great Leap Forward through judicious trimming and to vindicate it by launching more all-out efforts as soon as possible.

More conferences were convened between January and March. These included both Party and non-Party gatherings, capped by a Central Committee Plenum and a Supreme State Conference and National People's Congress. They carried on the task of assessing the damage and moderating the policies of the Great Leap. Mao took the lead in this retrenchment effort. In one meeting he went so far as to refer to himself as a "right opportunist" struggling against "left adventurists" on behalf of millions of local cadres and hundreds of millions of peasants.[21] As these remarks of Mao's suggest, there were now sharp differences of opinion about the success of the Great Leap Forward and whether or not to continue it. Advocates of retrenchment argued that excesses had to be reversed. By contrast, the directors of Party rural work departments at all levels, who attended a conference in January, 1959, had lost none of their confidence in the movement. They extolled the enthusiasm of the masses and called for a new "Leap" in 1959.

The general inclination during the spring and early summer of 1959 was to correct the mistakes of the Great Leap Forward, consolidate its achievements, and prepare for a new surge. This advance-and-retreat was a familiar pattern. Long experience had told the CCP leaders that campaigns led to excesses that then required readjustment. Even as the Great Leap was getting under way, they spoke of "saddlelike" development. They did not anticipate having to retreat so far that the advance would be virtually negated.

By June it appeared that the country could expect more relaxation. The top leaders were continuing to tour the provinces to assess developments. Various moderating resolutions and statements issued from the Party center. Mao's speeches emphasized going slowly, combining a practical spirit with revolutionary fervor, and setting realistic targets. The Party and government issued corrections of previously reported figures. Some of the more pragmatic leaders promoted this slogan, "The Whole Nation Is a Single Chessboard," in an effort to restore centralized economic coordination. Directives went down telling local Party cadres to quit monopolizing all governmental authority. Commune leaders were now directed to turn back land ownership, production decisions, and income allocations to the production brigades, which, in most cases, meant the former cooperatives. Agriculture was declared in need of a larger share of national investment.

A political change of uncertain significance also took place. Mao Zedong had been both the Chairman of the Party and formal head of state since 1949. He now decided that when his term expired in 1959, he would not stand for reelection to the latter office by the National People's Congress. This decision had been taken in early 1958 for the purpose of relieving him of ceremonial chores and allowing him to concentrate his energies on overall policy. Coming, however, during the contraction phase, Mao's replacement by Liu Shaoqi as head of state could be construed as a demotion. The center took great pains to reassure the Party rank and file and the public that this was not the case. But despite the appearance that political affairs were under control, a ferment was working beneath the surface. Deep dissatisfaction among some Party leaders and Russian opposition to the Great Leap Forward were the main ingredients in this leadership crisis, which erupted in July and August 1959. The key figure was Peng Dehuai.

## Showdown at Lushan: July 1959–August 1959

Peng Dehuai seems to have been an early critic of the Great Leap Forward, as his poem, cited earlier, attests. His dissatisfaction must have been compounded by Lin Biao's May 1959 promotion, over Peng's head, to the Standing Committee of the Politburo and by the summer Military Affairs Committee meeting that gutted his long-standing policies in national defense. There was also personal friction between him and Mao. The two men had a history of disagreements dating back to the war years. By contrast, Lin Biao struck an adoring posture toward Mao. During Mao's June 1958 speech at the Military Affairs Committee, for example, Lin interrupted the Chairman several times with fawning praise and echoes, such as the following comments when Mao said China must be more selective in learning from the USSR:

> Chief Lin said: "In political matters, such as Party leadership and in political work, our army has a fine tradition of its own. Our Party's Marxist-Leninist level is very high, not to speak of the Chairman's. The Chairman has said that our editorials are at a higher level than those of *Pravda*." [22]

Peng Dehuai, who at this stage in his life had become gruff and testy, may perhaps be forgiven if he felt not only professionally but also personally afflicted.

In the course of an April 1959 Politburo meeting, Peng criticized Mao for conducting the Great Leap Forward on his own authority and circumventing the other members of the Politburo Standing Committee. Mao, in return, criticized Peng. This exchange had no apparent immediate effects. But, in fact, the subsequent events suggest that on both sides personal and policy differences were pushing the two men to a confrontation. Peng, in his capacity as minister of defense, left China later in April for a tour of the Soviet Union and Eastern Europe. While he was gone, personnel changes in the armed forces removed some of his supporters. For his part, Peng appears to have tried in some way to enlist the help—or at least the sympathy—of the Russians in his disagreements with Mao. When he was in Albania, he met the Soviet premier and, as a hostile Maoist attack of several years later expressed it, he "informed baldheaded Khrushchev of the shortcomings of the Great Leap Forward, and the latter encouraged the former to go home and oppose Chairman Mao."[23]

Just how Peng hoped to use the USSR is not clear. Both he and Khrushchev may have believed that a Russian threat to withdraw military assistance would put irresistible pressure on Mao. If that was Peng's thinking, he miscalculated because, by colluding with foreigners, he was committing a cardinal sin of the CCP. This was the transgression for which Gao Gang had been purged in 1953. Just one week after Peng's return, the Russians abrogated their agreement to supply China nuclear military technology. We may assume that, upon his return, Peng advocated restoring the Russian assistance and that this involved some Chinese concessions.

Thus the stage was set for trouble. In July 1959 the Politburo met at Lushan for more discussion of Great Leap problems and countermeasures. The conference began on the generally positive note sounded by Mao:

The achievements are tremendous, the problems are numerous, the experience is rich, and the future is bright.[24]

But in small-group discussions Peng and others were outspokenly critical of the hectic campaign and the communes. They also seem to have done some personal lobbying for their position. Peng wrote and circulated a letter to Mao. Although the letter was temperate in its criticisms of the Great Leap Forward and explicitly exonerated the Chairman, it was read, probably correctly, as an attack on Mao's leadership. There was at least one other letter circulated, and there were several verbal expressions of agreement with Peng. The day after Mao received the letter, his Great Leap was the object of another attack, this one by Nikita Khrushchev writing in the pages of *Pravda*. The issue had now escalated to the question of the basic correctness of the Great Leap and to Mao's style of leadership. Peng was treading on dangerous ground.

A week after receiving Peng's letter, Mao counterattacked. In at least two different talks, he responded, not to the substantive issues, but to the challenge to his leadership. He charged the dissidents with anti-Party activity, conspiring in secret, and colluding with a foreign power. Mao played his trump card: that, above all, the Party must stay united behind him. Certainly, unity would collapse if Mao chose to oppose a majority of the Politburo, and more than once the Chairman threatened to break with his colleagues.

Probably Peng was looking for Mao to shoulder some of the blame for China's troubles and to relinquish active leadership to others. This would allow the pre-1958 policies to be reinstated, particularly Peng's military policies. But once the Chairman began to frame the issue in terms of Party unity and patriotism, Peng and his supporters were lost. During the next few weeks Peng and several supporters were isolated and attacked. In a vain attempt to salvage his position, he publicly criticized himself and also wrote a penitent letter to Mao.

Thus ended the career of one of the CCP's more colorful and capable leaders. Peng was dismissed as minister of defense, to be replaced by Lin Biao. Henceforth he received only minor assignments. Actually, he was treated rather gently, which reflected a widely held, if unspoken, belief that his criticism of Mao was just. In 1962 he attempted an unsuccessful political comeback. In 1974 he died in detention through cruel neglect.

## End of the Great Leap: 1960

Peng Dehuai's challenge at the Lushan meeting disrupted the normal wavelike pattern of the movement. Although a moderating phase had set in, Mao counterattacked politically to protect his position. Cadres in the ministries of defense and foreign affairs were organized to criticize Peng and the "anti-Party" clique. In the provinces, meetings were held to expose "rightist thinking, rightist sentiments, and rightist activities."[25] Many were purged. It appears that the rapid growth in Party membership of the preceding years reversed, as up to a million cadres were expelled. An anti-Rightist media campaign grew increasingly strident and began to suggest an insidious connection between the USSR, Peng, and anti-Party Rightist subversion.

A revival of the Great Leap Forward accompanied this political crackdown. Maoist credibility was linked with revolutionary modernization. When Peng challenged the program, Maoists reacted by reaffirming its correctness. Moderate commune policies were partially countermanded and abandoned as local cadres, fearful of appearing to be Rightist opportunists, swung back to radicalism. More mess halls and more mobilization were called for as devolution of management to production brigades was denounced. There was a push to establish urban communes, mainly among workers in light industry. By the summer of 1960, for example, virtually all the residents of Canton were organized into such communes.

This backlash was accompanied by increasingly bad feelings toward Moscow. The mutual irritation between the two sides over such issues as East-West policy, Taiwan, and the Great Leap was deepened when Mao perceived a Russian shadow behind Peng's challenge. Protests to the Soviet Union were presumably rebuffed. And then, as China's differences with India over the Tibet crisis and border issues grew sharper, *Tass* published an editorial that, far from backing the Chinese, struck an even-handed posture between the two sides. This amounted to a disavowal of China and has been considered by some to be "the first broadside in the Sino-Soviet dispute."[26]

Differences widened further in the wake of Khrushchev's visit to the United States. Although the Chinese cautiously supported the trip in the beginning, by late September 1959, Mao was extremely upset about Khrushchev. On the very day of the latter's arrival in Beijing to participate in the celebrations marking the tenth anniversary of the People's Republic, a vituperative criticism of Peng Dehuai appeared in the *People's Daily*. The Soviet leader returned this slap by lecturing the Chinese leaders on the subject of peaceful coexistence at their formal National Day reception.

Mao later complained that at this time high Party discussions were so preoccupied with foreign relations that domestic policy suffered. In April 1960, *Red Flag* published a long attack on Yugoslav revisionism. It was an open secret that the real target was the USSR. The passage of time only exacerbated the conflict. By the summer, Peng Zhen and Khrushchev were to be found trading insults at a conference of Communist powers. The culmination came in July, when Khrushchev recalled all Soviet technical advisers in China. No doubt, he thought that this would bring Mao around, but the effect was to alienate the Chinese even more. This split profoundly affected China's development. However inadequate Moscow's assistance may have been, it was now withdrawn completely. Beijing burned an important bridge at a time when no alternate support was at hand. That China would pay such a price for autonomy reflects the depth of Chinese nationalism.

The revived Great Leap Forward could not last. It was cut short by the same economic difficulties that had forced the earlier policy reversals. Weather conditions in 1960 were even worse than in 1959. The innumerable dislocations further hobbled production. So, by the summer of 1960, the Party was again adopting moderate policies. But the Great Leap came to an end without ever being explicitly repudiated. Indeed, the press continued to trumpet the correctness of Chairman Mao and the Three Red Banners more fervently than ever. Within the Party at all levels there persisted a current of pro-Great Leap opinion. The central icon for these elements was, of course, Mao, and their strongest organizational base was the PLA under Lin Biao. But these enthusiasts were opposed by many who, like Peng, were dismayed at the actual results of the Maoist policies.

The Great Leap Forward has had its apologists, who argued that its harm was exaggerated. They countered that, despite temporary economic problems, revolutionary gains were achieved. Old ways were shaken up. Market economies have setbacks, too, they said, and without the communes China would have experienced even greater difficulties in coping with the adverse weather conditions of the years 1959 through 1961. These arguments were most often heard in the late 1960s and through much of the 1970s. Since Mao's death, both the official Chinese view and the prevailing outside opinion have emphasized the damage caused by the movement.

While taking cognizance of this apologetic view, our own summary is that the Great Leap Forward, like the 1955 High Tide, of which it was essentially a massive revival, resulted in an economic disaster comparable to a major depression. The years 1960 and 1961 were particularly trying for the entire nation, with almost everyone struggling just to get food and millions dying from the effects of malnutrition. The economic aftereffects were felt for years, especially in agriculture. As a simple index of this, per capita grain production did not recover its 1957 level until 1973. Note also the downturn in national income in Figure 5.

Politically, the Great Leap produced increasing strife and disagreement within the Chinese Communist Party and ruined Sino-Soviet relationships, which had benefited China. Domestically, the difficulties forced the CCP to resort to intensifed indoctrination and coercion, thereby weakening the legitimacy of the regime. All the same, the Great Leap Forward must be regarded as a heroic failure, a colossal revolutionary drama that may have produced some intangible results favorable to modernization. If Maoist policies did not create a socialist utopia, it was not for want of trying.

# 5

# Depression, Recovery, and Struggle at the Top: 1960–65

The Great Leap Forward plunged the whole country into hunger, unemployment, despair, and lawlessness. Alarmed Party leaders had to abandon the radical policies. As a result, the hard times bottomed out in 1962, and the economy improved each year thereafter. But recovery also caused disagreements. Was the revolution being sold out in the name of economic production? Some, like Mao, said yes. Although he conceded that the Great Leap had flaws, he still embraced its central vision: achieving wonders through the determination of militant cadres and mobilized masses.

In late 1962, Mao insisted that the relaxation had gone too far and pushed for steps to revitalize the revolution. Consequently the Party launched a series of campaigns in the countryside collectively known as the Socialist Education movement. There were parallel campaigns in industry, education, and cultural life. But three years of developing and adjusting these programs produced deepening disagreements between a disgruntled Mao and his recalcitrant colleagues. By 1966 consensus among the Party elite fragmented into a great falling out.

# The Immediate Repercussions of the Great Leap

## Depression

The years 1960 and 1961 were a terrible ordeal. As one economist concludes, "The scale of fluctuation in this trough was almost unprecedented in the history of any country in peace time."[1] Grain production dropped to a level where the national reserves were being exhausted. China, which had recently exported grain, now had to purchase Australian and Canadian wheat to feed the cities. Across the land, people went hungry. Nor was the industrial sector spared. First consumer goods and then heavy industry followed into a steep decline. Fig. 5 in Chap. 4 dramatically illustrates the drop in in overall national income during the difficult years starting in 1959.

Millions who had poured into the cities during the Great Leap Forward and more millions of young people finishing school were thrown out of work. The birth rate slumped. The death rate surged. From recently released statistics it is estimated that between 1958 and 1962 there were 15 million to 30 million abnormal mortalities. China's population actually declined by 1.5 percent in 1960 and 0.5 percent in 1961. There are scattered accounts of popular unrest and even some armed uprisings.

## Adjustment

In 1960 a Chinese mountain climbing team scaled Mt. Everest. Drawing a lesson from their achievement, the Chairperson of the State Planning Committee hailed not only their daring but also their careful calculation. They

cherished the high ambition . . . [yet] they conducted scientific analysis . . . adopting decisions on the basis of seeking truth from facts. . . . [By contrast, although the Chinese people recently] . . . created many miracles unknown before in history, [there were nevertheless] shortcomings, . . . acting blindly, . . . and indiscriminately starting more and more projects [mistakes that required] certain sensible adjustments.[2]

This soberly optimistic note, so restrained by comparison with the tone of just a few months earlier, reflected a dawning realization of very serious economic trouble. The Party held a succession of top-level meetings starting in the summer of 1960 and culminating in a February 1962 conference attended by 7,000 Party officials. In the course of these eighteen months the consensus moved toward an increasingly sober and even alarmed appraisal. In response, the components of the Great Leap Forward were abandoned or modified. Posters still trumpeted, "Long Live the People's Communes," but the unspoken operative rule was this utterance of Deng Xiaoping, "Black cats, white cats, what does it matter? So long as they can catch rats, they are good cats!" Fig. 6 is a schematic representation of the modified commune system as it existed from the early 1960s into the late 1970s.

Two *People's Daily* editorials illustrate how successive adjustments in agricultural policy responded to the deepening concern. The editorial for November 20, 1960 advocated transferring decision making from the central commune administration to the smaller production brigades. Five days later the paper went even further. It argued for devolving authority onto the smallest subdivisions, the production teams. "Production teams . . . are the key in perfecting the people's commune system . . ."[3] They should have more cadres assigned to them and land and tools permanently turned over to them. As inducements to higher production, the teams should be offered contracts for fixed quantities of grain, with bonuses for overfulfillment. Individual team members should be compensated according to their labor. In addition, they should be permitted to make and sell handicrafts on open markets. The fact that some families would do better than others under these arrangements must be accepted. Such proposals read like a list of Great Leap heresies.

These measures were progressively implemented under the

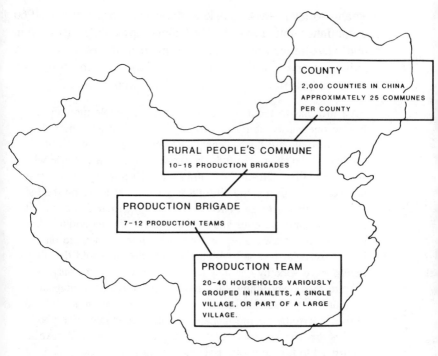

FIG. 6 The rural People's commune system: 1960–80.

leadership of some of the more pragmatic leaders, particularly Chen Yun, whom Liu Shaoqi raised again to a position of authority. A Party directive made production teams the basic accounting unit by March 1961. Chen Yun and Deng Xiaoping pushed an extension of private plots, free markets, and—by early 1962—even the "Anhwei responsibility system," a family-based farming arrangement organized according to production teams. It was getting very close to private farming. (This system was later widely adopted in the 1980s.) For the economy as a whole, Chen Yun undertook to lead the effort back toward more planning, more coordination, and even some reliance on private enterprise.

One urgent need was to get the unemployed out of the cities.

Programs to return these people to the villages began in late 1960 and continued into 1962. In 1961 alone upwards of 10 million people were moved away; and still more millions, in 1962. A Swedish observer who was then in Beijing gave the following account of how those who "went down" were chosen.

> Each firm has to report a certain number of people moving out. But no one can be compelled to go; the decision must be voluntary. Meetings are held evening after evening to consider these conflicting obligations. Everybody knows that the list of those who are to leave has already been drawn up. Everybody knows that the meetings will not end until those whose names are on the list have volunteered to go. This list is never mentioned. People all talk about patriotic duty and the welfare of the individual. But they all look at each other and wonder whose names are on the list. Those who feel safe volunteer—and are then told that they cannot leave. One by one they take the plunge, until the only ones left are those who know they have been chosen. Evening after evening the pressure is increased. Eventually it is impossible to refuse, but some people manage to find a loophole. Everybody notices this and knows what it means; someone else will have to go instead to fill the quota. Evening after evening these people sit facing each other, torn between conscience and self-interest, choosing the victims of the Chinese crisis.[4]

On the other hand, the heavy-handed treatment of the intelligentsia eased up. Khrushchev's withdrawal of Soviet advisers made China's own experts all the more critical. Their contribution could not be maximized in a repressive atmosphere. Consequently, not only technical, but also cultural areas were allowed to push Marxism into the background. Plays, articles, books, and films appeared that obliquely criticized the Great Leap Forward and, by implication its author, Mao. The year 1961 saw the staging of one particularly interesting historical drama about a Ming dynasty official named Hai Rui, of which more will be said later. There was also talk of strengthening the democratic parties. The National People's Congress and the Chinese People's Political Consultative Conference became more active.

Meanwhile, in the countryside it was necessary to consider both sanctions against cadres who had unscrupulously used the Great Leap to advance their own careers and restitution for their victims. Rectification of rural cadres began in late 1960. Even some provincial officials were dismissed. An overlapping campaign to "reverse verdicts" (i.e., rectify past injustices) culminated in early 1961 with a sweeping campaign of apologies, rehabilitation, and even compensation.

At such a critical time it was also prudent to minimize hostility in foreign relations. Consequently, criticism of the USSR abated. In June 1961, Liu Shaoqi gave a speech in which he paid "high tribute to the great Soviet people and the Communist Party of the Soviet Union."[5] Mao himself advocated solidarity with the USSR at a January 1961 Plenum. Even toward the United States a softer line was taken.

These policies enjoyed broad support. Although many leaders, including Mao, denied that the Great Leap was a mistake, they conceded excesses and accepted criticism. In June 1961 and again before 7,000 cadres at a conference in February of 1962, Mao admitted responsibility. He called for free discussion within the Party, including criticism of himself.

> No matter. Let everybody criticize us. As for me, I will not go out during the day; I will not go to the theatre at night. Please come and criticize me day and night (laughter).[6]

He told the lower cadres they could not duck responsibility: "You think that nobody will really dare to touch the arse of tigers like you? They damn well will!"[7] Opinions differed on just how much to blame the Party center. Some, like Liu, were prepared to suggest that 70 percent of the failure was attributable to human error and thus by implication to central policy. Many shared this view and even made veiled criticisms of the Chairman. At this time Peng Dehuai, the ousted minister of defense and archcritic of the Great Leap Forward, was hoping to make a comeback, and some Party leaders supported his rehabilitation. Not everyone joined the retreat. Lin Biao, the newly installed minister of defense, and Jiang Qing, the Chairman's wife, were prominent among those who continued to hymn the ideals and symbols of the revolution. Lin launched a vigorous program of making the PLA a revolutionary force. His military doctrine emphasized people over weapons in preference to Peng Dehuai's weapons-oriented professionalism. (The major exception was the new nuclear program, which produced a test bomb by 1964.) Lin gave ideological study and practice the top priority. At every echelon down to the company level, he installed a political officer or committee. To staff these positions, he recruited a quarter of a million new Party members within the army. Other programs complemented these efforts, including a rectification campaign among the officer corps.

Jiang Qing was virtually unknown in 1959. Because of lengthy illnesses and Mao's earlier commitment to keep her out of politics, she had stayed in the background, raising her daughter by Mao and Mao's daughter from his previous marriage. But during the retreat from the Great Leap Forward the ex-actress's interest in the performing arts began to converge with her political zeal. Attending the theater at Shanghai, she was appalled at the slack, satirical, degenerate quality of plays that were then being produced. She began a personal crusade to revolutionize the arts and to drive out all traditional, foreign, and bourgeois themes. She began to prevail on Mao to purify the arts, acting as his personal cultural watchdog. In 1960 she found young radical teachers and students at Beijing University who were anxious to subject plays, operas, and books to Marxist criticism and thus began to form her circle.

Lest one idealize either the left or the right as disinterested champions of rational views, it must be stressed that power, too, was at stake. The Great Leap had damaged Mao's authority. Although still Chairman, he retreated from the "first line" and resigned as head of state. He made only one public appearance in 1962. Mao was still peerless in his capacity to influence general policy. But the only way for him to implement his wishes was through the bureaucrats, and he could not help but chafe at the difficulty of getting them to carry out both the letter and the spirit of his policies. Also, in 1963, Mao would be seventy years old. Far from being invalided, he swam and rode horseback. But he wheezed from decades of chain smoking and gave signs of fading health. When he would go, no one could tell, but his passing would surely initiate some rearrangement of power. Against this day everyone was concerned to shore up the best possible position.

Liu Shaoqi moved into the opening created by Mao's semi-retirement. As head of state and CCP vice-chairperson, Liu assumed responsibility for the overall direction of Party affairs. He was widely considered to be Mao's successor. Deng Xiaoping, the Party's general secretary, and Peng Zhen, deputy general secretary and the Beijing Party boss, also assumed increased power and authority. These men favored policies that would enhance their position. As they performed their Party and state duties, they were daily strengthening their own bastions of power—"independent kingdoms," as Mao sometimes growled. For example, in 1960, Deng tightened the Secretariat's control over the provinces by establishing six regional bureaus. On the other hand, Lin Biao, who had little strength in the Party bureaucracy; Jiang Qing, who had no political network; and other persons whose ambitions outran their political connections embraced Maoism as a vehicle to advancement. They were paralleled on lower levels by cadres who had bettered themselves during the Great Leap Forward and who now were being undone by "reversals of verdicts."

## Recovery

Beginning in 1962 the economy steadily improved. In agriculture this was the result of good weather and changes in commune policy. It also came about as a result of the decision to invest more in agriculture and improve farm technology. The slogan used was this: "Take agriculture as the foundation and industry as the leading factor." Conferences were convened, such as the national agricultural science and technology conference held in the spring of 1963. Extension stations were set up. In 1963 and 1964 improved plows, seeders, land levelers, fertilizer sowers, and walking tractors were developed. Between 1962 and 1965, China imported several complete factories to produce chemical fertilizers and other agricultural inputs.

There was a dramatic increase in the production and use of irrigation pumps. Mechanical irrigation increased sixfold between 1961 and 1965 to 6.6 million hectares, mostly around Shanghai, Guangzhou (Canton), and Beijing. Several very successful high-yield areas were established in these three regions as well as in the central and the upper Yangzi. A rapid increase in petroleum production in the mid-1960s made this mechanization possible.

The result of all this was that from 1964 to 1967 grain production increased from 5 percent to 6 percent annually. Per capita availability of grain rose from a low of about 220 kilograms in 1960 to nearly 300 by 1966. (This was, however, still slightly below the pre-Great Leap levels.) The population growth rate, after its decline in the famine years, surged to 3.5 percent in 1963 and then dropped off toward 2 percent. In industry the picture was roughly the same. Indeed manufacturing assumed a typical rate of growth much higher than that of agriculture. Because of this industrial growth, the per capita gross national product in 1965 stood at 220 U.S. dollars in 1965 as compared with 190 U.S. dollars in 1957. Figure 5 in Chapter 4 illustrates the recovery of overall national income adjusted for prices.

## Political Crisis

By mid-1962 the worst days of deprivation seemed to be behind. The crops were better, and, with a new rationing system for consumer goods, the industrial situation improved. However, China was still poor as the rehabilitated Chen Yun was acutely aware. In the early months of that year he strongly urged holding to a steady, pragmatic, long-term course in order to achieve full recovery. "How many years are required for the recovery stage? In my personal opinion it requires about five years, starting from 1960."[8] But some economic planners with a bias for heavy industry did not accept Chen's willingness to downgrade investment in heavy industry for an extended period. Mao agreed. Moreover, he saw dangers that were just as urgent as food and fiber. He disapproved of the political price being paid for economic recovery and grew alarmed that his colleagues were happy to drift indefinitely with "peaceful coexistence in politics, the attitude of muddling through in organization, and the attitude of superficiality in economics."[9]

Mao was also alarmed about the deterioration of the Yanan ideal, which he believed to be the only truly revolutionary path. This ideal, it will be remembered, featured cadres whose commitment, ideology and self-sacrifice could mobilize the masses to storm all obstacles. But since liberation and especially since 1960, the cadres had all too often lost their Marxist-Leninist backbone and sometimes their basic honesty. This gloomy assessment was not groundless. Although the millions of cadres differed individually, they had come to constitute a many-layered elite. They had become modern equivalents of the mandarins of old, who valued their procedures and political connections more that the welfare of the people. Because almost everything in China was terribly scarce, many cadres habitually exploited their influence to obtain goods and special advantages for themselves and their families.

## The Tenth Plenum

In late July 1962, Mao summoned the entire Central Committee and several other central and provincial Party heads, more than two hundred in all, to a work conference at the seaside resort of Beidaihe. The agenda included agriculture and the economy, the government budget, class struggle, and other major questions.

The business of hearing reports, airing views, listening to speeches by Mao and other luminaries, and hammering out policy decisions lasted many weeks into September. Immediately thereafter, this same body constituted itself as the Tenth Plenum of the Central Committee to put the Party's official stamp on the various decisions. These deliberations launched a three-year effort to integrate Mao's revolutionary views into the recovery program.

Chen Yun, Liu Shaoqi, and others spoke up for the recovery adjustments. But the Chairman had not called this meeting to be given lessons in pragmatism. He shot back, heaping scorn on the Ministry of Finance, raising the great issues of revolution. Where is all this private farming leading? Is China not slipping back toward the restoration of capitalism and feudalism? Toward revisionism, like the Soviet Union? Mao coined another of his slogans: "Never forget class struggle." He admonished, "From now on we must talk about this every year, every month, every day."[10] The debates at Beidaihe may have grown heated. But when the Plenum convened, differences had been reconciled into a united Party voice. Although Mao conceded the importance of fostering production, cadre morale, and Party discipline, he forced the others to accept his conditions. In promoting these things, they should "never forget class struggle." They must take concrete steps lest China slide into revisionism.

Trouble was built into this compromise. Although the moderates recognized Mao's concerns, they were not prepared to push class struggle hard. They feared disruption that could plunge the country once more into economic crisis. Because they held the administrative levers and were prepared to hobble the very initiatives they were ostensibly promoting, Mao was bound to lose patience. Compromise was hindered by the situation in the countryside. Communes, production brigades, and production teams were laced with conflicts between demoralized cadres, corrupt cadres, ousted cadres, disgusted peasants, and free-wheeling private producers and traders. These tensions intertwined so tightly that to touch one affected them all. To placate peasant resentment would probably ruin cadre morale. To restore old cadres would embitter the new. To attack corruption and spontaneous capitalism would endanger production.

## The Socialist Education Movement

The Tenth Plenum launched the new movement to rekindle the socialist flame in the countryside. It had several phases and campaigns, but it has come to be known collectively as the Socialist Education movement. It ran its course for more than three years. The movement began in the winter of 1962–63. The first step called for careful examination of rural conditions and experimental solutions. Investigations confirmed widespread shortcomings among rural cadres. Logically, then, improvement of the commune system would depend on reforming these rural cadres. There were some pilot programs to clean up the local leadership through criticism, self-criticism, propaganda, and other measures. The phases through which the Socialist Education movement passed, marked by the succession of central documents, illustrate the growing difficulties encountered in attempting to make a society at once revolutionary and orderly.

*The First Ten Points.* In February 1963 the Party held a top-level conference to study progress to date. Mao praised the results in certain places. "Once we grasp class struggle, miracles are possible," he enthused.[11] These efforts led to the formulation of a central directive on the Socialist Education movement. This document, which turned out to be the first of four, is called the First Ten Points. To rectify the local cadres, it called for the formation of "Associations of Poor and Lower Middle Peasants" to help identify and correct cadre problems. This would require auditing the accounts and correcting irregularities. Cadres were also asked to spend some time working in production for the good of their proletarian consciousness. The campaign also included propaganda against landlords, exploiters, and other bad elements. The leaders, especially Peng Zhen, closely monitored the progress.

Unfortunately by the summer of 1963, the Socialist Education movement as a whole was falling short of the expectations. Local cadres were uncooperative. Some could not find the time to participate in labor. Others failed to publicize the rules on auditing accounts. Still others represented the Socialist Education movement as a campaign to promote production. No doubt the results were modest primarily because Party leaders on all levels hesitated to push too vigorously.

*The Second Ten Points.* Peng Zhen, whose star in the Party was rising rapidly, was chosen to draft another set of guidelines. The product of his labors came to be called "the Second Ten Points." He introduced work teams, a technique used in land reform, to guide the cleanup of local cadres. Squads of reliable, trained provincial and county cadres would go to selected production teams and brigades, "link up" with the peasants, and gain detailed knowledge of the local situation. In the early months of 1964 the Second Ten Points were implemented with moderation. The work teams walked a fine line between undermining the local cadres and mobilizing the peasants. Consequently, cadres with something to hide could still avoid exposure.

But this did not apply to cadres and rural entrepreneurs of Peach Blossom Brigade, located near the capital, for they came under the sharp eye of Wang Guangmei, wife of Liu Shaoqi. Wang took an active part in monitoring the Socialist Education movement, as did her husband and other members of the top elite. Her identity unknown, she joined a work team assigned to Peach Garden Brigade, where they investigated and rectified for many weeks. Wang was appalled by the extent of cadre corruption and rampant capitalism among the peasants. Her findings seem to have been considered representative and argued for a get-tough approach. In the summer, Liu, who had carried out his own investigations, and Mao, who seemed to share the alarm of Liu and his wife, agreed that stricter efforts were needed. They decided that local cadres and even provincial-level officials must be subjected to the criticism of the Associations of Poor and Lower Middle Peasants, led by the Party. At this juncture Liu took over the movement from Peng Zhen.

The result was a vigorous assault on local cadres in the second half of 1964. This phase of the Socialist Education movement was part of a year of heightened political conformity in all spheres of life. The Mao cult was being pushed as millions of copies of *Quotations of Chairman Mao* were published, and many cultural and educational figures came under attack. "Let politics take command!" was the operative motto.

*The Revised Second Ten Points.* The document ruling this phase of the movement was the third to be promulgated. It was drafted in September by Liu, and because it changed some of the points of its predecessor, it was known as the Revised Second Ten Points. This no-nonsense program to root out bad cadres rested on the premise that the movement under Peng Zhen had failed miserably. Liu's new approach called for large and aggressive work teams. No more tiptoeing around to protect local cadres. "Human sea" work teams would move in and take over a unit from its leaders. They would mobilize the peasants to struggle against the cadres.

The result was a sweeping purge of local Party personnel. Estimates vary, but the toll could have exceeded a million despite the fact that human resources only permitted the program to be carried out in about one-third of rural areas. This may have been the largest rural purge ever undertaken. Thus, Liu Shaoqi, ever the hard-boiled Party chief, sought to smash the problem of bad cadres.

The Revised Second Ten Points created an uproar, and Mao was not pleased. When he had agreed to a new approach, he meant that the Associations of Poor and Lower Middle Peasants would be free to criticize the cadres. But Liu's method was to control the peasants through the work teams. The big work teams also disturbed the peasants who wondered what new heaven-sent calamity was on its way. The cadres were even more upset and frequently refused to serve any more. This program threatened to weaken the newly recovering rural system once again.

Liu's case was further weakened by the fact that the work teams occasionally threatened people connected with other high leaders. One team moved in on Beijing University and mobilized students against the school administrators—who had close ties with Peng Zhen. Another attacked the agricultural unit that was fast becoming the model for all of China, the famed Dazhai Brigade in Shanxi Province. Investigators claimed that the vaunted self-reliance of this unit was a sham and that numerous irregularities had occurred. In desperation, Dazhai's leader wangled an audience with Mao, who had recently taken to praising him. He won Mao over completely, and the work team at Dazhai soon withdrew.

*The Twenty-Three Points.* The Chairman was thoroughly alarmed over this turn of events. Subsequently, a fourth and final phase of the Socialist Education movement began. In late 1964 and early 1965, Mao himself oversaw the drafting of yet another set of guidelines, the so-called Twenty-Three Points. This new document called for a more truly populist approach. "We must boldly unleash the masses."[12] Peng Zhen again took primary responsibility. Immediately, the aggressive rectification work teams were recalled to receive new instructions. But in the end Peng did not come much closer to Mao's intent than Liu. In fact, the peasants were not unleashed. Although the Twenty-Three Points called for county-level cadres to be criticized by the masses, this did not happen widely.

Thus, by mid-1965, after almost three years of pushing for a socialist revival in the countryside, Mao felt thoroughly frustrated. He was appalled by Liu's tough approach, which created fear and increased bureaucratism. His Twenty-Three Points dealt Liu a stiff—and certainly resented—rebuff, seriously affecting the relationship of the two men. On the other hand, Mao was disappointed with Peng's approach, which generated mostly words and motion without tangible results. To make matters worse, Mao's pique over the way his colleagues had handled the Socialist Education movement intermingled with other sources of discontent.

## Education

When Mao preached, "Never forget class struggle," he was concerned that forty years of revolution could be negated by the "ogres" of capitalist restoration.

> We must acknowledge that classes and class struggles still exist for a long time to come, and that the reactionary classes may stage a comeback. We must heighten our vigilance and successfully educate the young people, the cadres and the masses . . .[13]

This explains why the Tenth Plenum's agricultural program would include a "Socialist *Education* movement" and why Mao intended to radicalize the educational system as well. But what, specifically, troubled him?

In the post-Great Leap Forward crisis years, the policy for education paralleled the retreat in agriculture. Radical innovations were abandoned. Many of the work-and-study schools simply ceased to function. The Ministry of Education began to regain its grip. In July the labor requirement was eliminated for regular students. In December 1962 the Education Ministry identified a network of "key schools" ("little treasure pagodas," as their detractors called them) to educate China's brightest, from primary school to university. Deng Xiaoping and Liu Shaoqi oversaw these changes.

This marked a retreat from universal education. By 1962 the number of middle school students had declined to less than 15 percent of its earlier level. Not much more than half of all primary age children were in school. To address this problem, Liu began to develop two separate systems: a college and a vocational track. The renewed emphasis on expertise meant that the choicest opportunities went to those best equipped to pass the entrance exams and excel in class: urban youth, in particular children of intelligentsia and cadre families. It worked to the disadvantage of rural children and even offspring of factory workers, Marxism's cherished proletariat. There was a marked ideological relaxation as well. In late 1962, the blunt-talking foreign minister, Chen Yi, addressed graduating college students in Beijing. He downplayed political study and emphasized the need for technical expertise.

> Mei Lanfeng was a great artist, and as such had won honor for our country. Did he have to study political books thoroughly? No, he did not have to. But he had to perform for the people under the leadership of the Party.[14]

Upset by all this, Mao launched an attempt to reverse the liberalization in education following the Tenth Plenum. This effort enjoyed some success but, like the Socialist Education movement, was repeatedly watered down by established leaders who were prepared to beat the Maoist drum and march their own merry way. Admissions policies favorable to workers and peasants were reintroduced. Students met to "remember the bitterness [of the past] and think of the sweetness [of what the Party had achieved]." A new breed of PLA hero, the sincere, unassuming servant of others, was publicized for students to emulate. (See the next section.) Now secondary schools and colleges experienced an epidemic of students' sweeping the halls or secretly washing their comrades' bedsheets in an attempt to turn the difficult trick of standing out unobtrusively.

In 1964, Mao pushed for a reduction in college-preparatory emphasis and for wider access. As a consequence, there was soon more recruitment of worker and peasant students and even expulsions of students from "bad" (e.g., middle class or landlord) backgrounds. From 1964 on, students constantly heard of themselves referred to as the successor generation whose duty was to become true revolutionaries. There was pressure for greater equality between student and teacher, problem solving rather than recitation, and open-book exams. In interviews with his nephew and his niece, Mao scoffed at book learning and extolled independent, action-oriented thought. Students should sleep through boring lectures, he said, and rebel against school authority.

But although Mao's colleagues and the educational establishment acceded to some changes, they worked steadily to strengthen contrary policies. Their general approach was to expend most of the educational budget on secondary and higher education, that is, to train those who could contribute most to modernization. Universal primary schooling and irregular adult classes received lower priority and local financing. Aside from nourishing an elite system of "key schools," the Ministry of Education promoted conventional goals, methods, and materials. In the spring of 1964 the director of propaganda blocked a Maoist effort to reduce class time and cautioned against innovations that had not been tested out. In 1964 the old Ministry of Higher Education was reestablished. Liu Shaoqi, despite Mao's great interest in this sphere, became the leader most influential in educational policy.

The students themselves were not aware that these struggles were going on at the top or what political issues were at stake. Some responded fervently to the ideological appeals; others focused on getting ahead within this unpredictable system. But all lived under the shadow of the very restricted opportunities. Despite their relative advantages over peasant children, admitted students could not look forward to a steady climb up the ladder of success. Indeed, chances were against them. Not only were the places in secondary and higher education limited, but also the modern sector was not growing fast enough to provide jobs for all the graduates.

Consequently, only around 20 or 30 percent of high school graduates were accepted for further education. The rest were "sent down" to labor in the countryside. As they left, they were told that it was for a glorious, transforming purpose.

> Going to share the bitter and the sweet with the laboring people in the countryside, educated youths can gradually cultivate the habit of doing labor eagerly, establish a correct attitude towards phys-

ical labor, [and] reform their nonproletarian thoughts . . . an important guarantee for preventing themselves forever from being corrupted.[15]

One can imagine the uneasy mix of idealism and disappointment felt by the students. But their parents, while the Party official was thus preaching, were lamenting to one another, "Don't let this bright pearl of yours drop into a heap of ashes."[16]

## Culture

Mao's intention after the Tenth Plenum was to shake up writers, artists, and scholars, too. As usual, the Party responded but in a measured and controlled way. When Mao then pushed for a full-fledged cultural purge in late 1963, the response again failed to satisfy him. So in early 1965 he determined to circumvent the cultural establishment. This turned out to be the opening salvo of the Cultural Revolution.

After 1960, as the Great Leap Forward faded, two rival cultural camps emerged: radical and establishment intellectuals. The former have already been noted, particularly Jiang Qing with her faith in revolutionary transformation. The radicals seized eagerly on Mao's Tenth Plenum effort to tighten up the cultural realm. Most notably, Jiang Qing's circle took steps to reform the theater. Companies were encouraged to abandon traditional and foreign plays in favor of revolutionary themes. In 1963 the Party boss of Shanghai, a Mao supporter, appointed Zhang Chunqiao as head of the Shanghai Party Propaganda Department. Zhang, in turn, recruited Yao Wenyuan. The destinies of these two men were about to intertwine with Jiang Qing's as they constituted the avant guard against bourgeois culture.

Zhang Chunqiao (pronounced something like "Jang Chuncheeow") was in his early fifties, a thin-faced, bespectacled commissar. An active leftist since the 1930s, he had risen to become, in effect, Shanghai's "cultural czar" as head of the municipal Party's Propaganda Department and publisher of *Liber-*

*ation Daily*. His name had long been associated with the left, as he had strongly attacked "rightists" in the 1957 backlash following the Hundred Flowers campaign. During the Great Leap, he published an article advocating radical economic ideas, which caught Mao's attention.

Whereas Zhang was primarily a cultural bureaucrat, the younger Yao Wenyuan (pronounced "Yow One-you-an") was a talented polemicist, a leftist literary hatchet man. He too had taken an active role against "rightists" in 1957 even though his own father, an old-line leftist intellectual, had been stigmatized with the dreaded rightist label. One of Yao's articles that came to Mao's favorable attention attacked a newspaper for not placing the Chairman's words in boldface with banner headlines. Yao was one of several young writers recruited by Zhang Chunqiao. Round-faced with prominent eyes, he was later commonly rumored to have married the daughter of Mao and Jiang Qing.

The other camp, the establishment intellectuals, were scholars, writers, and cultural workers who occupied positions in the major schools and propaganda departments. Some of them became polemicists in a kind of high-level debate over the Great Leap Forward, Mao's leadership, and Peng Dehuai's dismissal. Because of the treatment Peng received, high-level airing of views on these issued was risky. Criticism then disguised itself in hints and allusions in the essays, fiction, theater, and academic debates of intellectuals who were patronized and protected by high Party officials.

One of these people was Wu Han, author of the play *Hai Rui Dismissed from Office*. He was not only a well-known member of the Chinese Academy of Sciences, but also a public figure with connections. He was a deputy mayor of Beijing, and his eminent friends included fellow bridge enthusiast Deng Xiaoping. Wu Han's direct patron was Peng Zhen, the Beijing Party chief and associate of Liu Shaoqi and Deng Xiaoping and of the director and deputy directors of the Party's Propaganda Department. These men sponsored scholars like Wu Han and controlled the major newspapers and periodicals in the capital.

Thus, when Wu Han dramatized a sixteenth-century official, he was not merely dabbling in theater. He was joining in the debate over the policies of the past three years. There were many other such Aesopian attacks on the Great Leap. Wu Han himself collaborated with two other writers in Peng Zhen's orbit to publish a series of short essays, some of which could be read as satires against the recent radical policies. In addition, a large number of films, novels, plays, and other artistic expressions, if they did not carry a hidden political message, at least avoided the heightened politics of the Great Leap and presented a more complex reality.

While the radical intellectuals hailed Mao's 1963 call to "never forget class struggle," the cultural establishment gave it a cooler reception. Some of the satirists sniffed danger and ceased publishing on the eve of the Tenth Plenum, and Peng Zhen's Beijing machine complied with a rather low-keyed program of criticism in the arts. But they undertook no thorough housecleaning. Moreover, in various forums and meetings, they encouraged the expression of moderate views and counterarguments.

By the end of 1963 it seemed as though Peng Zhen's cultural bureaucrats had made a fairly comfortable adjustment. A certain amount of tightening up had occurred. Some liberalization had been suppressed. At the same time, in the interests of fostering a creative environment, some diversity was tolerated. Perhaps representative of this were letters to the editor in which readers expressed their view of happiness, rejecting extreme self-sacrifice. As one of them wrote

> I think that happiness means leading a peaceful, pleasant life, not a life of struggle amid hardship . . . It is strange logic to equate hardship with happiness and enjoyment of creature comforts with bourgeois thought.[17]

Mao indulged this. But gradually, perhaps under his wife's influence and because of his growing hatred of Soviet revisionism, he lost patience with cultural laxity. From the winter of 1963 through the summer of 1964, he repeatedly nagged his colleagues about excessive liberalization. For example, traditional operas drew his fire. "Operas abound in feudal emperors, kings, generals, ministers, scholars, and beautiful women, but the Ministry of Culture doesn't care a bit." [18] In December he lashed out at "problems" in all forms of art: "Hence we should proceed with investigation and study and attend to this matter in earnest." [19]

In January 1964 ten of Mao's poems were published for the first time to great fanfare. Like almost all of his poetry, these selections were highly allusive and metaphorical, inviting diverse interpretations. But he may well have had liberal artists and writers in mind when he wrote:

> Away with all pests!
> Our force is irresistible. [20]

In the spring of 1965, Mao again expressed his impatience. He lashed out against the cultural bureaucrats, charging that they had "slid right down to the brink of revisionism." [21] And to leave no doubt about the seriousness of his intent, he linked liberalization to the bourgeois revisionism of the Soviet Union. In his polemic "On Khrushchev's Phony Communism and Its Historical Lessons for the World," published in July, he warned:

In socialist society, the overthrown bourgeoisie and other reactionary classes . . . sneak into the . . . cultural and educational institutions so as to resist or usurp the leadership of the proletariat. . . . In the ideological, cultural and educational fields, they counterpose the bourgeois world outlook to the proletarian world outlook and try to corrupt the proletariat and other working people with bourgeois ideology . . . [22]

Meanwhile Jiang Qing and the other radicals were at work. In December, under her urging, the Shanghai Propaganda Department organized an East China District Drama Competition to encourage the creation of new plays on revolutionary themes.

This was Jiang Qing's first big breakthrough. It was followed in June by a still greater triumph, the Beijing Opera Festival on Contemporary Themes. Thirty-seven new works were presented, along with numerous speeches by Party luminaries. Jiang Qing gave her first speech.

> Our operatic stage is occupied by emperors, princes, generals, ministers, scholars, and beauties, and on top of these ghosts and monsters. . . . The grain we eat is grown by the peasants, the clothes we wear and the houses we live in are all made by the workers, and the People's Liberation Army stands guard at the fronts of national defense for us and yet we do not portray them on stage . . .[23]

In December 1964 her stature rose another notch when she acquired her first formal position, delegate to the National People's Congress.

Mao's Party colleagues had little choice but to concur with his sentiments on culture. Over this period they responded with several efforts to implement his wishes. Most significant perhaps, the Secretariat, in May or June, formed a "Five-Person Group" to supervise a "cultural revolution." It was led by Peng Zhen. There were efforts to reform the arts and dispatch intellectuals to farms and factories for political "tempering." Several prominent writers and thinkers became the targets of criticism campaigns. There was a rectification campaign targeting cultural bureaucrats from the summer of 1964 to the spring of the following year.

But these efforts were decidedly less enthusiastic than those of Jiang Qing's circle. The Party leaders expressed reservations and attempted to keep reform firmly under the control of the established system. Peng Zhen's Five-Person Group contained only one Mao supporter. In December, although conceding that new dramas were needed, Liu Shaoqi suggested that feudal plays must continue to be staged because recent works were simply not as good yet. The cultural establishment kept the Jiang Qing's Beijing Opera Festival under its control as much as possible, omitting, for example, to publish her speech. The 1964 rectification was both sluggish and gentle by comparison with earlier antecedents. Its victims were selected from the second rank and escaped serious punishment. Wu Han was not attacked at all. In April 1965, the minister of culture declared the cultural rectification a success and terminated the movement. Not surprisingly, Mao took little pleasure in this result. He now responded to Jiang Qing's urgent suggestion to attack Wu Han.

## The PLA and Foreign Policy

Even in the period of retreat from the Great Leap Forward, Mao had good reason to be pleased with Lin Biao and the People's Liberation Army. In his demeanor toward Mao, Lin was the diametric opposite of Liu Shaoqi, Deng Xiaoping, and Peng Zhen. Whereas they dismantled the Great Leap and treated the Chairman as first among equals, Lin continued to defend the movement and glorify its author. He strengthened indoctrination and political structures in the army. So by the time of the Tenth Plenum in September 1962, the PLA's organization, morale, and commitment to Mao Zedong Thought were all strong. Lin became part of a radical faction around the Chairman. As Mao relinquished routine administration to Party headquarters, he gathered his own circle, some of high Party rank such as Chen Boda, some with little standing at all, like Jiang Qing. Lin Biao was a prized member of this camp as leader of the one powerful institution truly responsive to Mao.

As the Tenth Plenum met, military conflict was erupting on the Indian border over a rugged region called Aksai-Chin. Chinese generals considered it strategically vital because through it passed the one road between western Xinjiang Province and Tibet. Conflicting Chinese and Indian claims were stalemated although some believe that diplomacy might yet have won through. When fighting erupted during October and November 1962 the PLA troops sent Indian forces reeling backward and then withdrew to

LIN BIAO

defensive positions. Thus was another proud page added to the achievements of the armed forces and Lin Biao.

After 1962, Lin's PLA continued to stand out. There were tangible successes such as the testing of China's first atomic weapon in 1964. There were endless ideological campaigns featuring exhortations like the following.

Respond to Chairman Mao's Call to Learn Resolutely from Comrade Lei Feng. (1963)

Anti-Chemical Warfare Company in Canton [Guangzhou] Trains Successors in Hard and Meticulous Way. (1964)

Be Good and Do Good by Learning From Good People and Good Deeds; Look to Wang Chieh for Inspiration. (1965)[24]

The army published special materials, in particular the famous "Little Red Book," *Quotations of Chairman Mao*, and sponsored arts festivals on revolutionary themes. Political commissars were added and strengthened at every level. As the most revolutionary gesture of all, the PLA in 1965 abolished all military ranks and replaced Soviet-style uniforms with khaki fatigues for all.

The army also functioned as a model for society. Drawing on the Yanan days, when the troops intermingled with the people like fish in the sea, the PLA revived its role as exemplar. In addition to PLA literature and arts festivals, there were the emulation campaigns. The most famous model hero was Lei Feng, a young soldier whose family had suffered terribly before liberation. His boundless gratitude to the Party was such that he dedicated himself to "serving the people" in quiet humble ways. When he died in a freak accident (a telephone pole fell on him), the army published his diary as a paragon of quiet service to Chairman Mao. Lei Feng emulation campaigns were organized by the Communist Youth League and the Chinese Trade Union, with Mao personally scripting the slogan "Learn From Lei Feng."

By late 1963 Chairman Mao was calling for the whole country to learn from the PLA, by which he meant more than study groups. The idea was to replicate in the civil administration the ideological tautness of the army. To this end Lin and Mao wanted various ministries, especially those related to the economy, to have special political commissars assigned to them who would report to the PLA's General Political Department. This was in addition to the regular Party branch in every unit. The Party leaders complied with this plan, but they weakened it by insisting that the new "political departments," as they were called, should report to the Central Committee rather than to the PLA. There were other PLA intrusions into the civilian sector. In 1965 some army personnel were being used in Socialist Education movement work teams in the countryside. The PLA also involved itself to a limited degree in education.

The army played a role in foreign policy as well because important strategic issues had to be addressed. China was learning, as the French had learned in 1789 and the Russians in 1917, that great revolutions arouse great enemies. In this case, it was both of the superpowers. Would there be war with the United States over Vietnam? If so, should China commit massed armies as in Korea? Or should she prepare for invasion and Yanan-style guerrilla tactics? Was there an imminent Soviet threat as well?

Decisions on these questions had implications well beyond battlefield training. A guerrilla war strategy would not require heavy expenditures on sophisticated weapons and would thus permit sustained economic investment and independence from the USSR. It would require, however, some dispersal of industry to reduce vulnerability. On the other hand, a strategy of conventional war against the United States would require more investment in armaments, more concentration of industry, and better relations with Moscow, the source of military technology. It would also require the army to concentrate on defense and reduce its political role.

Perhaps the deciding factor in these deliberations was Mao's growing alienation from the USSR and his holy war against revisionism. As if to confound all the Western observers who considered the People's Republic another docile satellite of Moscow, China was in the process of fashioning a defiant new independence. By 1962 the great revolutionary friendship that was supposed to endure forever was rapidly disintegrating. China got little Soviet support in its dispute with India and criticized Moscow for backing down to Kennedy during the Cuban missile crisis. Nothing seemed to stem the tide: not the visit to Moscow by Deng Xiaoping and Peng Zhen, not Khrushchev's letter to Mao suggesting cooperation against imperialism (both in 1963), not efforts by Vietnamese and Japanese Communists to intercede, not Khrushchev's ouster in 1964. Not even imperialist U.S. bombs raining on Vietnam in 1965 reversed the downward trend.

Mao failed to see anything but revisionism in Moscow. As he said in his July 1964 diatribe "On Khrushchev's Phony Communism and Its Historical Lessons for the World,"

> The questions of whether revolution . . . and . . . the dictatorship of the proletariat should be upheld or opposed . . . are now

the focus of struggle between Marxist-Leninists the world over and the revisionist Khrushchev clique.[25]

Soviet leaders had betrayed Marxism-Leninism and their disease was communicable. Thus, Mao's battle with the Russian monster abroad and with capitalist ogres at home fed on one another—were in fact one and the same struggle. As he said rather poignantly to Zhou Enlai the year before they both died,

> You and I, old friends, can we just
> watch our efforts be washed away?[26]

In response to the military threat on two fronts, Beijing defined a new global policy. In 1963, China began to issue calls to the nonaligned countries, portraying herself as the model of a self-reliant people's liberation struggle. All peoples must join in resolutely rejecting Russian revisionism and defeating U.S. imperialism.

China launched a diplomatic offensive aimed at supplanting Russian influence in Asia and Africa. Although the Aksai-Chin conflict alienated India and damaged China's image elsewhere and although China's resources were limited, this new independent policy enjoyed considerable success. Between 1960 and 1965 diplomatic relations were established with fifteen new countries. Border issues were settled with five countries, from Burma to Mongolia.

In Asia, China participated in the settlement of the Laos conflict in 1962 and assisted the growth of an extremely powerful Communist party in Indonesia. In early 1965, China was joined by the parties of North Vietnam, North Korea, Japan, and Indonesia, as well as of Albania and Romania, in boycotting a Soviet-sponsored Communist conference. In Africa the effort to challenge Soviet influence led to extending nearly 300 million U.S. dollars in foreign aid between 1960 and 1965 to black nations. China began training guerrillas of several African states, most importantly the Congo, and participated actively in meetings of the Afro-Asian People's Solidarity Committee in 1960,

1963, and 1965. In 1965, Zhou Enlai and Chen Yi led an ambitious diplomatic mission to eleven African nations.

This new diplomatic thrust was not without its problems. Many African leaders resented Chinese efforts to export revolution. In 1964 the Beijing-supported Congolese rebels were defeated, and Burundi broke off diplomatic relations. Also damaging to Beijing's stature was its caution in Vietnam. Despite anti-American rhetoric, the Chinese offered little assistance to Hanoi. Only when the Tonkin Incident of August 1964 led to a widening U.S. involvement in the north did China begin to send military assistance. Even then a definite policy on Vietnam did not emerge until the fall of 1965. Despite these difficulties, the Chinese could compliment themselves on a successful new thrust in foreign policy. However, 1965 brought a number of serious setbacks, involving Vietnam, Indonesia, Africa, and Cuba, which helped worsen tensions among the leaders.

## The Crisis of 1965

In the summer of 1965 the average person had no inkling that there was trouble brewing at the commanding heights. The fact that on August 1 the PLA's *Quotations of Chairman Mao* was published for study in both rural and urban units did not seem particularly ominous. *People's Daily* readers saw a photograph of Mao and Liu out for a swim together, talking to children. Peng Zhen had recently been declared "Chairman Mao's Close Comrade-in-Arms." And there were many signs of normalcy. The economy had continued to grow since 1962, supplying markets with adequate food and consumer goods, at least by a poor nation's standards. In the countryside, cadres could relax as the Socialist Education movement moderated. A new rectification began in the fall for cadres at the county level, but it was superficial, resulting in very few dismissals. Such was the calm before the storm. Meanwhile, cut off from public view, a handful of critical disagreements were about to boil over, heated by the radicals' and Mao's dissatisfaction. These disagreements over defense, economic policy, education, and culture eventually stimulated a chain of events called "the Great Proletarian Cultural Revolution."

Vietnam suddenly became an important issue. In February 1965, President Johnson, authorized by the U.S. Congress's Tonkin Gulf Resolution to use military force against North Vietnam, ordered operation "Rolling Thunder," a program of sustained bombing. In 1965, American troop strength in the south stood at 70,000, then climbed to 125,000 with further increases on the way. Up to this time the Chinese had supposed that the United States would get tired and go home. But China now had to make decisions. The Americans, who had frequently charged that China was the source of the Vietnamese revolution, were assaulting a fraternal Marxist state. Parallels with Korea were too obvious to miss. Comradely instinct impelled Beijing to aid Hanoi. Indeed, when bombing of the north started, China sent a squadron of MIG-17s. By fall construction and engineering troops were being sent, eventually to total as many as 50,000.

This was a relatively modest contribution, for there were considerations pushing in the other direction. Washington did not want the war to spread to China and repeatedly signaled this in 1965 and 1966. Secondly, to the extent that embroilment would mean cooperation with Moscow, the Chinese hesitated because relations had become strained to the breaking point. Even the minimal cooperation required to send Russian aid through China succeeded only after prolonged wrangling. This created a third restraint on Chinese involvement: Alienated from Russia, China had no protection against U.S. nuclear weapons.

Still, a controversy did arise because Vietnam intertwined with domestic politics. The Maoists, led by Lin Biao, promoted a people's war thesis in order to keep the PLA off the battlefield and fully deployed in politics. Arguing that the anti-imperialist fight was a worldwide people's struggle, they held that every national liberation movement must rely on its own masses, a thesis that allowed China to remain relatively disengaged. The contrary view, too, had its supporters. They argued that China must actively aid Hanoi and prepare for American retaliation and that this required healing the breach with Moscow. The most prominent hawk was Luo Ruiqing, who had been named PLA chief of staff in 1959, when Lin became defense minister. He spoke for many PLA professionals who opposed some of Lin's policies. They wearied of Lin's Mao cult. They disliked the abolition of ranks, not merely because it removed their prestige, but also because it made them vulnerable; for, without ranks, they lacked any standing once deprived of a command. As professionals, they considered Lin's nostalgic guerrilla strategy a recipe for technological backwardness. Although their views sounded a little like the ousted Peng Dehuai's heresy, they received support from Liu Shaoqi and others bothered by Lin's growing prominence.

This issue came to a climax in September 1965. Lin Biao published an essay entitled "Long Live the Victory of People's War," which remained the classic Chinese statement on anti-imperialist struggles.

> . . . to make a revolution and to fight a people's war and be victorious, it is imperative to adhere to the policy of self-reliance, rely on the strength of the masses in one's own country, and prepare to carry on the fight independently even when all material aid from outside is cut off . . .[27]

At this same time, Luo Ruiqing delivered a contrary speech, arguing for a more positive policy and suggesting reconciliation with the Soviet Union.

> It is possible that U.S. imperialism may go mad in trying to save itself from its doom; we must take this into full account and make preparations against its expansion of the war of aggression in Viet Nam and against any war it may impose on us.[28]

This debate played itself out mainly behind closed doors, perhaps in the Politburo meeting that convened at this time. Details about this important meeting are extremely scarce, and observers differ about the participants' exact positions. However, it is clear that Lin Biao won the argument. China did not undertake massive defense preparations, reconcile with the Soviet Union, or extrude the PLA from politics. In December 1965, Luo Ruiqing was removed from office. He made a self-criticism but later retracted it and attempted suicide by jumping from a window. Thus, Luo became in a sense the first victim of the Cultural Revolution.

This Politburo meeting in September 1965 had to deal with other foreign setbacks. The Indonesian Communist party failed in an attempted coup d'état, which the Chinese had encouraged. Suppression of the attempt virtually obliterated the Indonesian party. Thousands of its members were massacred. In Jakarta, the generals who assumed control broke off relations with the People's Republic. A further fiasco was Zhou Enlai's unsuccessful effort to head up a second Afro-Asian conference in Algeria while excluding the Soviet Union from participation. In the end, China was unable to prevail and, to avoid rubbing shoulders with the USSR, insisted on scuttling the entire conference. At this same time, there were other setbacks in connection with the India-Pakistan conflict and in relations with Cuba. These setbacks in China's new Third World diplomacy cannot but have exacerbated an atmosphere of anger and frustration.

The Socialist Education movement, too, was a disappointment. After three years and numerous twists and turns, Mao's dream of the rural masses mobilized to help rectify the Party failed to come true. This source of friction was compounded by disputes over industrial policy. The economic planners considered the industrial decentralization of the Great Leap period extreme and counterproductive. Soon, under Liu Shaoqi's direction, they reversed the trend by setting up large, centralized, integrated industrial enterprises called "trusts." Several of these organizations had been created or were under development in 1965. This blatantly contradicted the radical slogan then being pushed: "In Industry, Learn from Daqing," Daqing being the name of the successful Manchurian oil field recently developed in a Maoist, mobilizational, self-reliant fashion. Education was another bone of contention. Mao and the radicals wanted to extend the work-and-study principle to all institutions. Liu was determined to continue two parallel systems. By late 1965, Mao was carping at this limited progress.

But the issue that triggered the catastrophe of 1966 was the politics of culture and, in particular, Wu Han's play, *Hai Rui Dismissed from Office*. It is impossible to be sure whether Mao equated Hai Rui with Peng Dehuai when the play was first published, but he had certainly come to that conclusion by the spring of 1965. Jiang Qing had long been pushing that view and asking permission to develop a Marxist criticism of Wu Han. Now, exasperated with the cultural establishment and its feeble feints at rectification, Mao acceded. He allowed her to have Yao Wenyuan, the aggressive Shanghai radical, write the article. But lest Peng Zhen's culture machine get wind of this and head it off, the project was kept confidential.

Little happened in the summer to soften the Chairman's feelings on this subject. Indeed, time only brought new confirmation of the Party leaders' balkiness in cultural renovation. They soft-pedaled the campaign to study Mao Zedong Thought and obstructed efforts to radicalize the arts. Consequently, Mao resolved to pressure them and decided to use an attack on Wu Han's play as the opening gambit. At the September 1965 Politburo meeting, Mao blasted the Party leaders' obstruction of the cultural revolution. Ominously he raised the question, "What are we to do about revisionism that crops up at the Party center?" [29] He insisted that Wu Han be criticized, and he gave the assignment to none other than Peng Zhen.

This was a favorite tactic of Mao's. By ordering Peng to criticize Wu Han, he put him in a ticklish position. If Peng condemned the play, he would have to discipline his own subordinate and weaken his Beijing political machine. Yet to exonerate Wu would be to risk criticism for whitewashing the affair. However, the issue did not seem to be too serious at that moment.

Deng Xiaoping continued to play bridge with Wu Han. Peng Zhen did essentially nothing.

Then in November 1965, Mao dropped a bombshell. He ordered a Shanghai paper to publish Yao Wenyuan's polemic on *Hai Rui Dismissed from Office*'' Unaware of Mao's connection, Peng was furious over not having been consulted. Did he not head the Five-Person Cultural Revolution Group specially assigned to examine the Wu Han play? How dare a regional committee take liberties over a writer directly linked to the Party center! He got on the phone with Shanghai, but his protestations had little effect. In contrast to Peng's spleen, other leaders sensed the need for caution. Certainly, Deng Xiaoping seems to have smelled trouble, for he cut off social relationships with Wu Han. But Peng, through desperation or foolhardiness, set out to protect his organization.

There followed four months of tactical moves. From November 1965 through February 1966, Peng tried to reassert Beijing's jurisdiction over the affair and to have the Shanghai group disciplined for breach of Party procedure. He blocked and countered Shanghai's efforts to proclaim Wu Han's guilt, arguing that the historian was participating in a purely academic debate. When he did permit the *People's Daily* to publish Yao's article on November 28, he added an introduction explaining that

> Our policy is to allow freedom of criticism and countercriticism; as for mistaken views we shall adopt the method of reason and persuasion, seeking truth from facts.[30]

Other papers throughout the country also carried this explanation, thereby demonstrating the hold Peng Zhen's group had over the propaganda apparatus.

In the course of his maneuvers, Peng summoned several meetings of his Five-Person Group and initiated two private audiences with Mao to explain his position and seek Mao's acquiescence. Mao remained out of Beijing, remote and difficult to figure out. Peng's specific object was to put the matter to rest with an official document that could be disseminated as Party policy. This document, called the February Outline Report, did receive Politburo approval and was sent down to Party committees. It called for open debate, equality before the truth (without appeals to Mao's authority), maintaining academic standards, and emphasizing construction over destruction.

But during these weeks, the radicals, too, were busy. Sniffing blood, they undertook to counter Peng's moves. Their greatest asset was, of course, Mao himself, who alone could proclaim holy writ. At a meeting in December 1965, the Chairman assailed Peng Zhen on the subject of Wu Han. Then in February Lin Biao commissioned Jiang Qing to convene a "Forum on the Work in Literature and Art for the Armed Forces." This meeting drafted a document, personally edited by Mao, frontally contradicting Peng's February Outline Report. It emphasized the importance of class struggle, the rejection of literature from the past, and the misdeeds of Wu Han and company. Finally, it advocated a "Great Socialist Cultural Revolution," a name that, with one alteration, was about to blaze across the pages of China's history.

Thus, into March 1966 the issue seemed to be at dead center, with Peng's report officially sanctioned and a rival document being promoted by the PLA. But then Mao intensified his attack by directly criticizing Peng and his Beijing machine at a Politburo meeting. It may not have been wholly coincidental that just at this time Chief of Staff Luo Ruiqing, a Peng Zhen ally, was being accused, interrogated, and dismissed. Nor did it help Peng's situation that at the crucial moment Liu Shaoqi departed on a diplomatic mission to Pakistan, Afghanistan, and Burma.

Politically, Peng was now mortally wounded. He tried to justify himself, but at a Secretariat meeting in early April 1966 Mao's men pummeled him with criticism. Deng Xiaoping and Zhou Enlai, who were present, sided with the radicals. Barely was this ordeal over when Mao personally convened the Politburo on Peng's case. He announced his intention of having the Five-Person Group disbanded. The final blow to Peng's career came in mid-May, as will be described in the next chapter.

Thus did several years of struggle and maneuver come to an end. But much is still unclear. Did all these grievances (USSR, agriculture, education, medicine, culture) vex Mao equally? Or were one or more of them decisive? Or did he simply espy behind all of them the great evil, revisionism? Did he at a particular moment, perhaps in early 1965 or September 1965 or January 1966, concoct a full-blown plan to decimate the Party center? Or did the sorry line of victims accumulate in an unanticipated way as events unfolded? And why was so much blood, both figuratively and literally, about to flow? Was it truly over policy issues, or were they just a smoke screen behind which loomed the great question, Who would succeed Mao?

# 6

# The Cultural Revolution: 1966–69

## Participants

The Great Proletarian Cultural Revolution took the whole world by surprise. Suddenly, China was at war with itself and at odds with just about everyone else. Nobody could quite understand what was going on or why, partly because systematic reporting was impossible. Millions of students were on the march; entire cities were festooned with wall posters; mighty leaders were wearing dunce caps; thousands of victims were dying in pitched battles; foreign embassies were being mobbed, even burned to the ground. And always words, a Niagara of rhetoric, slogans, accusations, denials, directives, and, above all, Mao Zedong Thought. Clearly, it was a power struggle. The fight seemed to be over ideological differences. Why did it drag on for so long, roughly from the spring of 1966 to the spring of 1969? What could explain the irrational extremism?

Mao Zedong occupied the center of this maelstrom. It was declared to be his personal revolution. The participants waved their Little Red Books and chanted his name while they savaged his own Party. This confirmed his foreign critics' view that he was mad or evil. Only gradually did it become clear that he had a rational purpose, albeit an audacious one, and pursued his goals with skill though he did not foresee all the consequences.

It has also become clear that one cannot understand the Cultural Revolution solely in terms of Mao's actions. He interacted with three distinct organizations: (1) the People's Liberation Army under Lin Biao, (2) the so-called Cultural Revolution Small Group under Chen Boda and Jiang Qing, and (3) the State Council with its central ministries under Premier Zhou Enlai. We may consider them as three factions protecting and promoting their own interests, sometimes cooperating and sometimes competing with one another in unstable coalitions. They reflected the personalities and objectives of their leaders.

Lin Biao had labored unremittingly to indoctrinate the armed forces and to promote the cult of Mao throughout society. This adulation of the leader was his unwavering theme and coincidentally enhanced his own stature as Mao's closest comrade in arms. The backing of Lin's disciplined military was an absolute prerequisite for Mao's attack on Party authority. The success of that attack, in turn, made the PLA the principal governing institution, causing many observers to speak of a military takeover.

Jiang Qing's faction was also notable for its dogmatism. One exasperated official remarked, "When the old hen begins to crow at sunrise, the honorable farmyard is in danger."[1] Her obduracy was, no doubt, the product of many causes: long, painful illnesses; the unwillingness of powers like Liu Shaoqi and Peng Zhen to take her seriously; and the disadvantages of being a woman. She and most of the Cultural Revolution Small Group were relative upstarts with narrow political bases. On the other hand, she was the Chairman's wife and made up the rest with zeal. Of the three factions, this one was the most idealistic and irresponsible. Jiang Qing and Chen Boda worked to foster revolutionary culture and radical populism. They were the closest to Mao's heart, but they lacked his balance and realism.

Premier Zhou Enlai was a practical administrator, not a zealot. His goals were actually closer to those of Liu Shaoqi. The Cultural Revolution was not his doing, but he went along with Mao from long habit of loyalty and an unerring talent for self-preservation. He took positions that were just radical enough to avoid destruction while he worked to minimize the chaos. His tireless negotiating skills became indispensable when civil strife and anarchy loomed in 1967 and 1968.

Because the three factions strove for different objectives, the directives emanating from Beijing changed as Mao favored one or another. Below there were other layers of power. A middle tier was made up of provincial and lower-level Party committees. Being responsible for the functioning of the system and jealous of their own positions and perquisites, they favored order and the status quo. Also at this level were the regional PLA commands. As these military leaders got dragged into the fray, they had to take up the reins of authority, and their attitudes became much like those of the officials they had displaced.

Down at the basic level in the cities, students of differing backgrounds and persuasions, graduates drifting back from the countryside, factory workers, temporary industrial workers, and suburban peasants created an astonishing array of organizations during the Cultural Revolution. Some were manipulated from above; some were spontaneous. All had a life of their own and were difficult to control. It was they that made the Cultural Revolution so explosive, hopeful, excessive, and ultimately tragic.

Disruption and relaxation followed one another in wavelike oscillations. Viewed broadly, the Cultural Revolution intensified in a long upsurge from May 1966 until September 1967. It then receded irregularly over a period lasting until the spring of 1969. Within this rise and fall, there were briefer pulses of turbulence and calm. The main reason for these waves was that Mao, although a true believer, was prepared to regroup when disaster loomed. Consequently, the Cultural Revolution repeated the familiar pattern (radical upsurge, unforeseen consequences, and adjustment) that had already appeared in 1955, 1957, and 1958.

When Mao attacked Peng Zhen and Luo Ruiqing in late 1965, he did not dream that he was about to decimate the Party. His target was revisionism and the few who tolerated it. But his policies had been repeatedly undercut. Ousting Peng Zhen did not solve the problem because Liu Shaoqi, Deng Xiaoping, and others continued to act in the same way. Finally, an aroused Mao charged personally into the fray and unleashed the student movement to give his colleagues a big lesson in mass politics.

## Tidal Wave

### Ominous Breakers: May 1966–August 1966

In May, June, and July 1966, Mao emerged from his semiobscurity to resume personal command in a way not seen since the Great Leap Forward. Prior to May he had not appeared publicly for months, and there were rumors of illness and even death. A May 10 newspaper photo showing him with an Albanian delegation dispelled some doubts. On July 16 he found a more spectacular way to dramatize his reentry. Accompanied by hundreds of youths, he swam the Yangzi River at Hankou, covering fifteen kilometers in just over an hour. Nationally reported in red ink headlines a few days later and greeted with drums, firecrackers, and congratulatory festivities, it was the first of many ecstatic communions between leader and masses.

By that time the Chairman had decisively strengthened his hand within the Party and started to push his program of cultural renewal. Most of the major logjams were cleared away in May 1966. *People's Daily* photos published at the time show that Mao was being supported by Lin Biao, Deng Xiaoping, and Zhou Enlai. He had isolated Liu Shaoqi. Actions taken at the enlarged Politburo meeting reflected new power realignments. Former Chief of Staff Luo Ruiqing's ouster was finalized, removing Lin Biao's rival in the PLA. Peng Zhen, together with his Beijing allies in propaganda and culture, was dismissed, which smashed the "independent kingdom" and gave Maoists control of the media.

A new conspiracy theory emerged: the anti-Party clique of Peng Zhen, Luo Ruiqing, and others, who were fingered by Lin Biao in his May 18 speech. Here was a "black line" that could be ascribed to one's enemies. The Politburo's "May 16 Circular" warned

> Those representatives of the bourgeoisie who have sneaked into the party, the government, the army and various cultural circles are a bunch of counterrevolutionary revisionists. Once conditions are ripe, they will seize power and turn the dictatorship of the proletariat into a dictatorship of the bourgeoisie. Some of them we have already seen through, others we have not. Some are still trusted by us and are being trained as our successors, persons like Khrushchev, for example, who are still nestling beside us . . .[2]

The task was now to carry out the Great Proletarian Cultural Revolution, which Zhou Enlai had proclaimed during the May Day festivities. The press carried criticisms of literature and culture, and the PLA promoted the living study of Mao Zedong Thought. On May 7, 1966, Mao sent a directive to Lin Biao. It came to be regarded as a kind of charter for the movement to unite all civil and military sectors in politics, production, and culture under the banner of Mao Zedong Thought.

The Maoist faction saw promise in high schools and universities. They encouraged radical students and teachers to carry out the Great Proletarian Cultural Revolution by criticizing Party leaders and administrators. The most famous of these early academic rebels was a philosophy instructor at Beijing University named Nie Yuanzi. On May 25 she and six students pasted up a wall poster indicting the president for suppressing student meetings, debates, marches, and posters. School heads throughout the country were thrown on the defensive by these attacks, particularly when Mao himself ordered the press and radio to report Nie's poster on June 1. In subsequent weeks many were dismissed from their posts, no doubt shocked and shaken at being assailed by their students. The following lines from a middle school poster convey the flavor of these assaults.

> Since we want rebellion, the matter has been taken out of your hands! We are going to make the air thick with the pungent smell

of explosives. Toss them over, grenades and stick bombs together, and start a big fight. "Sympathy," "all-sidedness," out of the way![3]

But the establishment had not entirely lost the capacity to protect itself. Various school administrators implored the Party center to send work teams to direct and contain the students. Liu Shaoqi responded by dispatching about 400 teams totalling 10,000 cadres to institutions in many cities. These work teams restrained the students' extremism. In this way, although Peng's anti-Party clique had been purged, the remaining leaders continued to frustrate Mao's mass politics. The structure of authority leading down from the Party center was still intact as was the habit of conducting affairs in privileged meetings and of shielding Party cadres from outside attacks.

Nevertheless, pressure from the left was intensifying. In early June 1966, *People's Daily* and other major publications ran a series of strident editorials to promote the Cultural Revolution with such titles as "SWEEP AWAY ALL MONSTERS AND DEMONS" and "CAPTURE THE POSITIONS IN THE FIELD OF HISTORICAL STUDIES SEIZED BY THE BOURGEOISIE."[4] At about this same time it was announced that college admissions were going to be determined by political criteria rather than by entrance exams and that this year's enrollment would be delayed for six months. A June 1 editorial proclaimed

The Great Proletarian Cultural Revolution is advancing with great rapidity and intensity. One group of monsters and demons after another has been exposed, and one reactionary bastion after another has been shattered . . .[5]

There is a Chinese saying which Mao now took as his motto: You must beat a vicious dog even if it has fallen in the water. Mao, furious at the work teams for suppressing the student movement, continued to swing his stick. Returning to Beijing after his swim, he intervened at Qinghua University, where the work team leader was none other than Liu's wife, Wang Guang-mei. Mao declared in favor of the students, and the work team withdrew. More shock waves pulsed across the country. Mao next summoned a work conference of Party leaders and berated them for opposing the students. He told them to drop their high and mighty posture and go learn from the students. Obediently, they trekked to various universities to talk with students. Liu Shaoqi's daughter later said, "I had never seen my father so upset."[6]

Next, to legitimize his moves, Mao convened the first Central Committee Plenum since the Tenth Plenum of 1962. Even at this point, Party leaders were balky, so he packed the Plenum with people from radical groups and the People's Liberation Army, and he excluded many Central Committee members. While it was in session, he held the Plenum's feet to the fire. On August 1, 1966, he published an open letter of praise to the Beijing middle school activists who made the poster partially quoted earlier. In this letter he used the designation "Red Guards" for the first time, and he praised their slogan, "Rebellion Is Justified!" He also published his May 7, 1966 directive to Lin Biao, mentioned earlier. Perhaps his boldest gesture was on August 5. On the door where the Central Committee met, he put up his own poster entitled "Bombard the Headquarters." In it he attacked the "fifty days" of work team tyranny in the schools and the "leading comrades" who had "enforced a bourgeois dictatorship and struck down the surging movement of the Great Cultural Revolution of the Proletariat . . . ."[7]

Under this pressure, the Central Committee took several important actions. It reorganized both the Politburo Standing Committee and the Military Affairs Committee, giving Maoists control of these key bodies. And it issued a directive for the promotion of the Cultural Revolution, called the "Sixteen Points." This document encouraged the creation of mass organizations to criticize the establishment. Its tone recalled the utopianism of the Great Leap Forward, proclaiming the birth of new institutions for mass participation.

> The cultural revolutionary groups, committees, and other organizational forms created by the masses in many schools and units are something new and of great historic importance . . . whereby the masses educate themselves. . . . They are an excellent bridge to keep our Party in close contact with the masses . . .[8]

It continued, evoking one of the sacred chapters in the history of Marxist revolutions.

> [They] should not be temporary organizations but permanent, standing mass organizations. . . . It is necessary to institute a system of general elections, like that of the Paris Commune, for electing members to [them].

Although this document was not published in the public media until a year later, it was sent to all important Party committees, and its contents were widely disseminated. It struck a radical new note by invoking the 1871 Paris Commune. This stimulated a further upsurge of mass political participation and raised hopes for a kind of Party-dominated democracy.

## Inundation: From August 1966 to the February 1967 Adverse Current

The August 1966 Plenum sounded the trumpets for the Great Proletarian Cultural Revolution. Beijing authorized students from "Red" families (cadre, military, peasant, worker) to form Red Guard organizations. They were to spearhead a purge of "capitalist roaders" (those taking the road of capitalism) at all levels and of "old" culture in every form. On August 18 a million Red Guards were brought to a rally at Beijing's huge Tian'anmen Square. At dawn Mao appeared to a tumultuous welcome and mingled with the delirious students for six hours. A middle school girl pinned a Red Guard armband on him, reportedly causing the participants to shout, "Chairman Mao is our supreme commander and we are his little soldiers."[9] Lin Biao was hailed as Chairman Mao's "closest comrade-in-arms." Zhou Enlai spoke as did Nie Yuanzi, the radical instructor from Beijing University. Next day, red-ink headlines breathlessly recounted the spectacle to the entire nation. Until cold weather intervened, millions more were brought to the capital to participate in similar events. The last rally in November 1966 reportedly numbered two and a half million.

Never since 1949 had China's youth tasted such excitement. Lauded by their government as "courageous and daring pathbreakers," both "vigorous in action and intelligent," [10] buoyed by adventure and idealism, and delivered from schoolwork and a future of exile in the countryside, they descended on Beijing in a great pilgrimage. Additional hordes, with government permission and free passage, jammed the railways to travel and "exchange experiences" with youths from other regions. Thousands more strode off on foot, bound for famous revolutionary sites in emulation of the Long March. Thus were China's successors being "steeled."

They wore a standard outfit of green PLA fatigues, a wide leather belt, and, most important, a bright red armband emblazoned in yellow with the words Red Guard. They might also wear a prized Mao button from Yanan, Jinggangshan, or other revolutionary shrines. Some changed their given names to more revolutionary ones. They sang "The Great Helmsman" and danced the Loyalty Dance to Chairman Mao. They carried always their *Quotations of Chairman Mao*, and some committed to memory every word of this 270-page catechism. They generated enormous quantities of communications, both from higher authorities and from their own ranks. The many factions published thousands of newssheets at government expense. Red Guard loudspeakers alternately blared propaganda and the strains of the "Internationale" into the small hours of the morning, driving the neighbors to distraction. Enormous energies went into creating and copying the thousands of "big character posters" pasted on walls, proclaiming every conceivable political message, perhaps none repeated more than Chairman Mao's audacious words of 1927:

A revolution is not a dinner party, or writing an essay, or painting a picture, or doing embroidery; it cannot be so refined, so leisurely and gentle, so temperate, kind, courteous, restrained, and magnanimous. A revolution is an insurrection, an act of violence by which one class overthrows another.[11]

In August and September 1966, the movement became harsh and violent. Assured that "Rebellion Is Justified," and that the "Four Olds" (old thought, old culture, old customs, old habits) must be destroyed, the Red Guards descended on the intelligentsia. Unceremonious bands burst into homes to confiscate books, musical instruments, Western clothes, paintings, and any other possessions considered old or foreign. The frightened intellectuals received verbal and sometimes physical abuse. In many cases, the victims even died from excitation, suicide, or brutal treatment. The young iconoclasts also defaced or destroyed thousands of temples, statues, gravestones, and monuments.

Another target was "power holders taking the capitalist road." From Beijing, Red Guards fanned out to other cities to launch wall poster exposés of cadre corruption and misconduct. But Party officials were better equipped than the intellectuals to withstand the attack. They were practiced at manipulating mass organizations, so nothing was more natural than to establish their own Red Guard units. The children of Party cadres often organized such groups. So long as they proclaimed their loyalty to Chairman Mao, waved their red books, and assailed revisionism, they could claim to be true children of the revolution. These "conservatives" would immediately find themselves in conflict with more radical Red Guards. In the capital the noisy assaults on government included demonstrations against the USSR. For two weeks in late August thousands massed in front of the Russian embassy, plastered the neighborhood with antirevisionist slogans, and blared forth accusations from their loudspeakers.

Mao seems to have been truly surprised by the virulence of the Red Guard attacks.

One big-character poster, the Red Guards, the great exchange of revolutionary experience, and nobody—not even I—expected that all the provinces and cities would be thrown into confusion.[12]

In October and November 1966 Mao and the Cultural Revolution Small Group took a milder tone and tried to steer the Red Guards along a more orderly restrained path. The youth were reminded that not all Party leaders could be capitalist roaders and that most of them could redeem themselves for past mistakes. Mao tried to reassure regional leaders in an October meeting.

> That which you never dreamed of has come to pass. What's come has come. I think that there are advantages in being assailed. For so many years you had not thought about such things, but as soon as they burst upon you, you began to think. Undoubtedly you have made some mistakes, some mistakes of line, but they can be corrected and that will be that! Whoever wants to overthrow you? I don't and I don't think the Red Guards do either.[13]

It is difficult to believe that they went away less nervous about his intentions.

At this same time, workers began to form their own revolutionary associations. In November young industrial workers organized in Shanghai. Beijing industrial contract laborers formed cultural revolution groups. There were organizations of former PLA personnel and of ex-students who had been sent down to the countryside. It was also decreed that students who were not of the "five red" classes could join Red Guard units if they demonstrated revolutionary behavior. These various organizations injected a complex new dimension to the Cultural Revolution. Their positions differed from the Red Guards and from one another. Although some were true Maoists, others attempted to use the upheaval to improve their condition (contract laborers, for example), and still others banded together to protect their interests (such as permanent factory workers).

Power relationships grew increasingly confused. The Cultural

Revolution Small Group, the Military Affairs Committee, and the State Council were supposedly in harmony, but in fact sometimes at odds. Mao supported now one and now another position. The cities pulsated with diverse student, worker, and other Cultural Revolution organizations. They tended to polarize into loose radical and conservative confederations although everyone claimed to represent the true left and swore that their opponents were rightists, ultraleftists, and counterrevolutionaries. Nervously caught in the middle were the central, provincial, and county Party leaders. They were urged ''boldly'' to take the lead in promoting the new mass politics. But recognizing a threat to their power, they strove to contain the damage and appear revolutionary at the same time. On the sidelines the regional PLA garrisons had orders to facilitate the great debate. It was the PLA, for example, that handled the logistics of the Red Guard rallies in Beijing. During this period Liu Shaoqi and Deng Xiaoping went into complete eclipse. Mao called a conference in October 1966 at which Liu and Deng delivered self-criticisms. By November they were the targets of wall posters and were seen at a rally sitting sullen and quiet. The Cultural Revolution Small Group took over Deng's base of power, the Secretariat.

In December 1966 and January 1967 the Cultural Revolution leaders lost patience with the evasive entrenched cadres. They decided to go after, not just a handful, but the entire Party leadership. This movement climaxed in the ''January storm'' under the slogan ''Seize power!'' For a few weeks Shanghai took the center stage. By year's end, two huge worker coalitions, one radical and one conservative, had stolen the limelight from the Red Guards in that city. In January, the radicals defeated their rivals, gained control of the media, withstood counterattacks from the entrenched cadres, and in a climactic meeting of one million workers, forced the Party leadership to resign. Through a complex series of events the ''Shanghai Commune'' was established in February. It seemed to some that the Shanghai Commune was precisely what the the Central Committees's ''Sixteen Points'' of early August 1966 meant when it referred to the Paris Commune. Radicals in other places also attempted to follow this model.

Zhou Enlai's State Council was also struck by the tide of power seizures. In January 1967, revolutionary rebels seized power in more than twenty ministries. The State Council soon numbered six active members, down from its much larger normal complement. Particularly ominous was the damage to China's foreign relations. On January 18, the Foreign Ministry was seized. Soon Chen Yi found himself before a struggle meeting of ten thousand reading a self-criticism. Even his wife was repeatedly "struggled."

These events affected relations with the whole world. China's ambassadors, with the single exception of the ambassador to Egypt, were called home. There were numerous international incidents, the most serious being altercations between the Moscow police and Chinese embassy personnel. In Beijing, Red Guards responded by massing outside the Soviet embassy. They belabored and harassed and, in some cases, manhandled Russian diplomats and their families. Moscow began to growl about limits to its patience. From this time Russia began to increase the number of Soviet army divisions stationed at various locations on the Chinese border.

Liu and the other fallen leaders were subjected to humiliating "struggle sessions," standing before Red Guards, a placard hanging from each of their necks, a dunce cap on each of their heads. There were many variations. The struggle session might be scheduled in advance, or the offenders might be jolted suddenly from sleep in the middle of the night. They might be paraded through the streets in a truck. The assembly might be small and relatively restrained, allowing the accused to respond, or there might be tens of thousands shouting accusations. And the victim's strength to cope with the ordeal varied. Crusty Foreign Minister Chen Yi drew laughter from the Red Guards when he asked permission to wear his dunce cap to lunch as he was growing rather attached to it. Others were not so resilient or protected. One of Chen Yi's subordinates cracked from the strain and killed himself.

By late January 1967, violence and chaos were increasing everywhere. Alarmed, Mao once again leaned toward moderation. He turned against the Shanghai Commune as a model. Summoning its leaders, Zhang Chunqiao and Yao Wenyuan, to Beijing, he dashed cold water on their creation just days after it had been celebrated by millions of Shanghailanders.

> [The demand heard in Shanghai to do away with all heads] is extreme anarchism, it is most reactionary. . . . In reality there will still always be "heads" . . .[14]

Mao favored developments in the northeast, where a coalition of radicals, "revolutionary" Party cadres, and regional PLA officers seized power. This "three-in-one" combination struck Mao as the pattern for the whole country. He disliked pure populism. "Democratic centralism," not "democracy," was his watchword. The three-in-one formula, with its inclusion of both organization and populism, corresponded more closely to the mass line concept. Immediately the media began promoting power seizures by three-in-one committees, emphasizing that not only the PLA but also cadres were important elements.

PLA commanders began ousting Party committees from power, forming three-in-one revolutionary committees in their place. The leading members were usually military officers. Surviving Party officials were supposed to supply the experience. Revolutionary rebel leaders would represent the masses. But although power seizures could be accomplished with relative ease, formation of revolutionary committees acceptable to all and their certification by Beijing, were processes made tortuous by the raging factionalism.

## Resurgent Tidal Wave: Summer 1967

For a brief period in February 1967, beleaguered authorities in Beijing and the provinces were able to take advantage of the new moderate line to shore up their positions. One ministry head staged a "fake" power seizure by revolutionary rebels loyal to himself. Chen Yi repudiated his earlier self-criticism. It was not long before this "February adverse current" was beaten back. Late in the month the Cultural Revolution Group organized rallies to protest the recapture of the government ministries. Simultaneously, the campaign against Liu Shaoqi intensified. Until now Liu's offense had been his Khrushchevite revisionist opposition to Mao. A serious problem, but he was still within the pale. Shorn of power, he lived in the Zhongnanhai compound, discredited but still in the Party.

An augury of worse to come had occurred in mid-January when Liu's son was arrested for allegedly selling state secrets to a foreign power. In late February the theme of treason made its appearance in editorials and wall posters. A "Preparatory Committee for Thoroughly Smashing the Liu Shaoqi Renegade Clique" was formed. It made the astonishing discovery that Liu had headed a secret traitorous conspiracy as far back as 1936. His wife, whose very name, Guangmei, meant "beautiful America" was unmasked as having been a U.S. spy during the civil war in 1947. Liu Shaoqi was now set up for political obliteration. In late March 1967, dozens of people with connections to him were arrested as members of his "renegade clique." Mao summoned a meeting of the Politburo Standing Committee, which divested Liu of all Party and non-Party offices (a legally dubious action). Editorial and wall posters blasted his famous book, *How to Be a Good Communist*. Wang Guangmei was not forgotten. A series of "struggle" meetings culminated in a huge daylong rally during which she received the Red Guards' derision dressed in high heels, a silk dress, and a necklace of ping-pong balls to represent the jewels she had worn as China's first lady.

During this period rebels were once more besieging the state ministries. Chen Yi again became the object of struggle. At the same time a minor diplomat who had been expelled from Indonesia came home to a hero's welcome and became a force in the Foreign Ministry. China's foreign relations deteriorated even more. Starting in May 1967, Hong Kong was wracked with disturbances instigated by mobs possibly acting under the orders of the Cultural Revolution Small Group or possibly under local leadership.

If the campaign against Liu was meant to dampen factionalism in Beijing and the provinces by setting up a common target for all, it failed. Bitter wrangling within and among cliques, groups, and confederations mounted daily. Because the PLA, a source of weapons, had been injected into the scene, the factions were no longer just hurling epithets. There was increasing violence unrelated to any goal other than destroying or not being destroyed. These trends reached a fever pitch in the hot months of July and August in 1967. In Beijing, Peng Dehuai, still paying for his impudence of 1959, was dragged out for a kangaroo trial. Outside the Zhongnanhai milled huge permanent crowds with posters, loudspeakers, and effigies, demanding that Liu Shaoqi, Deng Xiaoping, and others be dragged out for their own trials. This demand received partial satisfaction when a mass condemnation rally of one million was held as the offenders were being "struggled" against by smaller groups in their homes. On one occasion, even Zhou Enlai was beseiged for two days in the State Council offices and managed to fend off the Red Guard demands only by dint of his extraordinary persuasiveness.

Foreign relations hit a nadir. In a move to escalate the crisis over Hong Kong, the Foreign Ministry under its new leadership issued an ultimatum to the British chargé d'affaires concerning the riots there. Failing to get a satisfactory response, a mob broke into the British mission, terrorized the chargé d'affaires and some of his staff, and burned down the chancery.

Meanwhile, serious fighting raged everywhere out in the provinces. Guangzhou (Canton) was in chaos. Weapons destined for Vietnam were stolen and used. The Public Security forces simply gave up attempts to maintain order. There was anarchy and looting. Corpses were seen hanging from trees. Even more serious, if that can be imagined, was the situation at Wuhan in China's heartland. There the local military had supported a conservative worker coalition called "One Million Heroic

Troops," which closed down factories, railways, and bridges and assaulted radical groups. To bring this situation under control, the Cultural Revolution Small Group sent two of its highest members to order the military to support the radicals. In the stifling heat of July 14, 1967, a mutinous division occupied Wuhan, the two emissaries were seized, and one of them received a bad beating. This was serious, for with the Party in shambles the PLA was China's only cohesive organization. If it should fragment, national unity would be at risk.

The Wuhan mutiny was quickly brought under control by the dispatch of central troops. Its disgraced leaders were brought to Beijing for punishment (which was, however, lenient). And when the two emissaries from the Cultural Revolution Small Group returned, they were welcomed by gigantic rallies. This incident set off an even fiercer radicalism. Jiang Qing and others now began to call for the Cultural Revolution to be carried deeper into Zhou Enlai's State Council and into the one heretofore sacred institution, the PLA. "Pull out the handful of capitalist roaders in the army." Clearly the Cultural Revolution was threatening to career totally out of control. Toward the end of August Mao himself came to this conclusion. As he and others following his lead took steps to calm the waters, the great inward tide of the Cultural Revolution peaked and began to recede. But it was not a rapid or steady return to normal.

## The Flood Recedes

### Turbulent Reflux: September 1967–April 1969

On an inspection tour in September 1967, Mao reportedly exclaimed, "Some people say there is no civil war in China. But I think this is a civil war . . ."[15] He now repented his original faith in the students. His words seem harsh and ironic compared with earlier praise lavished on the "little generals":

the Red Guards . . . would certainly be toppled tomorrow if they were installed today. This is because they are politically imma-ture . . . [they] are incompetent; they haven't been tempered. We can't trust them with things of such major importance. . . . Pre-viously I had the intention to foster successors among the intel-lectuals but now this plan is far from desirable. . . . [They] em-brace the bourgeois world outlook. . . . They don't [rally under one banner under the Marxist slogan] . . .[16]

With the Chairman's blessing, Zhou, Lin, and others who hoped to restore order swung into action. On September 1, 1967, Zhou delivered a major speech demanding discipline among revolu-tionary groups and respect for the army. New orders went out to all revolutionary groups, cosigned by Chairman Mao himself, forbidding seizures of arms, requiring that arms already taken be turned in, and giving PLA commanders the right to return fire. To symbolize this return to militarily imposed order, all the old marshals of the PLA were to be seen with Mao atop the Gate of Heavenly Peace during the October 1 national celebrations.

As Lin's army and Zhou's organizational talents grew in-creasingly important, Jiang Qing and her Cultural Revolution Small Group struggled to protect their position. They toned down their rhetoric and spoke in support of Lin and Zhou. Jiang Qing began to assail a conspiratorial group behind the radical ex-cesses and the attacks on Zhou and the army. This heretofore unknown (and possibly nonexistent) cabal was called the "May 16 Corps." Some second level Cultural Revolution Small Group people were accused of being members. They were stripped of their positions in August.

Central to the new emphasis on normalcy was Mao's "Great Strategic Plan," announced on October 1, 1967. It was a far cry from "Bombard the Headquarters!" The target was no longer Party leaders taking the capitalist road but the rank and file of every unit, and the emphasis was on discipline. Under the slo-gan "Fight Selfishness and Criticize Revisionism," Mao's great plan called for factionalism to cease and for self-criticism all around. "Mao Zedong Thought Study Classes" were instituted with great fanfare. Although it seems astonishing that any Chinese would still require classes to learn Mao's thought, from across the country the new revolutionary committee leaders, many of them military officers, came to the capital to study texts, which they would take back and propagate among their colleagues.

But the genie of chaos was already out of the bottle, and even Beijing's authority, rhetoric, organization, and force could not easily put it back. Mao himself was still hesitant to abandon the radicals. In late January 1968 he allowed—or encouraged—Jiang Qing to renew attacks against various targets, including Zhou's State Council. Mao removed the PLA chief of staff and other high officers, one of whom two weeks earlier had tried to arrest one of Jiang's Cultural Revolution Small Group.

In the provinces, Jiang's call for militancy fanned smoldering fires. Factions and military units had been wrangling for months over representation on the three-in-one revolutionary committees. It was an intense fight because the losers could expect the victors to pay off old scores. By June 1968, partisan warfare reverberated again in the streets of Guangzhou (Canton). Even worse was the neighboring province of Guangxi, where a Red Guard alliance fought a worker-militia alliance, both supported by PLA elements. Weapons destined for Vietnam were again seized and used with bloody effect. Even tanks and artillery saw action. Numerous trussed-up corpses were tossed into the West River and floated past Guangzhou to the sea.

Students in other cities fought vendettas from their campus strongholds. Radicals, sensing repudiation, turned increasingly nasty. They fortified buildings and laid in supplies of bricks, stones, and firearms. Beatings and kidnappings punctuated incidents of gang violence such as the battle at Qinghua University, where fifteen students lost their lives. Among youth not in school, gang activity increased. This is not to say that all young people or workers participated in the ferment. It seems that, in fact, most students had left their schools and gone home, weary of loudspeakers, wall posters, and marches.

JIANG QING

Despite difficulties, order began to return in the summer of 1968. The PLA received tough, new orders to clamp down. They were to round up weapons and punish offenders. As for the students, Mao despaired over their factionalism and began to terminate the Red Guard movement. So-called Worker Mao Zedong Thought Propaganda Teams, usually under military leadership, moved onto high school and college campuses to restore order. Ironically, the student movement, which had begun with Mao's attack on Liu's work teams, was now suppressed by similar teams, dispatched by Mao himself. In late July 1968, Mao summoned the principal Beijing student leaders. Restrained and avuncular, he expressed his disappointment. He taunted a particular brilliant and aggressive student who had complained that a "black hand" was dispatching repressive teams to crush the students.

Who is the black hand [that has sent the worker teams to the universities to quell the students]? You still haven't captured him. The black hand is nobody else but me."[17]

Meanwhile, Zhou Enlai had been negotiating among contending factions over the formation of revolutionary committees. It was no easy task after two years of bitter division. Working province by province, calling the wrangling parties to Beijing to forge compromises and reconciliation, he was gradually able to fill the administrative map with functioning committees. On September 8, 1968, he announced to a huge gathering in Tiananmen Square that the last provincial committee had been formed. "Now the whole country is red." [18] Few revolutionary committees existed at lower levels, where innumerable grudges persisted. But a glimmering of authority was restored. At this same rally, Jiang Qing, apparently under compulsion, spoke a few words. It was her last occasion to address the Red Guards, whom she had incited to storm the heavens. For her it was a bleak finale.

The new system could now be formally established, and Moscow gave special urgency to the effort. On August 20, 1968, Soviet and Warsaw Pact troops had entered Czechoslovakia to suppress the "springtime of freedom" under Alexander Dubček's liberal regime. By late September the Russians announced the "Brezhnev doctrine" that socialist states had no right to abandon socialism—on pain of military intervention by other bloc countries. The Chinese could not be sure that the Russians would resist the temptation to invade them.

In October the surviving Party leaders, together with Cultural Revolution radicals, provincial revolutionary committee members, and, above all, the PLA officers, met as the Twelfth and last Plenum of the Eighth Central Committee to prepare for a Ninth Party Congress. A draft Party constitution was circulated naming Lin Biao, "Comrade Mao Zedong's close comrade-in-arms *and successor*," and revealing that the "number one person in authority taking the capitalist" road was none other than the "renegade, traitor, and scab," Liu Shaoqi. This plenum also saw a new development, of which the outside world was then unaware. With U.S. deescalation in Vietnam and the growing Soviet threat, Mao and others were beginning to rethink foreign policy. They considered normalizing relations with the United

States as a counterweight to their ominous northern neighbor.

In April 1969, after lower-level Party congresses had studied the relevant documents and selected delegates, the Ninth Congress of the Chinese Communist party convened. In the public eye the joyous official celebrations reflected the resolution of the issues raised by the Cultural Revolution. Maoism was triumphant in a framework of orthodoxy and order. Lin Biao, although looking frail and unhealthy, was Mao's named successor; and the PLA, a central force in administration and Party politics. The new Party constitution signaled continued Party rebuilding although Mao, Mao Zedong Thought, and mass supervision were supposed to make it a different Party from what is was before. But events were to show that the unity was only apparent.

As for the Red Guards, the range and depth of their feelings can scarcely be imagined. Little did it matter that they had trekked to the Gate of Heavenly Peace, Tian'anmen, for instructions from Premier Zhou or Vice-Chairman Lin or Jiang Qing or to touch the hand of Chairman Mao himself. It was of no consequence that they had served as the shock troops of the revolution, writing and reading the posters and struggling against Party leaders opposed to Chairman Mao. Never mind that they had defended their factions, sometimes to the death, against Chairman Mao's enemies. Now soldiers and former cadres controlled the revolutionary committees, occupied their schools, and had little use for student radicals despite all the three-in-one rhetoric. In any case, the entire educational system was in a shambles and would not recover for years.

They were a kind of lost generation, and the only place for them was where they least wanted to go: the countryside. In 1968 and 1969 millions were persuaded and coerced to go down to the villages. It may be doubted that many listened with the old thrill to Mao's encouragement:

> All people who have had some education ought to be very happy to work in the countryside if they get the chance. In our vast rural areas there is plenty of room for them to develop their talents to the full.[19]

Starting in October 1968, Party cadres experienced a rather similar fate. "May 7 Cadre Schools" began to be established all over the country. These were special farms set up, manned, and run by cadres of all ranks, assigned in groups for six-months to three years. The rationale was to carry out Mao's May 7, 1966, admonition that cadres, as well as soldiers, workers, peasants, and other groups, should work in other areas. A period of farm work under conditions familiar to peasants would give them a better understanding of the masses. Still, they were better off than the sent-down students because they continued to draw their cadre salaries ard, in most cases, expected to return to their old jobs.

## Final Assessments

"No Chinese with whom I have spoken has ever pretended to be able to explain the Cultural Revolution—or in any case not fully, not completely." So wrote a scholar who interviewed many survivors.[20] Small wonder that specialists, too, have struggled to comprehend it. So what should be concluded about this tumult? Describing the maneuvers in Beijing, the activities of Red Guards, and the like is the least difficult, but this does not mean that every incident can be known. Even the death toll is uncertain: Is it 1 million or 20 million?[21] Still, massive documentation exists and can be worked into a reliable mosaic of events. But the Cultural Revolution was so traumatic and so wounded the lives of perhaps 100 million persons that deeper questions linger: questions of cause, consequence, and meaning.

*Intentions and Goals.* Why did the people, from the high leaders down to lowly students and workers, do what they did? Many were reacting to threat, grasping to escape disaster, as in the case of beleaguered cadres. But for those who gave the impetus to events, a concept that may go far in understanding them is "frustration." One dimension of this frustration involved power. Mao fumed about his waning ability to control his colleagues. Lin Biao, Jiang Qing, and the other radicals also saw their road to power blocked by people like Peng Zhen, Liu Shaoqi, and Deng Xiaoping. This frustration also had an idealistic side. The Maoist revolutionary faith seemed compromised in every direction: economic policies, education, health services, art, culture. How could the many believers not feel exasperation?

Meanwhile across China, millions of people seethed with frustrations of another kind. Their situation mocked the bright future splashed on billboards and posters. For fifteen years, they had been led to victimize one another using class labels like landlord, rich peasant, and intellectual. Every person was restricted within the organizational walls of his or her unit, under the thumb of party bosses, a recipe for both dependency and resentment. In addition, people had learned by example that social and political goals were pursued through the coercion and violence of campaigns. This was the compound of frustration that exploded when Mao lit the fuse.[22] It was more acute among some elements of the population than others. Students were an especially volatile group. One scholar described the Cultural Revolution as "a rebellion of the dominated against the establishment . . . inspired and manipulated by the supreme leader."[23]

*Lasting Effects.* Another perspective asks what the movement achieved, for good or ill. As the following chapter shows, in the 1970s the Cultural Revolution was continuing, and the official assessment was upbeat. Mao called it

absolutely necessary and most timely for consolidating the dictatorship of the proletariat, preventing capitalist restoration, and building socialism.[24]

Many foreign commentators echoed these views, focusing on the movement's lofty goals and finding signs that a new society was being born. One called it

a nation-wide rejection of the Soviet model of socialism and a daring experiment with a new philosophy of continuous revolution.[25]

Then after Mao's death, the official line was reversed. The CCP declared that the Cultural Revolution was

responsible for the most severe setback and the heaviest losses suffered by the Party, the state and the people since the founding of the People's Republic.[26]

This condemnation has also become general among Western scholars, who concentrate increasingly on the awful suffering in these years. For example, a recent overview of China's modern history characterize the Cultural Revolution as "an immense and contorted movement that for years wrought terror and disorder on China."[27] It has also been demonstrated that far from liberating people from webs of dependency and "connections," the Cultural Revolution, by breaking down reliable rules and protections, ended up reinforcing such relationships.

But as with every disaster, one hopes that such a high price was not paid for nothing, and perhaps the Cultural Revolution did have some positive results. The very nightmare it became woke up people and leaders alike. "Never again!" said the entire nation, and this recoil opened up the way to pragmatic change. Indeed, an economist has argued that without the Cultural Revolution, China's bureaucrats, jealous of their power and control, would never have tolerated reform.

If the Cultural Revolution had not taken place the economy . . . would still have been a Soviet-style, centrally planned economy characterized by inefficiency, wasteful use of energy and declining real wages, and no one—not even Deng Xiaoping—would have had the political power to push the reforms through.[28]

A related point is that politically a generation lost its utopian dreams and its adoration of Mao. As will be discussed later, it was former Red Guards who, after Mao's death, initiated the "democracy movement," the protracted, spasmodic effort to change the one-party dictatorship. However, this result has had an unfortunate antithesis. The Cultural Revolution left China's rulers with a still deeper aversion to chaos; the specter of another uncontrolled upheaval has become their excuse for adamantly resisting political liberalization.

*Larger Meanings.* Finally, there is the impulse to seek the meaning of the Cultural Revolution in some wider angle of vision. Although it erupted from the aftermath of the Great Leap Forward, it can also be seen as one of many chapters in China's quest for economic and social transformation since the nineteenth century. This was not the first time that the modern assaulted the feudal, that the young assailed the old, that the powerless confronted the corrupt. The urgency was not new, nor was the desire to walk a uniquely Chinese way in defiance of the West.

The mid-nineteenth century had seen the Taiping Rebellion (1850–64), a quasi-Christian, messianic movement to install a new "Kingdom of Heavenly Peace." In 1900, the Boxers, a secret society, had launched an uprising to extirpate Christians and Western influence. After World War I, the May Fourth Movement tried to achieve a cultural transformation. Even though all these episodes differed from one another and from the Cultural Revolution, something linked them, aside from their all being strong responses to China's plight. They all ended with their goals unachieved, perhaps because they were so desperately bold.

# 7

# The Cultural Revolution in Retreat: 1969–76

There is some confusion about the term *Great Proletarian Cultural Revolution*. Its virulent phase began in the spring of 1966 and ended in the spring of 1969 with the move toward stability at the Ninth Party Congress. Strictly speaking, that was the Cultural Revolution. Because the movement was not declared over until after Mao died in 1976, the entire decade starting in 1966 is also commonly called the Cultural Revolution. In those final seven or eight years, triumphant Maoism was replaced by spasmodic radical attempts to stem the moderate tide.

After 1969 many ousted cadres reclaimed their posts in the Party and state bureaucracies. They revived the domestic policies of the early 1960s and initiated a new foreign policy. These "moderates" considered such measures a prescription for healthy modernization and for security in a fast-changing, dangerous world. The radicals, however, were not pleased with what seemed to them like a cancer eating at the soul of the revolution. They, too, held positions of power and did their utmost to resist these changes. Mao Zedong himself energized the resulting struggle as he repeatedly backed and encouraged the radicals. But with each episode the revisionist tide rose a little higher. When Mao died, the radicals lost their patron and were quickly overwhelmed.

# Failure to Consolidate Radical Rule, 1969–71

Throughout April 1969 the Ninth Congress of the Chinese Communist party convened in deep secrecy. The carefully selected delegates passed a new Party constitution very different from the one promulgated in 1956. Where the prior document ignored Mao Zedong Thought, the new constitution glorified his person and hailed his ideas as the Party's guiding star, the very perfection of Marxism:

> Mao Zedong thought is Marxism-Leninism of the era in which imperialism is heading for total collapse and socialism is advancing to worldwide victory.

The new charter also enjoined the Party to submit to the "opinions" and the "supervision" of the masses and named Lin Biao as "Chairman Mao Zedong's close comrade-in-arms and successor." [1]

As for the new leadership, it seemed that the Cultural Revolution gains had been secured. Most of the old Central Committee and the Politburo had been hounded out. Liu Shaoqi, being held in Henan Province was soon to die of pneumonia. Deng Xiaoping was under guard in Jiangxi Province, but permitted to labor in a tractor factory. Peng Zhen was also in confinement. The only nonradical member on the Politburo's Standing Committee was Zhou Enlai. In the vacated seats sat mostly Cultural Revolution radicals and military officers. On the Standing Committee were Lin Biao, Chen Boda, and another Maoist. Radicals in the Politburo included Lin Biao's wife, as well as Jiang Qing, and Jiang Qing's two Shanghai associates, Zhang Chunqiao and Yao Wenyuan. Finally, Lin Biao commanded the PLA, which was now the effective governing apparatus throughout the country.

But the triumph was fragile. Lin Biao's frail and sallow look as he addressed the Congress foretold his political future. Within two years he would be sliding toward oblivion on the heels of all who had occupied second place to Mao Zedong. The other radicals were to see power slip from their fingers leaving them able only to block and frustrate their opponents' policies as best they could. Even the PLA gradually drew back from its commanding position.

How could such triumph dissipate so quickly? The answer involves a paradox. The very hand that had beckoned these people to their main chance would not allow them to press their advantage. Mao Zedong lifted them up. But he fancied himself a dialectician. "One divides into two," as he liked to say. The left having prevailed and a new situation having obtained, it was now necessary to tack to the right. Moreover, conditions required a move away from the disorder of the Cultural Revolution. The most important were economic and social disruption, a new constellation of international power, a devastated Party, and the psychological-political threat from Lin Biao.

## Economic and Social Policy

First, the disorder in national life had to be addressed. The Cultural Revolution had adversely affected industry and agriculture and had caused foreign trade to decline. Figure 5 in Chapter 5 illustrates that, although the slump in overall national income was not as severe as after the Great Leap Forward, it was nonetheless substantial. The educational system was a shambles, particularly the colleges and universities. With few jobs or educational opportunities for youth, the cities were tinderboxes of unrest and lawlessness. Despite his revolutionary romanticism, Mao could not let this situation deteriorate.

The hope was to fashion a Maoist solution to these problems. This would mean putting politics first and fostering collective spirit, egalitarianism, participation, and self-reliance. In agriculture the epitome of these values was the Shanxi production brigade named Dazhai (pronounced something like "Dodge-eye"). As previously noted, Dazhai was already famous before the Cultural Revolution. It apparently thrived by emphasizing collective agriculture controlled by the production brigade rather than the smaller production team, moral over material incentives, relatively equal distribution of income in preference to payment according to work, grain self-sufficiency over diversified crops, and locally generated investment funds rather than borrowing from the state. In 1970 a big campaign was launched under this slogan: "In Agriculture, Learn from Dazhai." Industry, not to be outdone, had its own Maoist model. It was provided by the newly developed oil fields at Daqing (pronounced "Dah-ching"). Here again a collective spirit, egalitarianism, and a self-sufficient, "can-do" attitude provided an example for other industrial enterprises. So the Dazhai slogan had its industrial counterpart: "In Industry Learn from Daqing."

Education was supposed to embody these same values. Schooling should be proletarianized. Rather than by admissions exams, students in higher education would be selected by their fellow workers and their revolutionary committees. The curriculum should de-emphasize pure academicism to stress practice and production. This would mean regular participation in productive labor, no exams, and no grades. Every school either had its own shop or maintained connections with one or more enterprises where students worked part-time. School life should be political, emphasizing the collective spirit and self-sacrifice. Most middle school graduates were to be mobilized to "go down to the countryside" to make a life as peasants. By the spring of 1976, 12 million had done so.

Although programs after 1969 did embody these values, bits and pieces of pragmatism also began to emerge—always dressed in Maoist rhetoric. Revolutionary committees in industry came under the control of the Party or army secretary, thereby promoting a return to economic discipline. National policy began to favor material incentives, centralized control, less grain self-sufficiency, more economic diversity, and more foreign trade. In December 1971 the Party Center issued a directive against slavishly copying Dazhai.

## A New Global Strategy

The importance of economic growth was underlined by new dangers and new opportunities in the world. In the Cultural Revolution, Lin Biao pushed the "Maoist" line that the Third World revolutionaries must oppose both the Tweedledum of Russian "hegemonism" and the Tweedledee of American "imperialism." Now what if Moscow were emerging as a mortal threat, hell-bent on world hegemony while Washington had lost its grip on empire— but remained a useful source of technology? Was it unthinkable to abandon the Maoist doctrine, so fervently promoted in the 1960s, and make peace with bourgeois imperialism?

It has been noted that, during the virulent stages of the Cultural Revolution, Moscow began a large-scale buildup of troops across China's borders. Countervailing forces were placed on the Chinese side. Before long, tensions grew very serious. In 1969 border clashes between Chinese and Soviet troops occurred in the west and in the northeast. Beijing charged that Russia had provoked 429 border incidents in June and July 1969. In August and September the Soviets began to hint at preemptive strikes against Chinese nuclear installations and later allegedly sounded out the American SALT negotiators about joint action against possible Chinese provocation. Both sides strengthened their border armies, and the Chinese began a vast campaign to build urban air raid tunnels.

Fortunately, both countries exercised some restraint. In September 1969, Soviet Premier Aleksei Kosygin stopped off in Beijing. The degree of iciness is reflected in the fact that Mao would not receive him, and Zhou met him only at the airport. Nevertheless, the two came to some sort of understanding about future negotiations and military restraint. Border incidents declined. Still, a hostile tone continued. Moscow denied any plans for a preemptive strike and accused the Chinese of preparing for war. At the same time, Russian frontier forces swelled to formidable proportions.

In April 1970 the Chinese published their most vehement denunciation ever of the Soviet Union, charging their former friend and ally of being even more aggressive than the United States. Although polemics receded somewhat in the second half of 1970, when Chinese and Soviet ambassadors returned to their respective posts, by 1971 the two sides were once again trading recriminations. The brief war between India and Pakistan in December of that year set Russians and Chinese editors into a new round of charges and countercharges.

This extremely serious hostility was one side of the new international equation facing the People's Republic of China. It was counterbalanced by a shift in Sino-American relations. By 1968 and 1969 the Chinese realized that the United States presence in Vietnam would soon end, and concluded that American power in Asia was waning. In June 1969 the first stages of American withdrawal got under way. The following month President Nixon articulated the "Nixon Doctrine" that U.S. allies would henceforth be more responsible for their own defense as Washington reduced its world police officer's role.

Before long, there were increasing hints and signs from both sides that some rapprochement would be welcome. Ambassadorial talks at Warsaw were resumed in January 1970 at about the same time that China hinted it would welcome admission to the United Nations. For the first time ever an American diplomat publicly spoke the words "The People's Republic of China." At the October 1, 1970, National Day celebrations, Mao personally sent a signal. He invited Edgar Snow and his wife to stand beside him on the reviewing stand. Snow was the reporter who had interviewed Mao in 1936 and who had since written sympathetically about China. A photograph of Mao and the Snows appeared on the front page of *People's Daily*, which also carried this statement by Mao: "Peoples of the world, including the American people, are all our friends."[2] President Nixon sent a secret message suggesting that a high American official might like to visit China.

The reconciliation did not proceed entirely smoothly. The United States was still in Vietnam, and Nixon wanted to get out with a minimum loss of face. Consequently, intransigence from Hanoi was answered with U.S. counterattacks and bombings. In May 1970, American forces abruptly invaded Cambodia in the hope of rooting out enemy command centers. Quite aside from the furious public reaction inside the United States, this move prompted a strong personal condemnation from Mao. Again in February 1971, an American-backed South Vietnamese thrust into Laos threatened to expand the conflict, but fortunately for Sino-American relations it failed. In December 1971, American planes flew heavy bombing raids against North Vietnam troop concentrations.

Nevertheless, U.S. disengagement was unmistakable, and the advantages of rapprochement impelled both sides forward. In the course of 1970 and 1971, Washington made a number of gestures. Nixon, too, used the friendly term ''People's Republic of China.'' Travel restrictions for Americans visiting China were eased. The trade embargo was lifted. Washington indicated that it would no longer oppose Chinese admission to the United Nations.

From China came responding signals. In April 1971, the American table tennis team, then visiting Japan, received an invitation to play in China. Thus began the famous ''ping-pong'' diplomacy, as the journalists accompanying the team reported a warm Chinese welcome. In June 1971, President Nixon's foreign security adviser, Henry Kissinger, secretly flew to Beijing to negotiate a Nixon trip, and a week later the president himself announced that he would soon visit China. When in October the UN took up the question of China's admission, the United States made only a token (and unsuccessful) gesture to preserve Taiwan's General Assembly seat. Thus, both sides—Nixon, the fierce anti-Communist, and Mao, the archfoe of capitalism—had executed a dramatic about-face.

## Party Rebuilding

Accompanying these domestic and foreign developments was a shift in political leadership. Many observers, noting the military men on the Ninth Central Committee and Politburo, concluded that the army was "taking over." It was also reasonable to assume an important role for the "three-in-one" revolutionary committees. However, neither expectation proved correct. The revolutionary committees quickly lost out to Party or PLA leaders. The military began to be supplanted by a revived Party structure much sooner than might have been expected.

How could a party, so decimated, ever recover? Leninist "democratic centralism" was deeply ingrained in Chinese communism. Mao dealt the CCP a terrific blow in the Cultural Revolution, but he never intended to annihilate it. In 1967 he had rebuffed Zhang Chunqiao's and Yao Wenyuan's Shanghai Commune precisely because it included no commanding role for the Party. As for Party-army relations, Mao's own famous adage encapsulates the CCP tradition: "Our principle is that the Party commands the gun, and the gun must never be allowed to command the Party."[3]

There are other reasons as well. One is brute numbers. The armed forces, numbering about 4 million, could hardly supplant the 28 million (by 1973) Party members even if every soldier gave up military duties. Moreover in mid-1969 it was urgent to get things back to normal. Revolutionary committees had proved to be fractious and unstable. In turn, they stimulated popular unrest. In the summer of 1969, serious conflicts erupted in Shanxi. Contemporary sources described a serious situation where "a handful of class enemies and bad leaders" who had "wormed their way" into mass organizations and organized armed combat teams assaulted the PLA; sabotaged railroads, highways, and bridges; looted banks, warehouses, and stores; and sabotaged industry and agriculture.[4]

During the two years following the Ninth Party Congress, Party rebuilding proceeded slowly and tortuously. It was necessary to rehabilitate veteran Party cadres and recruit new members. Radicalism had to be diminished. At the top, Jiang Qing's and Chen Boda's Cultural Revolution Group was phased out. In the provinces some leftists were purged. There was an early-1970 witch-hunt of members of the alleged ultraradical May 16 Corps. During this period the PLA continued to assign officers to schools, enterprises, and communes across the country.

It was necessary to reconstitute provincial and lower-level Party committees. The first provincial committee was established in Hunan in December 1970; the last, in August of 1971. Yet rebuilding was still not complete because at the county level only about one-fifth of the Party committees had been rebuilt. Still, the process was well under way. Simultaneously with Party revival, Zhou Enlai was rebuilding the state bureaucracy.

Some new faces emerged during this restoration process. One was a man named Hua Guofeng (pronounced "Hwah Gwo-fung") who headed the new Hunan committee mentioned earlier. Hua was about fifty at this time. Of northern peasant extraction, he had joined the Communist guerrillas as a young man during the anti-Japanese struggle. At the time of liberation, he found himself a cadre in Mao's home province of Hunan. He gradually worked his way up through the Party organization, occasionally coming to Mao's attention for his defense of the High Tide and of the Great Leap Forward. He also had personal responsibility over Mao's native district, which he favored. Hua was a combination Maoist, pragmatist, opportunist with a certain bent for conciliation. He was tall, jowly, and rumpled in appearance, an obscure provincial functionary about to be thrust into the national limelight.

## The Fall of Lin Biao

To the radicals, all these changes were unsettling. But they were mere pinpricks compared to the devastating blow of September 1971: Lin Biao's disgrace and death.

How did the Cultural Revolution's greatest beneficiary, the man who shared Mao's sacred niche above all other mortals, suddenly turn traitor? How could the Chairman again choose a successor whom he had to destroy? What caused the falling out? Who turned on whom? These questions elude ready answers, to say nothing about the plain facts as to what happened. An embarrassment of this magnitude brought out the full artistry of the official obfuscators. Almost all available information was released weeks or years after the event. It is full of improbable allegations and gaping omissions and cannot be verified—a tantalizing puzzle, but an important one in view of Lin Biao's standing and the consequences of his ruination.

Some facts are reasonably certain. Lin Biao and Chen Boda, who had become allies, came into conflict with Mao at a Central Committee Plenum in August 1970. Mao struck back immediately at Chen, the lesser of the two, and abruptly ended his fellow theoretician's career. It is also fairly certain that Mao took a series of actions in the months that followed to weaken Lin's position. Several generals and even Lin's wife were forced to make self-criticisms. Important regional military commanders were shifted around. In August 1971 Mao toured southern and central China, getting support. Immediately on the Chairman's return, Lin Biao met his death, together with his wife, his son, and several others, including altogether five members of the Politburo. A wave of arrests rounded up scores of Lin supporters in the PLA.

Almost all the rest of the story must be reconstructed from alleged facts and inferences. Lin could not rest easy in his high position. Moderates such as Zhou opposed his economic views. His revolutionary global strategy was at stake if the United States should cease to be an enemy. If China abandoned guerrilla warfare for professionalism, his position would also be undercut. Domestically, his military power base weakened as the Party revived. Lin's fall was also tied in with power struggle. There are those who argue that Mao was never able to tolerate a near rival and exhibited a deeply ingrained pattern of turning on his second-in-command.

Lin's difficulties probably began as early as 1969 over policy disagreements. Then at the 1970 Plenum Lin and Chen took two actions that for some reason infuriated Mao. In connection with a state constitution then being drafted, Lin proposed reviving the office of head of state. Since Liu Shaoqi's disgrace, the position had, in effect, been abolished. In addition, Lin and Chen Boda proposed that the Party formally endorse the theory of "genius," the theory that Mao Zedong was the kind of genius that appears only once in several centuries.

It would be easier to believe that these two suggestions had been made, rejected, and forgotten than that they had caused the ruin of two such powerful men. But the unbelievable is closer to the truth. It would seem that Mao considered their head-of-state initiative as an attempt to ease him from active power or else as an effort to secure the job for Lin himself. The genius theory was probably Chen Boda's. Although the intention was, no doubt, to honor and flatter Mao, there may have been a fairly transparent ulterior motive, namely, to strengthen the positions of Lin and Chen, who naturally would be the head priests in charge of interpreting Maoist scripture for other mortals.

Was this paranoia in the mind of Mao? Did Lin see, or imagine, that his position was at risk and take desperate action? Was Lin always a cunning schemer, unmasked only at the last minute? The authorities alleged that Lin desperately drew up a plan to assassinate Mao and, when it failed, fled with his closest conspirators. Some have bought this story more or less as offered. Others have refused to believe part or all of it. The plot was too cuckoo to be the work of a great battlefield tactician and experienced politician. It had to be the work of his profligate twenty-seven-year-old son. But would even a twenty-seven-year-old concoct a plan that called for the use of dynamite, bazookas, artillery, exploding oil storage tanks, aerial bombs, and assassins? Surely, Lin Biao fathered a more subtle offspring than this? Still, that is the story.

On finding their plan foiled, the plotters are said to have dashed for the airport, hotly pursued. After a hair-raising takeoff in Lin Biao's personal Trident, they headed for Russia, the inevitable destination of all traitors. But the fuel tanks ran dry, and they had to attempt an emergency landing in Mongolia, where the aircraft burst into flames. There were no survivors. A plane did, in fact, crash in Mongolia. But just who the passengers were, why they were on it, and where they were going remains part of the great puzzle.

## The Uneasy Regime of the Moderates: 1972–75

### The Radicals Lose Ground

For four years after the fall of Lin Biao, from 1972 through 1975, the rhetorical side of the Cultural Revolution retained great strength whereas actual government policies in most spheres moved increasingly in the direction of the "moderate" thrust of the early 1960s. On the surface, China remained a thoroughly Maoist society, a self-proclaimed model for other peoples hoping to mitigate the social problems of modernization. But underneath, the majority of China's rulers were attempting to modernize in an un-Maoist fashion. Behind them was a broad consensus of veteran cadres at all levels, military commanders, the intelligentsia, sent-down youth in the countryside, permanent industrial workers, and middle peasants.

Trying valiantly to force or cajole that multitude in the direction of equality, justice, and heroic self-dedication was a smaller group strongly attached to the principles of the Great Leap Forward and the Cultural Revolution. Besides radicals like Jiang Qing, they included poorer peasants who benefited from rural egalitarianism, workers without secure employment, and younger cadres who saw their futures limited by entrenched incumbents. Their leaders claimed the revolutionary moral high ground, which they defended in the *People's Daily* and the other propaganda and cultural institutions under their control. Most important, they had Mao's protection—and sometimes his backing.

From 1972 through 1975, these two broadly defined forces engaged in a to-and-fro that had some peculiar qualities. The rhetoric of both sides sounded roughly similar. But behind the words and rituals, the larger side was steadily promoting pragmatic modernization. The other side, with little bureaucratic power, used its ideological weapons and its Mao connection to frustrate this reverse course whenever possible. The result was the familiar seesaw of "moderate" and "radical" policies.

Aftertremors of the Lin Biao affair shuddered through the Party and army for months. In addition to the destruction of Lin's personal faction, well over a hundred central and provincial military commanders were purged. With them fell nearly fifty provincial Party leaders. The Party rank and file must have gaped with amazement as they read top secret directives informing them that Lin was dead after plotting to blow up the Chairman's train and further revealing that Lin had for years opposed Mao and carried on counterrevolutionary conspiracies. Heads must have been shaking as Party committees rounded up Lin's portraits, his calligraphic inscriptions, his books and pamphlets, and even the Party constitution to forward to higher authorities for destruction. "Mao Zedong's close comrade-in-arms and successor" was now that "swindler like Liu Shaoqi," sometimes compared to "dogshit." The *People's Daily* New Year's editorial for 1972 almost pleads, "Practice Marxism, and not revisionism; unite, and don't split; be open and above board, and don't intrigue and conspire."[5]

The October 1, 1971, National Day celebrations had to be canceled. The whole affair was deeply embarrassing not only inside China but also in the world at large at a time when China was being admitted to the United Nations and Henry Kissinger was paying his secret visit. For months, the Chinese leaders could think of no better course than to say nothing. Only in mid-1972 did the official story begin to be released.

Lin's fall and Chen Boda's disgrace undercut the position of the remaining radicals. The stigma on their policies could be partly removed by claiming that Lin and Chen were ultrarightists only feigning to be left. More serious was the fact that the Maoists now had no one of great prestige and institutional power to champion their point of view. Jiang Qing was powerful, principally because of her ties to Mao. Even that relationship eroded in 1972, when Mao learned that, without authorization, she had granted a series of interviews to an American professor, Roxanne Witke. After this the husband and wife stopped living in the same house, and he is known to have rebuked her on several occasions.

Among Jiang Qing's "Shanghai Group," the only person with any credibility as a Party leader was Zhang Chunqiao. However even he was only a figure of provincial stature. Zhang's associate, Yao Wenyuan, was principally a radical propagandist with no claim to broad expertise. The fourth member of the group, Wang Hongwen, had been a security guard at Number Seventeen Cotton Mill when the Cultural Revolution began. In the upheavals, his ability to organize workers was put in the service of Zhang's and Yao's Shanghai Commune. Suddenly in 1969 this handsome young worker was named to the Central Committee, and by the early 1970s, thanks to Jiang Qing's patronage, he had "helicoptered" to the top. Nevertheless, being only in his late thirties and with no great revolutionary prestige or bureaucratic base, he was vulnerable.

## Zhou Enlai Takes Charge

In inverse ratio to the radicals' uncertain standing, Zhou Enlai's influence reached a pinnacle. Having spent over a quarter of a century as number three or four in the hierarchy, he now occupied the riskier second spot. The depth and breadth of his political authority were unmatched, in some ways even by Mao. Premier since 1949, Zhou oversaw the State Council and its entire spectrum of administration and planning. He played a particularly prominent role in foreign affairs until 1958 as foreign minister and even thereafter. His legendary capacity for work had been put to the supreme test during the Cultural Revolution, when he kept the central administration together single-handedly. Many Party and military leaders owed their survival to his protection during those trying times.[6]

Lin's sudden disgrace allowed Zhou to push ahead with the

ZHOU ENLAI

modernizing programs already under way. Central to this effort was economic development. The Five-Year Plan and all the activities that took place under its aegis from 1971 through 1975 are a vast and complex subject, not easy to characterize in a few words and not without faults according to more recent assessments. Generally speaking, in all sectors the principles Zhou pushed were pragmatic management, central planning, material incentives, and interdependence, all of which contradicted Lin's (and Mao's) emphasis on decentralization, moral incentives, self-reliance, and politics first.

Zhou got results. Industrial production, which had slumped briefly during the Cultural Revolution, rebounded and moved upward through the 1970s. As for agriculture, already in December 1971, with the wreckage of Lin's presumed escape plane still smoldering in Mongolia, the Central Committee was admonishing cadres against pushing the Dazhai approach. More criticisms followed in succeeding months, even as the slogan "In Agriculture Learn from Dazhai" continued to be plastered all over the country. These signals from the center only strengthened tendencies that were already at work. Not the Dazhai spirit but practicality was the order of the day, and results showed it. Grain harvests, which had slumped during the Cultural Revolution, increased smartly through 1975 with the sole exception of 1972, a year of bad weather. By 1975 the per capita availability of grain finally recovered to levels that had been reached back in the 1950s on the eve of the Great Leap Forward. Figure 5 in Chapter 4 represents the recovery in overall national income during this period.

The massive program of sending down young people to the countryside continued. Radical insistence on "tempering" China's youth converged with the pragmatists' interest in limiting the growth of urban population and attendant unemployment problems. Consequently, this program never flagged until after Mao's death. By the end of 1972, the number of youths who had gone down to the villages since the end of the Cultural Revolution totaled 7 million.

Even education, which the Maoists had adamantly insisted should shake off bourgeois influences, began to be drawn back into more conventional patterns. The radical rhetoric continued, as did the practice of intermixing labor with academic study, selecting college students from candidates recommended by fellow workers or peasants and favoring categories such as workers, peasants, and women. Underneath, a gradual return to academic emphasis and even entrance examinations were creeping in. The government was particularly anxious to rebuild scientific and technical education and research as absolutely essential for economic modernization.

Under Zhou the new thrust in foreign affairs, which Lin had opposed, continued to develop. The most sensational moment came when Richard Nixon, in the *Spirit of '76*, touched down at Beijing airport in February 1972. The famous "Shanghai Communiqué" signed by Nixon and Zhou on February 27 established the basis for improved relations between the two countries by sidestepping the Taiwan issue as a problem that would be solved among the Chinese themselves in due time. Meanwhile, economic, cultural, and other contacts could move ahead. The spring of 1973 saw a high point in the relationship when the two countries established liaison offices in each others' capitals. This was a step toward full diplomatic relations, which, however, did not come about for another six years.

Formal recognition was forthcoming from many other countries. Shortly after Nixon's visit, Sino-Japanese relations changed dramatically. In September 1972, the same Chinese leaders who one year earlier were railing against Japanese militarism and expansion received Prime Minister Tanaka and established diplomatic relations between Beijing and Tokyo. Altogether sixteen more countries granted formal recognition to the PRC in 1972. Fourteen had done so in 1971. In the UN, China took up its role with great seriousness and responsibility and won the general respect of the other delegations. These breakthroughs were part of a broad redefinition of foreign policy. As we noted earlier, Beijing was abandoning the substance, if not always the rhetoric, of encouraging people's liberation movements against both American imperialism and Russian "hegemonism." The new "Three Worlds" thesis divided the world into two superpowers, other developed nations, and undeveloped nations. Of the superpowers, only the USSR was a truly dangerous enemy. Against Russia, China was prepared to join all countries without concern for their revolutionary credentials.

Hostility toward the USSR continued unabated although fears concerning a preemptive Russian strike declined, and border incidents became rare. Large concentrations of troops were still arrayed on either side of the world's longest frontier. By late 1972, perhaps one-third of the Soviet army was there, well supplied with mechanized divisions, air support, and tactical nuclear weapons. But China's own nuclear program had also been making progress. In addition to long-range bombers, medium-range (1,500 miles) and intermediate range (3,000 miles) ballistic missiles were already deployed, and intercontinental ballistic missiles, capable of reaching European Russia, were being rapidly developed. In addition, the tunnels under the cities afforded at least a psychological sense of protection against Russian attack. With these developments, China's sense of security was growing.

The new diplomacy allowed China to tap foreign technology, especially from Japan, Europe, and the United States. Once again, as in the 1950s and the early 1960s, complete "turnkey" plants were imported. From late 1972 to the end of 1974, over 2 billion U.S. dollars' worth were purchased, in large measure thanks to funds available from a reduced military budget after Lin's fall and to export earnings from China's rapidly expanding petroleum exports.

Finally, Zhou's program included further rebuilding of the political and administrative system. Party reorganization continued. The political role of the radicals decreased proportionately. Mass organizations that had been destroyed during the Cultural Revolution (trade unions and the Communist Youth League) reappeared. The Mao cult moderated, and the catechismlike recitations from the Little Red Book ceased with a movement to study complete Marxist classics, including Mao's theoretical essays. Large numbers of former cadres were rehabilitated. In August 1972, at the annual Army Day reception, the two leaders of the 1967 Wuhan mutiny appeared. The hubbub that this caused was small compared with the stir over Deng Xiaoping's reemergence in the spring of 1973. An Australian visitor observed the electric response of movie audiences when the once familiar face of this former capitalist roader, second only to Liu Shaoqi, reappeared in newsreels.[7]

In August 1973, some 1,200 delegates were gathered for a short and secret Tenth Congress of the Chinese Communist party. This was necessary to formalize the changes since the Ninth Congress of 1969. Lin Biao, now named by name, and Chen Boda were both formally denounced and expelled from the Party, the former as a "bourgeois careerist, conspirator, counterrevolutionary, double-dealer, renegade, and traitor" and the latter as a "principal member of the Lin Biao anti-Party clique, anticommunist Guomindang element, Trotskyite, renegade, enemy agent, and revisionist.''[8] A new Party constitution was written, removing Lin as Mao's designated successor.

The new leadership hierarchy emerged. Rehabilitated Party members appeared on the Central Committee, most notably Deng Xiaoping. One of the new faces in the Politburo was the fast-rising Hunan Party chief Hua Guofeng. Military representation was down although by no means insignificant. Only two speeches were delivered at the Congress so far as is known. One of them was Zhou Enlai's. In his section on the economy, after paying lip service to several Maoist slogans, he argued that ''planning and coordination must be strengthened, rational rules and regulations improved, and both central and local initiative further brought into full play . . .''[9]

## Persisting Radical Influence

Yet Zhou Enlai did not have it all his own way, nor were the radicals ready to be counted out. One new factor was that Zhou had been diagnosed as having stomach cancer in 1972. In May 1973, he entered the hospital, emerging on rare occasions such as the Party Congress. With his days numbered, it was not clear whether he would be able to solidify the modernization programs sufficiently before his death. This was surely one of the main reasons for rehabilitating the able pragmatist Deng Xiaoping.

Secondly, the radicals were not without support for their views. Mao, of course, remained the ultimate fountain of revolutionary values. Presumably, with his backing, the Shanghai Group all had places on the eighteen-member Politburo, and two of them (Zhang Chunqiao and Wang Hongwen) were on its Standing Committee. Wang, in particular, had made a spectacular rise and was now ranked third just after Zhou Enlai. Increasingly, he was talked about as a possible successor to Mao.

The Shanghai Group were not prepared to see moderate programs continue unopposed. They had succeeded in inserting Cultural Revolution principles in the new Party constitution: the need for periodic cultural revolutions, the duty to criticize revisionism, and the revolutionary spirit of "daring to go against the tide." The phrase was emblematic of the leftists as a brave minority against the organization-minded majority.

Immediately after the Tenth Congress, the left began to strike back. As they did not control the administrative machinery at any level or have influence in the PLA, their main instrument was the propaganda and culture apparatus. Consequently, they launched a big campaign to "Criticize Confucius." This would seem innocuous enough, given that Confucius died more than 2,000 years ago. It was political code. "Confucius" meant Zhou Enlai, and the "Criticize Confucius" campaign took aim at his programs.

Actually, there had been a steady tattoo of radical criticism, and it is hard to pinpoint when the campaign began—probably about September 1973. It is also hard to establish just what Mao's connection was. Did he initiate the movement as some claim? At least it would seem that he was in the mood for a dialectical turn away from moderation. At the end of November 1973, when the *People's Daily* quoted him as saying, "Every seven or eight years monsters and demons will jump out," the radicals took this as a signal. The demons and monsters were, of course, revisionists who require to be beaten back periodically with cultural revolutions. Soon a vast amorphous campaign was under way, attacking such diverse evils as *Jonathan Livingston Seagull*, bourgeois music, and material incentives.

The Shanghai Group were not the only ones who knew how to use the media. Early in 1974, Zhou Enlai or his supporters complicated things and deflected the criticism by grafting a "Criticize Lin Biao" campaign onto the existing one. In this complicated way, it became a "Criticize Lin, Criticize Confucius" movement. On one side, the *People's Daily* and other radical-controlled media flailed this improbable pair as rightists while the moderates, in publications such as *Red Flag*, excoriated Lin and Confucius as leftists. Consequently, the campaign lurched forward in a contradictory and ill-defined fashion, it not always being clear to Chinese or to foreigners just who was the target of a given attack. Although no deep inroads were made into the modernization programs, the campaign did have the effect of slowing and, in a few cases, obstructing Zhou's programs.

By July 1974, the campaign to criticize Lin Biao and Confucius had run its course. Possibly because the moderates could point to lagging economic performance and signs of popular resistance since the onset of the campaign and perhaps because the radicals could see they weren't getting very far, the Politburo decided to wind it down. The *People's Daily* editorial for July 1, marking the Party anniversary, proclaimed:

> Of the Party, the government, the army, the mass organizations, and the cultural and educational institutions . . . , it is the Party that exercises leadership in everything. The current movement to criticize Lin Biao and Confucius must be conducted under the centralized leadership of Party committees. Only when Party leadership is strengthened is it possible to organize the various forces and attain UNITY IN THINKING, POLICY, PLAN, COMMAND, AND ACTION . . .[10]

On this same day, the Politburo issued a directive, "The Central Committee Notice Concerning Grasping Revolution and Promoting Production," which ordered work stoppages to cease, production to resume, and wage and management disputes to be deferred. The campaign sputtered on for a few months, but its force was spent.

Late 1974 and early 1975 saw the rehabilitated Deng Xiaoping rise once more to the top, protected by the ailing Zhou Enlai. This caused no little anxiety among Deng's enemies. The radicals launched several ineffectual and slightly desperate initiatives to regain influence. Mao having left Beijing for the south in July 1974, they launched a campaign to build up Jiang Qing's stature as "Expounder of Mao Zedong Thought." But he frowned on her presumption and purportedly scolded her for sticking her nose into everything, lecturing people, and pursuing personal ambition. Also, in October 1974, Wang Hongwen is said to have visited Mao to complain that the radicals had too few high posts and to charge that Zhou, Deng, and others were plotting against the Chairman. Mao took little notice.

The capstone of Zhou's and Deng's efforts, in a formal sense, was the long overdue Fourth National People's Congress in January 1975. Zhou Enlai left his sickbed to preside. Perhaps the most remarkable thing about this Congress is the rebound in the status of Deng Xiaoping that it marked. Languishing in oblivion just two years previously, he now occupied commanding positions in each of the three institutional hierarchies. As ranking vice-premier, he was effectively in charge of the State Council in Premier Zhou's absence. As a vice-chairperson of the Party (an appointment made by a Central Committee Plenum just prior to the Congress), he once again belonged to the Politburo and its Standing Committee. And as chief of staff of the People's Liberation Army, he commanded the military services.

Also noteworthy was the way this Congress formalized the planned program of development. Zhou's keynote address, although hedged with radical rhetoric, was essentially a call to forge ahead with the long-range plan of achieving

the comprehensive modernization of agriculture, industry, national defense, and science and technology before the end of the century, so that our national economy will be advancing in the front ranks of the world.[11]

This broad objective came to be referred to as the "Four Modernizations." To realize them, Zhou said that the State Council would draw up China's fifth Five-Year Plan (1976 to 1980), together with long-range and annual plans. The new constitution proclaimed

the planned and proportionate development of the socialist economy, taking agriculture as the foundation and industry as the leading factor . . .[12]

In agriculture, the document reaffirmed the production team as the prime unit of ownership and management and guaranteed peasants their right to have private plots, engage in sideline occupations, and market their products.

However, as was characteristic of this period generally, the Congress was not a unified love feast for pragmatic policies. Despite the importance of this meeting, Mao did not attend, probably signaling his disapproval. It was unlikely that he was ill because he was able, while the Congress was in session, to receive West Germany's Franz Josef Strauss. Aside from Mao, the important radicals were prominently in attendance. Sitting at the rostrum before the 2,800 delegates with Zhou, Deng, and some of their supporters sat the Shanghai Group: Jiang Qing, Zhang Chunqiao, Wang Hongwen, and Yao Wenyuan. Zhang, the most experienced of them, was awarded positions in the State Council, the army, and the Party just subordinate to Deng Xiaoping—perhaps as part of the deal when Deng's promotions were negotiated. Also at the dais was Hua Guofeng, the Hunan leader, who had been named sixth-ranking vice-premier and head of the sensitive Ministry of Public Security.

In the months following the Fourth National Peoples Congress, Deng continued to push the development program. In virtually every sector of the economy, excellent growth was recorded for the year. In addition to current production, the State Council was absorbed with completing the new Five-Year Plan to start in 1976. A number of conferences were organized to determine the needs of agriculture, industry, science and technology, and national defense. Deng called Military Affairs Committee meetings in May and July 1975, where he advocated efficiency, professionalism, better weapons, and Party control. To direct the modernization program, he rehabilitated none other than Luo Ruiqing, the chief of staff in the early 1960s who had opposed Lin Biao, had joined Peng Zhen as the earliest victim of the Cultural Revolution, and had tried twice to commit suicide under radical pressure.

As usual, much of this was anathema to the radicals. The rehabilitation of people like Luo Ruiqing (not to mention Deng!), the downgrading of the human factor in warfare, and the renewed emphasis on technology and expertise all offended against Maoist doctrine. Consequently, it is not surprising that, as had happened after the Tenth Party Congress of 1973, the period following the Fourth National People's Congress saw a surge of radical propaganda and efforts to undercut Deng's program.

Again, it is not clear just how central Mao's role was. A case can be made that, in his dissatisfaction with the Fourth People's Congress, he attempted to sponsor a swing back toward the Left. After returning to the capital in January 1975 (somewhat unusual for a man who preferred to winter in the south), he wrote a new admonition that was featured in the *People's Daily* editorial for February 9. He said:

Lack of clarity on [exercising proletarian dictatorship over the bourgeoisie] will lead to revisionism. This should be made known to the whole nation.[13]

Here again was Mao's theme of politics in command. In March and April 1975, both Zhang Chunqiao and Yao Wenyuan of the Shanghai Group published attacks on Deng's approach. Zhang warned against the bourgeoisie who assured China's youth that material incentives "like 'stinky' bean curd, smells awful but tastes good."[14] Yao, too, decried material incentives. Zhang urged that, in agriculture, efforts be made to increase the importance of brigades and communes at the expense of the smaller production teams. This propaganda campaign buzzed over the heads of Deng's bureaucrats as they went ahead with their plans.

This radical sniping continued into the summer and fall of 1975, with Mao taking an unpredictable position. In May it seems that he had chastised the Shanghai Group for factionalism and sectarianism. They all wrote letters of self-criticism. But late August found him initiating further attacks on Zhou and Deng through criticism of a popular traditional novel, *Water Margin*. The novel's hero, a stand-in for Deng, was charged with "capitulationism'' (and hence revisionism) to the emperor, that is, to Zhou Enlai presumably. A number of articles echoed this theme, orchestrated no doubt by the Shanghai Group. Yet once again the net effect of the leftist initiatives was marginal. They were unable to reverse Deng's course, but they did force the moderates to dress up modernization with revolutionary rhetoric. In some places, their opposition to material incentives sparked a backlash of industrial unrest. Their patron, however, was growing weaker by the day. Foreigners who visited him during 1975 found a man of sound mind but physically almost as helpless as a baby.

## Mao's Final Months and the Arrest of the Gang of Four: 1976

By the end of 1975, the nation had experienced four years of a fluctuating moderate-radical stalemate. The moderates had the advantage in their control over the Party and state systems. Cadres concerned to get on with the job typically had little use for the radicals. In agriculture, even when the Dazhai system was being promoted, thousands of production teams went their own way by underreporting their output, allocating extra private plots, using collective vehicles and facilities for private gain, sending weaker family members to do collective labor while the more vigorous worked on private enterprises, and leaving the village in slack season to work in the cities. A February 1976 report on the situation in Fujian Province complained:

The restoration of capitalism in the district of Changle has assumed extremely alarming proportions. In reality, the situation there is about the same as during the period of the rule of the Guomindang. The only thing which is missing is the Guomindang flag. . . . There are thirty-five groups of people who produce exclusively for their own benefit. . . . They have distributed the arable land to the individual households and have made the individual households into a distribution organ. . . . In an entire [county], everybody, cadres as well as the population, [is] busy with speculation. . . . On top of all this, they put on performances of classic Fujian operas."[15]

The radicals' bureaucratic resources were fewer; and their popular support, smaller. Yet there were many cadres who had risen during the Cultural Revolution and other elements, as, for example, students selected under the academically less rigorous criteria, whose interests or idealism aligned them with the Shanghai Group. There were brigades who did, in fact, emulate the Dazhai model. And the radicals' criticism of bureaucratism and elite privilege certainly sounded a responsive chord. But for the most part this camp could do little more than obstruct the moderates through the propaganda media and with Mao's fluctuating support.

At this time, at least a few figures were emerging at the top who might be considered a compromise group between the hardcore radicals and Deng's moderates. Most prominent among them were Hua Guofeng, the Hunan Party chairperson recently promoted to high posts (including the Security Ministry), and Chen Yonggui, the peasant leader from Dazhai. These men had good Maoist credentials, but they were more pragmatic and less confrontational than the Shanghai Group.

Toward the end of 1975, politics heated up. Mao's Parkinson's disease and Zhou's cancer were closing in on their victims. Any day could bring fateful news. Now the succession problem, which had figured in political struggles for years, became acute. The departure of one of these men could leave his protégés fatally exposed. The Shanghai Group reacted to this heightened uncertainty by launching shrill attacks on Deng toward the end of 1975. Already at midyear Jiang Qing had been railing against "friendly gentlemen like Malenkov," by which she presumably meant Hua Guofeng, "but above all people like Khrushchev are still right in our [midst] . . . ," alluding, of course, to Deng.[16] By November the radical media were criticising the "right deviationist wind," which was "reversing correct verdicts," that is, rehabilitating victims of the Cultural Revolution.[17]

At the turn of the year, it got even more intense. Presumably with Mao's support, the radicals launched a campaign against creeping revisionism in education. On New Year's Day the *People's Daily* carried this Mao quote: "Stability and unity do not mean writing off class struggle. Class struggle is the key link and everything else hinges on it."[18] This term, "key link," became a constantly repeated theme.

And then, from Deng's point of view, the worst possible thing happened. Zhou Enlai died on January 8, 1976. Suddenly, the entire nation was in deep and emotional mourning. Zhou's remains were cremated, and a casket containing his ashes was placed in one of the buildings in the Imperial Palace. In subzero temperatures, thousands of mourners stood on line for hours to pay their last respects. For days the airwaves carried nothing but funeral music and tributes to the departed leader. If the people had lost their great folk hero, Deng Xiaoping may have lost his lifeline.

Deng gave the eulogy at the memorial ceremony at the Great Hall of the People, attended by some 5,000 mourners. As it turned out, this was his last public utterance (for the time being). The radical attack now unleashed its full fury against him. A campaign of oblique attacks on the "unrepenting capitalist-roader inside the Party" and on the modernization program now began, with Mao himself adding a barb or two, such as this view of his carried by *People's Daily*: "That man's never been interested in class struggle."[19] Shorn of Zhou's protection, Deng was unable to resist, despite his high positions. He disappeared from view in February or March, 1976. To the complete astonishment of observers inside and outside China, the new acting premier was not Deng, but the virtually unknown Hua Guofeng, whom Mao nominated in January, 1976 as a compromise candidate.

Then a succession of events in early April brought the political struggle to a climax. Several indications point to the conclusion that organized or individual Deng adherents had been working to counteract the radicals. A March 25 Shanghai newspaper article disparaged Zhou, saying that a certain "capitalist-roader in the Party wanted to put back in power a capitalist-roader who had been toppled and is unrepentant to this day." [20] This triggered thousands of protesting telegrams and letters. No doubt convinced that Deng adherents would take advantage of the upcoming Qing Ming Festival to honor Zhou (and thereby Deng), the authorities sent out a directive to all workplaces discouraging participation in any activities, but in vain.

Sunday, April 4, 1976, marked Qing Ming, a traditional holiday for cleaning and repairing family graves. Thousands of Beijing residents came to the massive square at Tian'anmen to express their affection for the departed premier. They came here because his ashes had been scattered, and no grave or monument honored his memory. For some days wreaths had been appearing at the large cenotaph that commemorates heroes of the Revolution. By Qing Ming there was an enormous accumulation of them, reportedly accumulating thirty feet high. People also attached paper slips bearing poems or statements to the nearby hedges. Some of them were barely disguised denunciations of Jiang Qing, the Shanghai Group, or even of Mao himself. Such free expression of dissent was not to be tolerated.

In the early morning hours of April 5, on orders from the highest authority, city officials removed the wreaths. When dawn came and the public discovered this fact, a huge demonstration developed, the famous Tian'anmen Incident. Tens of thousands milled around the square in great agitation. Foreign observers were roughly sent away. Harangues were delivered, slogans chanted, police officers were scolded, scuffles broke out, and some people were beaten. A loudspeaker van was overturned, two or three cars were set on fire, and the police headquarters bordering the square was put to the torch. Finally, in the evening, as the crowds thinned, militia moved in with clubs and cleared the square, with numerous arrests. It was a daylong riot that was answered by demonstrations elsewhere in the country.

Ironically, the Tian'anmen Incident sealed Deng's fate (for the time being). His extraordinary career, just recently revived, ended in a second disgrace. Blaming him for the unrest (on no known evidence), the Politburo stripped him of all offices. He retained only his Party membership. The anti-Deng campaign heated up even more, with extensive wall poster displays detailing his manifold revisionism. At the same time, the radicals began to push again for Dazhai policies in agriculture.

It was not a complete victory for the radicals. Although they ousted Deng, they lacked the power to capture effective leadership for themselves. It was the dark horse candidate, Hua Guofeng, who, with Mao's backing, stepped in as a compromise. He succeeded Zhou as premier and became ranking Party vice-chairperson second only to Mao. Moreover, Deng's removal was a solitary demotion, not a sweeping purge. The whole system of cadres and military leaders, many of them Deng supporters, remained in place. Deng himself was taken out of Beijing under the protection of one of the regional military commanders. He is said to have met with several key PLA leaders to work out strategy for the future.

Soon after the Tian'anmen Incident, Mao's health took a turn for worse. Foreign visitors who were received by him in April and May 1976 found a man barely capable of moving and speaking. A May 27 *People's Daily* photo with Pakistani Prime Minister Bhutto showed him scarcely able to sit up. On June 15 the president of Madagascar left China without having had an audience, and shortly thereafter it was announced that the Chairman would no longer receive foreign dignitaries. Mao's deteriorating condition exacerbated the already strong tendency for an inner palace court to form. Increasingly, those who informed the Chairman and transmitted his will to the outside world were in a position to manipulate him. Jiang Qing's influence rose. Mao's nephew, Mao Yuanxin, seemed to function as palace chief of staff. The commander of the Central Guard Division, PLA Unit 8341, which numbered perhaps 40,000 well-armed troops became an increasingly important element in succession politics.

As Mao lay dying, natural disasters revived traditional notions about the fall of dynasties. The old "Mandate of Heaven" belief said that prodigies signaled Heaven's displeasure with the ruler and anticipated the withdrawal of the divine "mandate" to rule. In the spring and summer in 1976, several provinces suffered severe drought. Two major earthquakes struck the southwest in May. In late July a major earthquake hit Tangshan, not far from Beijing, a second quake then striking the capital itself. The Tangshan quake was a disaster of vast dimensions, perhaps the worst in centuries. Internal documents claimed that over 655,000 people died and a million were left homeless. Other sources put the toll at 250,000. In either case, the losses were staggering. "Mandate of Heaven" talk became so common that the Party launched a small campaign to stop it.

Mao died on September 9, 1976. Naturally, the nationwide mourning was deep and prolonged. Visitors testify that the mood was more reserved and formal and less emotional than when Zhou Enlai died. Despite the reverence in which he was held for his early revolutionary leadership, there was a broad, if unspoken, view that his excesses had not served China well. As one writer expresses it, "The very success of Mao's revolution had produced a generation that passed him by . . . [He] was like a speaker addressing an audience that has left for its next engagement." [21] Or as a commonly heard formula of the 1980s stated: His founding of the Republic was meritorious; his antirightism was mistaken; his Cultural Revolution was criminal.

The day that had been dreaded and anticipated for over fifteen years had finally arrived. Once the giant memorial service was over and the decision made to display Mao's embalmed remains in a memorial hall, the big questions were: Who would inherit Mao's authority, and what direction would the country take? The short-term answers were soon given. Hua Guofeng teamed up with the PLA contingent in the Party and arrested Jiang Qing's faction on October 6, 1976. With their mentor gone, the radicals' position collapsed totally. Now excoriated as the "Gang of Four," Jiang Qing, Wang Hongwen, Zhang Chunqiao, and Yao Wenyuan entered the last phase of their careers as scapegoats for virtually every evil, natural or human, that had afflicted China for the last decade. Incarcerated in Qincheng Prison in the suburbs of Beijing, they would be dragged out for public trial four years later, together with Chen Boda and others.

Now Hua Guofeng seemed to emerge on top. He was appointed to be head of all three major hierarchies: chairperson of the Party, premier of the State Council, and chairperson of the Party's Military Affairs Commission. From October 21 through October 24 in 1976 a series of giant rallies were organized in Beijing and other cities to celebrate the ascent of the new leader.

## An End and a Beginning

September and October in 1976 cut a line across modern Chinese history that is equaled only by one other momentous transition. On October 1, 1949, Mao had proclaimed the end of insurgency and the beginning of nation building. Twenty-seven years later, his death terminated an era dominated by Maoism. His preserved flesh and his edited words became holy relics manipulated by others as they addressed problems more complex and daunting than he had been prepared to comprehend.

It has been seen that in 1949 a great challenge faced Mao's talented team of revolutionaries—to organize and develop the world's largest nation. After a phase of copying Soviet formulas verbatim, they had to deal with a Mao-inspired effort to incorporate the spirit of Yanan in the process of modernization. Since 1955 an uneasy tension separated "Maoists" who refused to accept modernization that was not "Red" from a diverse opposition who were prepared to sacrifice some "redness" as the necessary price for modernization. In all that quarter of a century, this issue was never decisively settled. The final episode from 1969 to 1976 saw "radicalism" and "pragmatism" wrestle indecisively back and forth. With Mao's departure and the quick elimination of Jiang Qing's radicals, "Maoism" became, not orthodoxy, but a barely defensible minority position.

# 8

# Crossing the River, Groping for the Stones: Reform in the 1980s

Mao Zedong's remains were soon to be laid out in a crystal coffin in the Chairman Mao Memorial Hall on Tiananmen Square. His revolutionary vision was about to be embalmed as well. China under Deng Xiaoping took up the less romantic work of economic development: to modernize a vast system of communes and state enterprises. This project achieved impressive but uneven results. Just as Mao's dreams had collided with material facts, now in the 1980s Deng's economic pragmatism stirred up political resistance.

## Power Struggle

*September 1976*

Mao's death occasioned solemn ceremonies across China. The national leaders held a mass memorial at Tiananmen Square, but behind their eulogies a struggle was shaping up. Jiang Qing and Wang Hongwen were on the dignitaries' platform, representing true Maoism. Also conspicuous was Hua Guofeng, recently appointed premier. He possessed a slip of paper on which the departed Chairman had written, "With you in charge, I am at ease." Hua promised to keep faith with Maoism and denounced the purged and conspicuously absent Deng Xiaoping. Among other things, Hua was in charge of building a mausoleum in Tiananmen Square to enshrine Mao's remains in a crystal coffin, after the fashion of Lenin and Ho Chi Minh.

What about the mood in the streets? Perhaps people should have been happy that China had "stood up" in the world and addressed its many problems. Nonetheless, there was much disenchantment. Average peasant living standards and per capita grain output were stuck at the level of the 1950s; poor villages struggled for just enough food, fuel, and clothing to survive; and the countryside overflowed with laborers forbidden to migrate to the cities. Although the cities were better off, they too were bleak. The planners, who always favored "heavy" industries over housing and consumer products, had managed to invest massively without raising living standards. Accordingly, goods were shoddy and scarce, and services were poor. People were jammed into tiny apartments. Unemployment (although officially nonexistent) swelled, even as overstaffing was rampant. Scientific and technical personnel numbered merely 60,000. Meanwhile, Chinese citizens were learning about the prosperity in Taiwan, Hong Kong, and Singapore; social and political dissatisfaction bubbled below the surface. Twenty years of extolling the "great Chinese Communist Party" could not hide abuses of power, corruption, and bureaucratism.

## Transition: October 1976–December 1978

October 1976 brought a sensation. A mass rally summoned to Tiananmen Square learned that Jiang Qing's faction had been arrested. The capital and other cities burst into delirious celebration, marked, it was said, by the "three empties" (empty liquor stores, empty fireworks stores, and empty hospital beds). Now derided as the "Gang of Four," their fall was total. Nine months later, the Party expelled them, calling Jiang Qing a "renegade," Zhang Chunqiao a "Nationalist special agent," Yao Wenyuan an "alien class element," Wang Hongwen a "new bourgeois element," and all of them "bourgeois careerist, conspirator, counterrevolutionary double-dealers."[1]

It seemed that Hua Guofeng was moving up to become Mao's successor. This formerly obscure bureaucrat in Mao's native province was brought to Beijing in 1971 and was "helicoptered" to high position, taking the post of acting premier when Zhou Enlai died and becoming full premier when Deng Xiaoping was cashiered in April 1976. A month after Mao's death, Hua joined a cabal of military, security, and Party elders to arrest the Gang of Four. Now mass demonstrations were organized to hail him as chair of the Party and head of the Military Affairs Committee.

Yet Hua's position remained shaky. Former targets of the Cultural Revolution knew that he had been advancing his career while they were locked up in "cowsheds." To polish his image, he launched a propaganda campaign. Hundreds of publications praised him as the "wise" leader. Posters and billboards depicted him sitting with Chairman Mao. Hua even adopted Mao's hair style, called for fidelity to Mao, and criticized Deng Xiaoping. In February 1977, a supporter editorialized in *People's Daily:*

> Let us hold still higher Chairman Mao's great banner and implement Chairman Mao's revolutionary line still more consciously. We resolutely defend *whatever* policies Chairman Mao has formulated and unswervingly adhere to *whatever* instructions Chairman Mao has issued.[2]

Hua's faction thus came to be called the "Whateverists."

Official propagandists blamed the Gang of Four for all of China's problems. But "wise" Hua Guofeng would have to provide real solutions. Unfortunately, his approach was a contradictory mix of orthodox central planning, technological transformation, and Maoist mobilization. He revived the "Four Modernizations" goal that had been set by Zhou Enlai in the 1970s: the modernization of agriculture, industry, science and technology, and national defense. There was to be a new "leap forward" under Mao's old slogan, "Let us go all out, aim high, and achieve greater, faster, better and more economical results in building socialism."[3] Hua's Ten-Year Plan of February 1978 envisioned technologically advanced communes all growing grain while industry made massive investments. Defense would modernize. China would catch up with the developed nations by the year 2000. Familiar dreams.

Meanwhile, the political challengers were circling. Since 1973 many purged cadres and victimized intellectuals had been rehabilitated, and Hua could not block the return of more veterans, even though many blamed him for their persecution. Deng Xiaoping cast an especially long shadow, as he was widely respected for his work under Zhou Enlai and had innumerable connections in the Party, the government, and the army. By late 1976 Hua no longer openly criticized Deng.

Ordinary citizens of Beijing also played a role in events. In January 1977, crowds came to Tiananmen Square to remember the departed Premier Zhou. On the temporary fences surrounding Mao's mausoleum, then under construction, they put up posters, some calling for Deng's return. Small bottles were hung from trees, bearing the words *very good*. Everyone understood this pun, since the words *xiao ping* (small bottle) sound like the *Xiaoping* in Deng's name.

High Party leaders also backed Deng's return and in March 1977, he reappeared in the State Council and was soon formally rehabilitated by the Central Committee. Deng took charge of the campaign to criticize the Gang of Four and also restored the Party's Organization Department under Hu Yaobang. Through these means, radicals were expelled and Deng supporters were recalled.

Hu Yaobang (pronounced something like "Who Yaow-bong") was then in his early sixties. From peasant stock, he probably had never graduated from primary school. Short like Deng, he was a blunt-talking, chain-smoking veteran of the Long March. Hu worked under Deng during the Anti-Japanese war, and from then on their fortunes were linked. For fourteen years, as head of the Communist Youth League, Hu acquired extensive Party connections. Although he fell during the Cultural Revolution, he rebounded (with Deng) in the early 1970s to become head of the Chinese Academy of Sciences, where he worked to better the lot of intellectuals and scientists. In 1976 he again lost his position when Deng fell. Rehabilitated once more by late 1978, Hu had caused Party shake-ups in every province.

Deng's group also attacked Maoism. In August 1977, soon after his public reappearance, Deng cautioned the delegates of the Eleventh Party Congress:

> We must revive and carry forward the practice of seeking truth from facts. . . . Deed and word must match and theory and practice must be closely integrated. We must reject flashiness without substance and every sort of boasting. There must be less empty talk and more hard work.[4]

"Seeking Truth from Facts" became the slogan of Deng's pragmatists, a challenge to the "Whateverists." In May 1978, Hu Yaobang sponsored the publication of an article entitled "Practice Is the Sole Criterion for Testing Truth," which stimulated sympathetic responses across the country. This was a potent message: If practice were the criterion of truth, then even Mao's words must pass the test of experience. Deng supporters published Mao's own 1962 remarks concerning the Great Leap, in which he admitted, "When it comes to productive forces I still know very little. . . . Haven't we done many foolish things during the last few years?"[5] In view of this, how could China follow *whatever* Mao said?

## The Famous Third Plenum of December 1978

In late 1978, the Eleventh Central Committee formally convened its Third Plenum. Hua Guofeng's star was sinking: "Our

wise leader Chairman Hua'' became plain ''Comrade Hua Guofeng.'' His ''Whateverists'' criticized themselves and were soon
to be dropped from the Central Committee.

Peng Zhen (the Cultural Revolution's first senior casualty) reappeared. Thousands of victims of the 1957 anti-Rightist campaign were exonerated or released from detention. Chen Yun,
Hu Yaobang, and two other Deng supporters entered the Politburo. New organs were created to outflank Hua, notably the
Central Discipline Inspection Commission, under Chen Yun, with
authority to police the Party. Finally, the Party posthumously
rehabilitated Peng Dehuai, who had died in 1974.

The Third Plenum is considered the great watershed of post-
Mao China, opening the way for big changes in every corner of
society. In the following sections, economics, the heart of the
reforms, will be considered first, followed by politics and other
issues.


## Socialist Economics with Chinese Characteristics

### Economic Change After the Third Plenum

Hua Guofeng's economic plan, launched earlier in the year, called
for heroic investments in industrial projects like iron and steel
complexes, nonferrous metals mills, coal mines, oil and gas fields,
power stations, trunk railways, and harbors. The resulting
scramble of projects overloaded China's financial and raw materials capacity. To cool this down, special economic commis-
sions were established under Chen Yun and other Party elders.
A retrenchment plan reduced investment and allocated more to
agriculture and consumer goods.

Fresher ideas began to emerge as well. From the newly established Chinese Academy of Social Sciences and elsewhere came
repudiations of Maoist economics, which held that no society
can flout economic ''laws.'' The ''law of planned proportionate
development'' is violated by overinvestment in heavy industry
at the expense of light industry and agriculture. The ''law of

value" says that prices must reflect costs of production. "Self-reliance" should not exclude acquiring technology from abroad or international trade, or even foreign borrowing. Workers should be paid according to what they produce. Class struggle is no longer the key problem.

At the same time, to cope with poverty and bad weather, a few provincial officials were allowing peasants to circumvent the commune system. In Anhui and Sichuan they directed production teams to contract out land to individual families. One of these reformers was Zhao Ziyang, who was soon to be elevated to become, along with Hu Yaobang, Deng's apparent successor.

Zhao Ziyang (pronounced something like "Jao Dz-yang") was born to a Henan landlord family in 1919. He was in his teens when Henan got embroiled in fighting the Japanese and Zhao joined the Communist Party and became a local cadre. After Liberation, he went to Guangdong Province as part of land reform and remained there, rising to become Guangdong's second-ranking Party official. During the Cultural Revolution he was sent to Inner Mongolia. He returned to Guangdong by 1971, where he soon became first secretary of the Party and a member of the Central Committee. He supported Zhou Enlai's and Deng Xiaoping's pragmatic policies. In 1975 Zhao moved to Sichuan, a vast province that was in crisis stemming from the Cultural Revolution. The agrarian and industrial reforms that Zhao had introduced temporarily stalled in 1976, when Zhou Enlai died and Deng Xiaoping fell. But by mid-1977 Zhao's program was back on track, and Sichuan's economy rebounded rapidly. Harvests increased, giving rise to the peasant jingle *"Yao chi liang, zhao Ziyang"* ("If you want food, find Ziyang!").

## Conventional Reform, Bold Reform

Great economic changes followed the Third Plenum, relentlessly pushed by Deng Xiaoping. The system's defects must be corrected, he urged, or "people will say: 'Why is the socialist system incapable of solving problems that the capitalist system has already solved?' "[6]

Even though all the new leaders rejected Maoist economics, they differed on the nature of reform. One school might be called "conventional reformers," with Chen Yun as its senior figure. As the architect of the First Five-Year Plan, he advocated socialist central planning that promoted steady growth across all sectors and regions. In 1978, Chen's moves were welcomed by all of Deng's coalition, and in 1979 the government curtailed foreign purchases and reduced investment as part of the "readjustment, restructuring, consolidation, and improvement."

A second approach could be called "bold reform," which spread among the economists and experts in the new planning agencies. Many ideas came from Eastern Europe and from Western development studies. Bold reformers argued that the economy needed individual and collective ownership, markets, and prices. To orthodox ears this sounded suspiciously "capitalistic," but its supporters finessed such ideological concerns by calling it "socialism with Chinese characteristics."

With Deng's backing, Zhao Ziyang and Hu Yaobang became the leaders of reform and emerged as Deng's apparent successors. Bold reformers staffed several research organizations reporting to the State Council. Zhao, with his Western suits and dark-rimmed glasses, was appointed to the State Council in 1980 and became the patron of these policy analysts. In September the National People's Congress named him premier, supplanting Hua Guofeng. Hu Yaobang, too, supported bold reform, although he was more active in cultural and political affairs.

The early reforms were both feasible and popular. Most important of all were the rural policies. The Third Plenum declared that there would be no more mass movements and class struggles. While praising the communes, it sanctioned the Anhui and Sichuan experiments of turning production over to small groups, awarding bonuses for exceeding quotas, and encouraging specialized households and sidelines. Grain prices were raised and investment in agriculture increased, with harvests improving in 1978 and 1979.

In the early 1980s, farmers were further spurred by the "responsibility system," which spread rapidly. There were several variants, but essentially it entailed parceling out village land to families who agreed to sell an amount of grain to the state. The family could earn more by exceeding its quota or from cash crops or sidelines. These measures created incentives for peasants to work hard and undercut collective farming. Soon even the commune governmental functions (schools, welfare, etc.) were transferred to the restored "townships." In January 1983, the *People's Daily* proclaimed that "the people's commune in the old sense no longer exists." [7] The communes died as swiftly as they had been born.

Although 1980 and 1981 were unexceptional, bumper grain harvests came in 1982, 1983, and 1984. Cotton and other crops surged too. Peasants eagerly took up sidelines such as pig raising and vegetable growing, forestry, transportation, and construction. By 1987, over half of the rural economy consisted of nonagricultural activities. Despite some problems, the villages prospered as never before.

Far from the villages, China's cities were the realm of state enterprises whose workers enjoyed the "iron rice bowl" of permanent employment, subsidized food and housing, and pensions. Socialism supposedly provided work for everyone. Even the word *unemployment* was avoided in favor of *daiye* (waiting for work). But the already overstaffed enterprises could not employ everyone, especially as school graduates were no longer sent to the countryside. Total reliance on the public sector had to be abandoned.

In 1981, the state announced the end of guaranteed employment and gave permission to set up private or collective businesses, such as restaurants and repair shops. The press proclaimed that it was all right for some to "get rich first." Consequently, many who could not get state jobs grasped the new opportunities. State enterprises still dominated, but collective and private operations thrived, especially in service and retailing and particularly in southern coastal cities. Already in 1981 collectives were employing about 25 million (typically women). By 1984 they created jobs for 7 million more. Private businesses grew from 1 million in 1981 to nearly 3.4 million in 1984, another relatively easy reform.

A third big change was consumption. The earlier policy based on Mao's self-denying proletarian was replaced by a view of the worker motivated by pay and bonuses. But money works as an incentive only if there is something to buy. Thus the reforms took a different attitude toward consumer goods, and the media began to speak of a "socialist commodity economy." Wage hikes in 1979 stimulated consumption. Output and sales of cloth and bicycles jumped. Visiting overseas relatives from Hong Kong and elsewhere were allowed to bring in TVs and appliances. Books and entertainments, both traditional and foreign, multiplied. Relaxed trade restrictions led to a flood of consumer durable imports in 1979 and a second in 1984. Food and cloth rationing stopped in 1982 and 1983, and the consumption of meat, vegetables, beer, and tobacco increased. Chinese began to look less like Mao's "blue ants" and more like people elsewhere, eager to satisfy contemporary fashions. They bought wrist watches, bicycles, radios, cameras, sewing machines, TVs, cassette players, washing machines, and refrigerators. Housing expanded. Motorcycles became more common, and taxis began to proliferate. In a few years, Guangzhou, Shanghai, and other cities developed traffic problems.

A fourth area of relatively easy reform was the "open door" to trade, technology, investment, and tourism. Eager to catch up to Hong Kong, Taiwan, South Korea, and Singapore, China's leaders sought foreign technology. But this required hard currency, which meant exports—which in turn required joining the global economy. From 1978, commodity trade grew rapidly, pausing only in 1982 and 1983. By 1987, it had quadrupled. Tourists were welcomed in increasingly large numbers.

In 1980, Deng pushed through the creation of four "special

economic zones'' (SEZs) whose purpose was to promote exports by providing enclaves and inducements for foreign investment and joint ventures. The largest SEZ was Shenzhen, across the border from Hong Kong. A second SEZ bordered Macao, and the third and fourth, farther up the coast, looked across the water to prosperous Taiwan. It was hoped that the SEZs would pull the rest of China toward modernization. Although they grew slowly at first, Shenzhen in particular soon began to show results, and within a decade it mushroomed into a large city.

Hainan Island, an undeveloped part of Guangdong Province, received special privileges in 1981 and was later elevated to full provincial status. In 1984 the government announced that fourteen coastal cities could also offer concessions to foreign investors. Thus export-led development met an eager response in the coastal provinces. Guangdong, with its three SEZs and links to Hong Kong, led the parade, together with Zhejiang and Jiangsu in the lower Yangzi region.

The "open door" also featured a Foreign Investment Joint Venture Law to improve the legal climate. China joined the World Bank and the International Monetary Fund and participated in international deliberations. Zhao, Hu, and other senior leaders began regularly to visit Western nations and welcome their heads of state to China. Hundreds of organizations and departments sponsored visits by foreign experts. Thousands of Chinese specialists, scholars, and students traveled abroad: Between 1979 and 1987 the United States alone issued 56,000 visas for students and scholars, of whom 20,000 had returned home as of 1988.

## Emerging Problems

The early reforms, involving easy moves and benefiting eager constituencies, had immediate results, but in the mid- and late 1980s, circumstances grew more complex. The reforms yielded diminishing benefits, or contradicted one another, or created unanticipated problems. Complaints increased.

Average peasant incomes trailed far behind those of urban workers. Remote places remained extremely poor, since prosperity depended on access to a market. Other problems persisted. Alarmingly large areas of farmland were being lost to urban expansion, erosion, and salinization. Neither the farmers nor the state was investing enough in land improvement, irrigation, and other agricultural assets. Peasants, needing money and no longer controlled by commune leaders, were felling forests at a calamitous rate. Education, health, and welfare systems were in jeopardy as the communes disappeared.

The state was groping for a satisfactory grain policy. The great harvest of 1984, capping two bumper years, swamped the granary system, and the authorities responded by changing procurement rules and prices. The resulting price structure greatly favored cash crops, and so farmers again had to be coerced to grow grains. As a result, grain harvests dropped off; only sideline occupations and cash crops enabled rural incomes to continue rising. The new grain system also created fiscal woes. By the mid-1980s, government prices to farmers had climbed (although not enough to make growing grain truly attractive). The urban grain stores kept prices low, since state wages were also low. The gap between what the state paid to farmers and what it got from urban sales contributed to the ballooning budget deficits.

The state sector struggled with other problems common to Soviet-type systems. Enterprises had never needed to make profits (a meaningless concept anyway, when prices are administratively set), and they never went bankrupt, no matter how much they lost. Consequently, most were stodgy and inefficient, controlled by Party secretaries who might or might not be good managers. In 1979 thousands of enterprises were transferred from central ministries to provincial and municipal governments, presumably to make them more independent and entrepreneurial.

In 1983 a new incentive was introduced, whereby rather than turn over profits to the state, enterprises could keep them and pay taxes instead. Another policy attempted to shift authority from Party secretaries to professional managers.

But the state enterprises did not become lean and efficient; control only shifted from central bureaucrats to local bureaucrats. Perversely, ministries and municipalities scrambled to establish new ventures (tourist hotels were a favorite). The excess investment created inflationary pressures while draining investment funds for transportation, energy, and agriculture. Although some enterprises made good returns, many operated at a loss and required constant infusions of state money. The management reforms had little effect on the power of Party secretaries.

In October 1984 at a Central Committee Plenum, the bold reformers pushed to accelerate urban reforms, despite resistance from the conventional reformers. The "Decision of the Central Committee on Reform of the Economic Structure" decreed a "responsibility system" for managers in state enterprises. Party committees would relinquish day-to-day direction. Laws would regulate the Party's role. The number of state-set prices was reduced, and allowing enterprises to go bankrupt was proposed. These measures would have dramatically affected the economy. But although managers welcomed the "responsibility system," the Party secretaries had no intention of moving to the sidelines. Few state enterprises went bankrupt because they could protest that their losses were caused by irrational prices or forces beyond their control. For social and political reasons, therefore, it was unlikely that a big factory, with its welfare obligations to workers and support staffs of drivers, teachers, and cooks, would be permitted to close.

The "open door" also created difficulties. The periodic bursts of consumer and machinery imports created foreign exchange problems. The SEZs also were slow to meet expectations: Although they absorbed investments in roads and facilities, they failed to generate trade surpluses. Investors in Shenzhen concentrated on high rises and resorts and products for China's domestic market. The other three SEZs were even more sluggish, and heated debates flared over whether the SEZs were a good idea. "Opening" also created opportunities for smuggling, currency trafficking, and bribery. In 1985 a scandal broke in Hainan Island: Officials had used foreign exchange not for investment projects but to acquire 90,000 trucks and cars, 120,000 motorcycles, 250,000 VCRs, and 3 million TVs, which they peddled on the black market across China.

Inflation was another unwelcome guest. Under Mao, China had boasted of having no inflation, unlike the situation in capitalist countries. But now as price controls eased and the money supply increased to accommodate runaway investment, inflation made an appearance. It was moderate at first. Starting in 1985, however, the combination of nongrain food increases, ballooning subsidies, higher urban wages and bonuses, unchecked local investment, and the banks' willingness to increase the money supply to accommodate all this produced double-digit inflation.

Although the positive results noted earlier bolstered Zhao Ziyang, Hu Yaobang, and their patron Deng Xiaoping—especially from 1982 through 1984—the conventional reformers and the remaining more orthodox Marxists deplored what was happening, for it was undermining the planned socialist system. One conservative, for example, visited the SEZs in 1984 and complained, "Apart from the five-starred red flag, everything in Shenzhen has turned capitalist." [8] Others were offended by the "spiritual pollution" seeping in through the "open door" from Hong Kong and the West.

In various ways, the reforms threatened central planners, Party ideologues, the poorer internal provinces, and the military. Party committees in state enterprises saw their control threatened; state workers feared for their "iron rice bowl"; and peasants disliked having to grow grain and to have to adhere to strict birth control policies. Everyone fumed about corruption. The bold reformers were stymied in many directions, sometimes able to enact only limited experiments. The reforms were stop and go, never consolidated in a comprehensive package. As Zhao Ziyang said in early 1980, "In China, we have a saying—'When you cross the river, you grope for the stones.' But you must cross the river. You can't just jump over it. Sometimes things don't work and you have to start again."[9]

## Political Dilemmas

Until Mao's death, the people's democratic dictatorship was strongly (if imperfectly) enforced. There was one truth: Marxism-Leninism Mao Zedong Thought. One party exercised dictatorship in the name of the masses. All institutions were controlled by Party committees. Everyone belonged to a "unit": the factory, the school, the production brigade from which he or she received income and other life benefits and to which he or she was subservient. China was a vast web of authoritarian relationships.

The power of this system was immense. It remedied many problems that had plagued China for a hundred years. On the other hand, its stifling side effects (the stagnant economy and corruption of power) became increasingly apparent. It seemed that the system had to become less totalitarian and more tolerant. Indeed, this was the direction that things took in the 1980s, as official intrusion in people's private lives diminished. Hobbies, pets, stylish clothes, and disco dancing were now permitted. Visitors noted the more relaxed tone of life. But this produced a dilemma. Those with power, from the village cadres to the Central Committee elite, resisted sharing it. The whole structure might crumble if dictatorship were seriously questioned. Rather than introduce "bourgeois democracy," the approach was to cleanse and streamline the system, to loosen restraints on people's private lives, and to permit controlled discussion. Success depended on keeping people from going too far. Inevitably, some did test the boundaries, but it was not the peasants, poorly educated and preoccupied with their daily labors, nor the state workers, cocooned in their units; rather, it was the youths, students, and intellectuals. The first episode is known as the Democracy Wall.

## The Cry for "Democracy"

In late 1978, a poster containing the following appeared on the gray brick wall in front of Beijing's municipal bus station, not far from Tiananmen Square:

> Try and ask yourself the question: How could Lin Biao rise to such power without Chairman Mao's support? . . . Did Chairman Mao realize the true nature of Jiang Qing? . . . How could the Gang of Four start an anti-Rightist campaign to topple Vice-Premier Deng from power without Chairman Mao's knowledge? . . . How could the Tiananmen incident get labeled a counterrevolutionary act without Chairman Mao nodding his head? [10]

Curiously, the police did nothing. But such tolerance was no oversight; criticism of the past was being encouraged. In the secret Central Committee meetings just then in session, Deng Xiaoping's group was in the process of pushing Hua Guofeng aside. In this struggle, popular criticism of the Cultural Revolution and Maoism were useful. For a year, the official media had invited the airing of grievances. The *People's Daily* urged criticism of corrupt officials. Another newspaper condemned Yao Wenyuan's 1965 attack on *Hai Rui Dismissed from Office* (the first salvo of the Cultural Revolution). A wave of "wound" literature telling of the Cultural Revolution was being published, and the Beijing Public Security Bureau was quietly exonerating several hundred "counterrevolutionaries" jailed after the 1976 Tiananmen demonstrations.

Democracy Wall became a sensation, especially when the word spread that Deng approved of it. Crowds gathered, read, copied, and criticized the diverse posters. Activist groups sold mimeographed journals, the first unofficial publications since the Cultural Revolution. Concurrently, authorities tolerated the thousands of peasants pouring into Beijing and other cities to plead for redress of their grievances. The press criticized the Cultural Revolution and Maoism. The *Liberation Army Daily* published the story of Peng Dehuai's death: His nieces and nephews described how in 1974, even as he died, his guards denied him books and newspapers, pen and paper, and even sunlight. In January 1979, the Party declared that Lin Biao and the Gang of Four were not really *rightists* pretending to be left. Rather, they were ultra*leftists*. Now "left deviationism" was as bad as rightism.

In February 1979, a speech by an editor of the *People's Daily* circulated in the Party, condemning Mao on several accounts. There were veiled attacks on Hua Guofeng for calling the Gang of Four "rightists" and for helping purge Deng in 1976. In Guangzhou (Canton), a stir was created when three notorious men were released from prison. Collectively known as Li Yizhe, they had been jailed in 1974 for writing a poster, "Socialist Democracy and the Legal System," a lengthy criticism of the Party and a defense of the rule of law.

The Democracy Wall posters proliferated, and the boundary of the permissible began to be tested. Among them was the "Nineteen-Point Declaration" of an accountant named Ren Wanding, calling for free elections, independent courts, a multiparty system, limitations on the privileges of Party members, and more freedom of information. Bolder yet was Wei Jingsheng. This Party cadre's son, a former Red Guard and PLA officer, had been deeply disillusioned by the Cultural Revolution. He denounced the system in posters and in his journal *Explorations*. His long poster, "The Fifth Modernization," warned that the Four Modernizations could not succeed without a fifth: democracy. Without it, "modernization of production and livelihood is impossible, all pledges by any Great Man to the contrary notwithstanding." [11] He invited people to consider that

> according to the definition of the Marxist ancestors, socialism means that the people, or the proletariat, are their own masters. Let me

ask the Chinese workers and peasants: With the meager wages you get every month, whose master and what kind of master can you be?[12]

Notoriety also came to Fu Yuehua, a municipal worker who earlier had been raped by her superior. When she brought charges, she was the one who suffered ostracism while he went scot free. Now her indignation caused her to take up the cause of the peasants who had come to Beijing. She led their marches and chants, hoping to shame the bureaucrats into action.

Domestic access to world news was increasing. Foreign journalists were being granted greater freedom. China was welcoming thousands of overseas Chinese and foreign tourists. Official tolerance of all this may have been influenced by the improving United States–China relations. As formal diplomatic recognition was being restored in January 1979, signs of liberalization dressed up China's image. When Deng visited the United States in January 1979, Chinese TV showed marvels like Disneyland and their leader donning at Texas ten-gallon hat.

## The "Four Cardinal Principles"

Deng Xiaoping might find the Democracy Wall useful, but he would not tolerate threats to the Party's power. At this time another crisis erupted, involving urban youth returned from the villages. Many were home for the Spring Festival (lunar New Year), some illegally. During the first half of 1979, around 5 million returned to the city. Rumor had it that the program would terminate, but what would happen to those already sent down? In February, several hundred thousand defiant Shanghai youths refused to go back. They demonstrated and seized the railroad station. Similar outbursts erupted elsewhere.

It was time for the state to "kill the chicken in order to warn the monkey," as the saying goes. Fu Yuehua was arrested. In March, Wei Jingsheng gave a foreign journalist a Defense Ministry document relating to China's invasion of Vietnam. Although the information was inconsequential, because, like all official documents it was classified, Wei was arrested for breaching national security. In early April Ren Wanding was taken in for protesting Wei's arrest. Other activists in several cities met the same fate. In March, Deng Xiaoping announced the "Four Cardinal Principles." People were not permitted to question socialism, the proletarian dictatorship, Communist Party leadership, or Marxism-Leninism Mao Zedong Thought. This formula became the rhetorical cornerstone of party dictatorship. [13]

Wei and Fu were tried in October. Both defied the rule of "leniency to those who confess, severity to those who resist" and defended themselves, which was, of course, futile. The prosecutor invoked the Four Cardinal Principles, stating, "There exists no freedom to violate them but only the freedom to uphold them." [14] Wei got fifteen years, and Fu Yuehua got two years. In 1993 Wei was languishing in prison, reportedly suffering mental distress (a charge denied by authorities). Fu's sentence was later doubled. Ren Wanding also was tried and convicted, spending most of the next four years in a cell ten feet square, covertly writing long political essays on toilet paper. Although he was released in 1983, he was again tried and imprisoned in 1990.

The authorities closed the Democracy Wall in December 1979 and suppressed private publications. There were more arrests and sentences. Police harassed and threatened Chinese who maintained contacts with foreigners. In January 1980, Deng Xiaoping called for removing from the constitution Mao's "Four Great Freedoms" (speaking out freely, airing views freely, holding great debates, and writing big-character posters), and the National People's Congress obediently did so at its next meeting.

The Four Cardinal Principles and removal of the Four Great Freedoms only reflected political reality. Nevertheless, the rulers could not ignore the need for a less-coerced society, and therefore they used limited means to protect Party power, far short of the mass reprisals of the 1957 anti-Rightist movement. And they still tolerated minor protest. Peasants remained in Beijing in the fall of 1980. Beijing University students demonstrated against the continued military occupation of certain school buildings. Local people's congress elections went forward under rules allowing activists in Changsha, Beijing, and at least ten other cities to run as candidates. Some won against dogged local Party resistance, although their victories meant little. In September 1980, at the National People's Congress, some delegates even cast some negative votes.

A few private publications survived, more or less underground, despite hard-liners clamoring to suppress all "illegal" journals and election challenges. In late December 1980 at a Party work conference, Deng himself criticized "bourgeois liberalization" and "illegal" organizations and publications, thereby launching a campaign that led to many arrests in April 1981. For example, in Guangzhou, the three authors of "Socialist Democracy and the Legal System" were returned to jail, and the elections of dissidents to people's congresses were nullified.

## The Trial of the Gang of Four

Even Mao (with Hua Guofeng) was under attack. A reevaluation of him was debated in top Party circles and delivered in September by the PLA's senior marshal. It blamed Mao for the Cultural Revolution, "a calamity for our people," and it redefined "Mao Zedong Thought" as a collective rather than a personal achievement, "the product of his comrades-in-arms, the Party and the revolutionary people . . . the crystallization of the collective wisdom of the Chinese Party." [15] Hua Guofeng's allies were assailed. For example, Dazhai, the model production brigade, and its famous leader (and Hua supporter) Chen Yonggui came under attack, because Dazhai's miracles were allegedly the result of subsidies and bogus bookkeeping. Furthermore, during the Cultural Revolution, Dazhai had witnessed excesses under Chen Yonggui himself; even his son was corrupt. The once ubiquitous slogan "In Agriculture Learn from Dazhai" disappeared.

As for the fate of the "Gang of Four": After four years of detention without charge, on November 20, 1980, thirty-five special judges convened, with a corps of prosecutors, some defense counsel, and a handpicked audience (no foreign reporters). Escorted in manacles were Jiang Qing, Zhang Chunqiao, Wang Hongwen, and Yao Wenyuan, as well as Chen Boda and five of Lin Biao's generals. The court announced that Lin and his wife and son would also have been on trial if they were not already dead. Long clips of the proceedings were televised.

The defendants were charged with plotting against the Party, persecuting hundreds of thousands during the Cultural Revolution, and causing nearly 35,000 deaths. The Gang was additionally indicted for plotting a military coup after Mao's death, and the generals, for conspiring to assassinate Mao in 1971. Witnesses described horrible crimes, played tape recordings of groaning victims, and claimed that Jiang Qing had a private torture chamber.

Jiang Qing matched the official theatrics: She projected first confusion and innocence and then scorn and defiance. Claiming to have acted on Mao's directives, she scorned her spineless accusers: "For thirty-eight years [I] was Mao's wife. . . . In the war years, I was the only woman with Chairman Mao at the front. Where were you hiding then?" Zhang Chunqiao doggedly refused to acknowledge the tribunal or say one word. The others groveled and appealed for mercy. Broken old Chen Boda, long presumed dead, declared that the firing squad would be too good for the likes of himself, who deserved beheading.

In the end Jiang Qing and Zhang Chunqiao received death sentences, which were postponed for two years to allow for repentance. Wang Hongwen got life, the others from sixteen to twenty years. (The death sentences were later commuted indefinitely, and Chen Boda and the generals were released because of failing health. In 1991, Jiang Qing reportedly committed suicide while on medical release.) The trial was another blow to Maoism and Hua Guofeng. The prosecution blamed Mao for the Cultural Revolution and for Lin Biao and Jiang Qing, adding, however, that the masses would never forget his great revolutionary contributions.

The trial sheds interesting light on the legal reforms then under way. The Great Leap Forward and the Cultural Revolution had gutted the judicial system, leaving criminal and civil matters to be handled administratively or through informal mediation. But a modernizing China looking for international business could not continue to depend on informal processes. In 1980, new codes and procedures were being developed under the direction of Peng Zhen, chair of the National People's Congress's Standing Committee. The Ministry of Justice was reestablished, and the courts and criminal justice apparatus reconstituted. Law schools began to expand. But the law remained weak. Party committees operated above the law and interfered routinely in the judicial system. Criminal procedures were stacked hopelessly against the accused. The crime of "counterrevolutionary activity" remained on the books for the handy prosecution of dissidents. Journalistic independence was limited, and "illegal" organizations and publications were monitored and restricted. The state sometimes even refused to publish new statutes, lest citizens and foreigners make use of them.

As a judicial proceeding, the trial of the Gang of Four was not reassuring. The accused were proclaimed guilty in advance. Defense counsel made no objections, cross-examined no witnesses, and presented no evidence. Deng's own outburst to the Italian interviewer Oriana Fallaci on the eve of the trial typifies the show-trial atmosphere:

> She is a very, very evil woman. She is so evil that any evil thing you say about her isn't evil enough, and if you ask me to judge her with the grades as we do in China, I answer that this is impossible, there are no grades for Jiang Qing, that Jiang Qing is a thousand times a thousand below zero.[16]

Still, Jiang Qing and Zhang Chunqiao salvaged the small victory of defiance. Jiang was last seen being dragged from the courtroom, shouting the Cultural Revolution slogan: "To rebel is justified!"

## The Reforms of 1981–86

The Eleventh Central Committee's Sixth Plenum, meeting in June 1981, sealed the transfer of power. Hua Guofeng surrendered the Military Affairs Committee chair to Deng and the Party chair to Hu Yaobang. Earlier he had turned over the premiership to Zhao Ziyang. It may be wondered why Deng did not personally take the top offices. This question, however, is almost irrelevant in Chinese politics, in which a leader's prestige and network of supporters—not his or her office—determine power. With his vast connections and his control over the military, Deng was the most influential person in China. His intent was to groom Hu Yaobang and Zhao Ziyang as successors for an orderly transfer of power.

In addition to the economy, high priority was given to government reform, a more competent Party and administrative bureaucracy, and a better way of linking the leaders and the people. The results were mixed. Although there were positive outcomes such as the recruitment of a new generation of leaders, on the whole, the reforms were ragged and inconclusive. The reformers disagreed about what should replace Maoism. Conventional reformers like Chen Yun groomed their own younger leaders, notably Li Peng, who would ultimately displace Hu Yaobang and Zhao Ziyang, while the few remaining ardent Marxist-Leninists fought to preserve socialist principles, but the immensity of China and thirty years of socialism made changing the system as difficult as turning around a supertanker.

## Leaders and Their Views, 1981–86

Leadership changes into the mid-1980s reflected this uneven process. Deng wanted to bring in a new generation, but age was not synonymous with conservatism, nor youth with reform. Old

ZHAO ZIYANG

Deng was bold in economic reform, whereas certain younger leaders were conservative. Thus even as new leaders emerged, the old hung on. As the bold reformers pushed their plans, the conventional reformers (and outright enemies of reform) remained powerful.

These changes were reflected in key Party meetings: the Twelfth Party Congress of 1982, a "National Delegate Conference" of 1985, and the 1987 Thirteenth Party Congress. Although Deng Xiaoping, Chen Yun, and other elders retained some positions as well as enormous informal influence, there was a changeover to younger leaders. For example, in 1982, the Politburo and its Standing Committee were purged of Hua Guofeng supporters. Zhao Ziyang and Hu Yaobang were added to the Standing Committee, and in 1985 several older veterans left the Politburo as younger members were added. By 1987 the old leaders had ceded the entire Standing Committee and virtually the whole Politburo. Hu Yaobang was the Party's general secretary until early

1987, and Zhao Ziyang was the premier (and the Party's general secretary from 1987). These younger leaders also included conventional reformers, such as Li Peng and the not-so-young Yao Yilin, both associates of Chen Yun, who entered the Politburo Standing Committee in 1987.

Wide differences continued to separate the bold and conventional reform camps. Whereas the bold reformers had some tolerance for disruption, political innovation, and Western ideas, the conventional reformers and orthodox ideologists disliked the consequences of bold reform, particularly those that weakened the Party. They were suspicious of markets and Western influence and decried the "spiritual pollution" that crept in with the reforms. Above all they feared "chaos."

Numerous debates pitted bold against conventional reformers. One involved "alienation." For Marx, alienation was a capitalist disorder: the workers' separation from their products and from the reigning politics and ideology. Chinese theorists followed this doctrine. But in March 1983, a top cultural official made the remarkable concession that although socialism is naturally superior to capitalism,

> that is not to say that there is no alienation at all in socialist society. In the past we did many stupid things in economic construction . . . this was alienation in the economic field. Because democracy and the legal system were unsound, public servants sometimes made indiscriminate use of [their] power . . . this was alienation in the political field. . . . As for alienation in the ideological field, it was typified in [Mao's] cult of personality.[17]

The basic purpose here was to work toward a more credible Marxism. The conventional reformers were appalled, however, and got the editor of the *People's Daily* fired and forced the article's author to criticize himself.

In the fall of 1984, Hu Yaobang created another stir when he stated that Marxism cannot solve China's problems. To placate the outraged orthodoxy, he quickly added that he meant that Marxism cannot solve *all* the problems.[18] Deng Xiaoping himself seemed to support Hu when in early 1985, he was quoted by the *People's Daily:*

> I am afraid that some of our old colleagues have this fear: after a generation of socialism and Communism, it is unacceptable to spout some capitalism. It cannot harm us. It cannot harm us.[19]

As noted previously, in 1980/81 the conservatives were able to launch a campaign against "bourgeois liberalism" in literature and art, culminating in a crackdown on the remnants of the Democracy Wall movement. In 1983 they spearheaded a campaign against "spiritual pollution." Peng Zhen defined this as

> various decadent and declining ideologies of the bourgeoisie and other exploiting classes and the spreading of . . . distrust regarding . . . socialism and communism and the leadership of the Communist Party.[20]

At the 1985 Party conference, Chen Yun strongly criticized the economic problems that he blamed on the reforms. At that time, a campaign was launched against "unhealthy tendencies" such as vulgarity in art, economic corruption, and public extravagance. None of these movements equaled the campaigns of old, and all ended rather quickly. Nevertheless, the conservatives were repeatedly able to stir up inner-Party efforts against artistic license, extravagance, unorthodox ideas, and other novelties.

## Institutional Reforms, 1981–86

The reformers took steps to rejuvenate the bloated Party and state bureaucracies, partly in order to weed out opponents. Zhao Ziyang launched a massive replacement of personnel. Older officials retired to make way for the younger and more educated. By mid-1986, more than 2.5 million pre-1949 cadres had resigned, including many (but not all) senior leaders. In 1981 and

1982, Zhao announced a restructuring of the State Council, a turnover of ministers, and limits on terms for top officials. Party Central Committee offices were reorganized. In 1982 military budgets were cut, and in 1985 Hu Yaobang initiated reductions of 1 million military personnel.

In 1983, reorganization moved to the provinces and countryside. There was a big turnover in the leadership. The communes were dissolved and reorganized as townships. As noted in the preceding section, steps were taken to ease central Party control of state enterprises, and Party committees were required to loosen their grip over professional managers. But this proved difficult.

To combat leftism, factionalism, and corruption, the Party launched "rectification" efforts. The biggest was a three-year campaign beginning in late 1983. It was a low-key affair so as not to hurt cadre morale. Still, 300,000 cadres were disciplined, and in early 1986 two children of high cadres were executed for corruption. These efforts seemed impressive, but they failed to cure bureaucratism and corruption.

Under Zhao Ziyang, the policy process was broadened to include wider consultation. Experts in the new policy study groups under the State Council began to exert influence through their data and reports. The leaders circulated proposals and solicited reactions. The non-Communist parties were permitted to recruit new members and operate schools. By the mid-1980s there were some remarkable cases of public coalitions' addressing important policies, for example, the effort led by the outspoken woman journalist Dai Qing to block construction of a mammoth dam and hydroelectric project in Sichuan.

## Foreign Policy

In Mao's waning years, China's foreign policy was dominated by fear of the Soviet Union. Beijing's grievances dated back to the pullout of Soviet advisers in 1960 and Moscow's tilt toward India in the 1960s. The Soviet invasion of Czechoslovakia in

1968 and the border clashes with China the following year made relations even more volatile. Moscow deployed over thirty army divisions, 2,500 aircraft, and 1,200 nuclear missiles along the Chinese border and assembled a Pacific fleet.

Beijing responded in the early 1970s by improving relations with the United States. But President Richard Nixon's visit hardly opened the door to close Sino-American relations. Domestic politics in both countries precluded this, as did the continued U.S. recognition of and military support for Taiwan. In the 1970s China portrayed itself as a member of the Third World and called for vigilance against superpower "hegemonism."

The death of Mao and world events began to loosen this stalemate. Deng Xiaoping had a long-standing commitment to pragmatic moderate foreign policy toward the West and increased trade with developed countries. Meanwhile, the USSR actually increased its power in Asia, including its ground, missile, and naval forces, and moved into Southeast Asia by building a close relationship with Vietnam.

## "Punishing" Vietnam

China's most dramatic international action in the reform period was the invasion of Vietnam. At the heart of it were China's relations with the Soviet Union. During the Vietnam War, Moscow and Beijing bickered while jointly aiding Hanoi. The Chinese had long assisted Ho Chi Minh, but there also was a long history of Vietnamese–Chinese antagonism. Indeed, Hanoi was not amused when Zhou Enlai and Richard Nixon signed the Shanghai Communiqué in 1972.

In 1975 when South Vietnam collapsed, Beijing feared Soviet influence in the area and badgered Hanoi to line up against Moscow. But because the USSR had more resources to aid the Vietnamese, in late 1978 they signed a mutual defense treaty with the Soviet Union. To Beijing this was gross ingratitude for China's military assistance against the United States.

Then developments in Cambodia inflamed the situation. In

1970 that unfortunate land was dragged into the war by a coup under the anti-Communist general Lon Nol. In April 1975, when the South Vietnamese government collapsed, Lon Nol fell to an insurgency led by Pol Pot and his Khmer Rouge, a radical Communist movement. To the Chinese, who had ties to the Khmer Rouge, this augured well. Cambodia (renamed Democratic Kampuchea in January 1976) could be China's counterweight to Soviet regional influence, even though it was much weaker than Vietnam. Beijing thus announced its support for Kampuchea and promised large-scale economic and military aid. Chinese arms and advisers flowed in. Pol Pot, however, turned Kampuchea into a "killing field," herding the entire city population to the countryside and there murdering hundreds of thousands of them. Refugees poured west into Thailand and east into southern Vietnam. Pol Pot's mistreatment of ethnic Vietnamese and his belligerence also alienated Vietnam. By the spring of 1977, Kampuchea and Vietnam clashed, and Hanoi learned of China's support for Pol Pot. In January 1978, Vietnamese troops thrust briefly into Kampuchea, followed in December by a full-scale intervention by 100,000 Vietnamese and 20,000 Kampuchean allies. Phnom Penh fell in January 1979.

Sino-Vietnamese relations were further poisoned by Hanoi's discriminatory policies toward its ethnic Chinese minority. Finally in the summer of 1978, Beijing, in a replay of Khrushchev's 1960 pullout from China, withdrew all aid and technical assistance to Vietnam. Soon refugees were streaming into China from northern Vietnam and fleeing the south by boat despite high seas, rickety vessels, and pirates.

On February 17, soon after Deng's return from his American visit, 75,000 to 85,000 PLA troops "counterattacked" at twenty points along the Vietnamese border. They expected to repeat their successful 1962 surgical strike into India and to force Vietnam's withdrawal from Kampuchea. Although they did capture frontier positions and provincial towns, their casualties were high, and Vietnamese forces remained in Kampuchea. By mid-March China terminated the operation, claiming to have taught Hanoi a lesson. But the real lesson was that the PLA was deficient in modern warfare and could not chastise even a small, war-weary nation.

Even though the Soviet Union did not intervene, the Soviet–Vietnamese alliance survived. And when neighboring Laos sided with Vietnam and expelled its Chinese advisers, Beijing's influence in Indochina dwindled to nothing, though armed hostility persisted along the Vietnamese frontier into the late 1980s.

## Taiwan, Hong Kong, South Korea, and Singapore

In the early days of the People's Republic, it would have seemed laughable that China could be challenged by Taiwan, Hong Kong, or South Korea. Taiwan (population 11 million in 1960, 19 million in 1984) and Hong Kong (3 million in 1960, 5.4 million in 1984) are ethnically Chinese. Taiwan and South Korea (population 41 million in 1984) were dependent on the United States, as was Hong Kong on Britain. Their governments were not very liberal or democratic, although none equaled China's "totalitarianism." All three achieved rapid, sustained, export-led economic growth by the 1970s and enjoyed living standards far superior to China's. Their ability to prosper under authoritarian rule was seen by many, both inside and outside China, as a model for the mainland. They became important trading partners and sources of investment. (See Figure 7 in Chapter 10 which compares China's growth with these societies plus India.)

Beijing insisted that Hong Kong and Taiwan were merely parts of China. Its power to reclaim Hong Kong was greater, since the colony is attached to the mainland. Simply cutting off water would jeopardize its survival. But because Hong Kong is China's economic link with the rest of the world, its value is inestimable, and so to ruin it would entail heavy economic costs. In any case, part of Hong Kong was scheduled by treaty to revert to China in 1997, meaning that as a practical matter, the entire colony would come under Chinese control. The challenge here was to negotiate an orderly transfer.

Taiwan's separation from the mainland made it far less vulnerable. It is doubtful that back in 1950, even with no Korean War, Mao's armies could have successfully invaded the island. By the mid-1950s, moreover, Taiwan was much strengthened by its American alliance. Beijing's challenge, therefore, was to advance a future unification while sustaining its claims. It also had to undermine the Taiwan independence movement. Fortunately for Beijing, the Nationalist government also feared and suppressed this movement. For many years, China interjected the Taiwan issue between any Sino-American rapprochement. The unique feature of the 1972 Shanghai Communiqué, signed by Richard Nixon and Zhou Enlai, was that this issue would be finessed, with both parties stating their position and declaring that it was a matter to be decided by "the Chinese."

South Korea was not Chinese, but the Korean War had solidified the bitter division of the country, by which China became closely allied with the North and regularly excoriated South Korea as a tool of American imperialism. China also insisted on Korean reunification under the North and the withdrawal of American troops from the South.

By the 1980s, the economic growth of Taiwan, Hong Kong, and Korea had begun to overshadow geopolitical and nationalistic considerations; and China's approach to all three entities changed significantly. In 1984 Beijing and London negotiated an agreement according to which Hong Kong would be reunited with China in 1997 but would retain its social and economic system for at least fifty years. This was known as the "one country, two systems" principle, which China also hoped to apply to the Taiwan case. But many in Hong Kong and Taiwan remained skeptical of Beijing's trustworthiness in upholding an agreement that limited its own powers.

Taiwan figured importantly in the normalization of relations with the United States. Washington agreed to withdraw its recognition from Taipei and, by mid-1979, to withdraw all military forces from Taiwan. On the other hand, informal U.S. relations and even weapons sales to Taiwan were tolerated by the Chinese.

The Taiwan Relations Act, signed into American law in early 1979, made it clear that United States–China relations would not end American involvements with Taiwan. Beijing also accepted the participation of Taiwan in international organizations, for example, the Olympics and the Asian Development Bank. Moreover, people from Taiwan were permitted to visit the mainland, and tourism and especially investment were encouraged.

South Korea became increasingly interesting to China because of the emergence of giant industrial combines that might be the sources of technology transfer and investment. Thus, despite declarations of support for North Korea, China began to build up indirect trading relationships with the South; and in 1992, the two states agreed to establish formal diplomatic relations.

Singapore should also be mentioned here. Although more distant from China, it resembles Hong Kong and Taiwan in being ethnically Chinese and economically successful. Singapore is ruled by a personalistic authoritarian regime devoted to economic growth. In the reform period, China also began to invite tourism, trade, and investment from Singapore.

## A Diplomacy of "Independence"

In late 1979, Soviet armies intervened in Afghanistan, a prolonged campaign that caused the most alarm to the Middle Eastern powers. China, however, with its own Muslim population and a long-standing friendship with Pakistan, considered it a third Soviet threat, added to the Soviet armies on China's borders and Moscow's Vietnamese alliance. These came to be called the "three obstacles" to reconciliation with the Soviet Union.

Also in the late 1970s, the United States was signaling its readiness to rethink its links with Taiwan (in late 1976, China had indicated that it was prepared to settle the Taiwan issue through negotiation). Consequently, in 1978 and 1979, as Deng was consolidating his influence, Sino-American relations began to warm. The establishment of full diplomatic relations was announced, and Deng made an unprecedented visit to America. Immediately upon his return, China invaded Vietnam.

This Sino-American rapprochement had its limits. Conventional reformers like Chen Yun opposed friendship with the West and hoped to improve relations with the USSR. Moreover, Ronald Reagan's inauguration in 1981 installed an American administration openly partial to Taiwan. Consequently, the relationship, which appeared in 1980 to be moving toward an alliance against Russia, was seriously strained, as China strongly protested American arms sales to Taiwan. However, China had no wish to intensify hostilities with either superpower; rather, its great need was for a peaceful context in which to pursue economic development: to foster investment, technology, and trade with the developed economies. In 1982 Beijing and Washington therefore worked out an agreement by which the United States would gradually reduce and then end sales of weapons to Taiwan. Some in Washington hoped that the Chinese would join in closer cooperation against Moscow, although through the mid-1980s, the Chinese preferred to follow a policy of "independence," which meant better relations with Washington, though short of an alliance against the USSR.

Sino-Soviet relations seemed to be going nowhere, as Beijing insisted that the Kremlin first remove the "three obstacles." Actually, however, the situation was not stagnant. Its Afghan war and a troubled economy weakened the Soviet Union, just as American military strength was increasing—developments which made Moscow increasingly pliant. China and the Soviet Union began negotiations in 1982, expanding trade and cultural exchanges. In 1984 under Mikhail Gorbachev, the USSR launched a reform process not unlike China's in 1978, but with far more disruptive political consequences. By 1990 every Central European country had overthrown its Marxist-Leninist system (not always with happy results) and had escaped Moscow's control. The Soviet Union itself fragmented into several countries. In this context Chinese leaders were forced to temper their alarm over the collapse of socialist regimes and to adopt a pragmatic diplomacy toward the new realities of Europe and Asia.

## Chinese Society Under Reform

### *Family and Population*

The previously discussed changes, especially the economic ones, could not help but profoundly affect every corner of Chinese society. The diverse ramifications defy brief generalization, but broadly speaking, the communes and the centralized economic apparatus, with their hierarchical chains of authority, gave ground to a more complex and diverse society. This transformation brought not only liberation, novelty, and improvement but also loss and disarray. These crosscurrents can be seen in the institution of the family. After Liberation, the household became just a place where people ate and slept and sheltered children and grandparents. Work and income were controlled by team, brigade, commune, and urban unit. Benefits such as provision for old age, and health and education were mainly supplied by collective structures. Family and clan ancestor worship were suppressed in favor of state doctrines centered on Marxism-Leninism Mao Zedong Thought.

Under reform, as the communes disappeared, and, to a lesser extent in the cities, as collective and private enterprises flourished, families and individual assumed greater importance. Village traditions reemerged. Kinship regained its importance as a basis of cooperation (and conflict). With the rural family once again a production unit, the head of the household reclaimed some of his old authority, although when family members went outside to work, authority relationships became more complicated. Communities increasingly chose their own cultural pursuits. Many villages resurrected old religious customs, and especially in the cities, individual leisure activities proliferated.

Most people welcomed less state control, more amusements,

and traditional cultural practices. But there were negative sides, too. In the villages, disparities grew because some families had more working adults and other assets for making a living. Cadres and former cadres could use their political connections and insider knowledge to make money. All this generated complaints and even physical attacks. The state attempted to moderate these resentments by promoting the idea that "remuneration according to work . . . also involves encouraging part of the people . . . , by working more and getting more, to become prosperous first."[21]

Equally contentious, especially in the countryside, was the nation's birth control policy. By the late 1970s, the government saw that the population growth rate, although lower than that in many other developing countries, was a huge problem, given China's total size. Consequently in 1979, a one-child policy was introduced, which in its sternest form allowed just one child per couple. Such a policy would quickly trim the growth rate and cause the population to level off in the early twenty-first century. But the program was never strictly or universally implemented; minority groups were exempted, and there were many ways it could be flexibly implemented or circumvented, especially in the countryside. Nevertheless, for villagers, because of the importance of sons as income earners and providers in their parents' old age (daughters married into other families)—not to mention traditional preferences for male offspring—the one-child policy was the most disliked feature of the reforms.

Another evil was the reemergence of abuse of women and children. Whereas the collective system had promoted gender equality, however imperfectly, the reforms (not always, but frequently) undermined this egalitarianism. Since the bride normally left home to live with her husband, her natal family now required a "bride price" to compensate for the loss of her labor. Child labor and the practice of taking children out of school to work (especially girls) became more common, and female infanticide became a serious (albeit hidden) problem, as families, under pressure from the one-child policy, desperately attempted to get a son.

## Education and Health

Education and health also reflected the complex effects of the reforms. China's universities and intellectuals had been devastated by the Cultural Revolution, and at the time of Mao's death they were only beginning to recover. What accelerated this was the reformers' recognition that the Four Modernizations needed science and technology, and so they stopped sending students to the countryside and began to rebuild the higher education system. Intellectuals were declared to be members of the working class, no longer to be stigmatized as the "stinking ninth category."

By the mid- to late 1980s, much progress had been made in rebuilding higher education. "Key" universities were designated as elite schools with special funding and staff. Radio and TV universities serviced those unable to get into regular institutions. Students were admitted through competitive exams, and their numbers steadily climbed. Graduate programs were reestablished and began to award masters' and doctors' degrees. Research was professionalized and somewhat freed from politics. Professional societies were reestablished and began to interact with their international counterparts, and some scholars and students were allowed to seek training abroad.

Education still had many shortcomings, however. Building libraries and laboratories was a slow process. Access to higher education remained very limited relative to China's population. Politics still dominated many parts of the system. Although they paid no tuition, students had to put up with poor food and housing, tight restrictions on their personal and academic lives, and job assignments decided by their schools. Not surprisingly, the "brain drain" of students and scholars to the United States and other countries grew quickly. Its effect on development has been debated, some arguing and others disputing that it was a serious loss. The new generation of college students were less scarred by the Cultural Revolution and were more consumption minded and self-indulgent. Surveys of students revealed that few retained much belief in communism.

Primary and secondary education deteriorated in many poorer and remoter villages, as the collapse of the communes often left rural schools strapped for funds. Families withdrew their children for work, and anyway, rural children seldom had access to "key" schools, located in the cities. National surveys found surprisingly high rates of illiteracy, with females comprising the majority of those unable to read. Teaching was a low-status field, and few teachers wanted to go to rural areas. In the cities, the good news was the development of good-quality "key" primary and secondary schools. Unfortunately, students educated in the ordinary school system had little chance of entering universities.

The reforms also had an ambiguous effect on health care. Already China was enjoying one of the major achievements of the Maoist era: a pattern of disease and mortality more typical of developed than of undeveloped countries. Especially in the cities, heart disease, cancer, stroke, and lung and digestive diseases became leading causes of death, replacing the epidemic diseases more characteristic of developing nations. This was the result of egalitarian distribution of health services and massive efforts to eliminate epidemics. The reforms also dismantled much of the old commune health system, the barefoot doctors, clinics, and commune hospitals. Although they created greater inequality, they also introduced up-to-date professionalized medicine and better hospitals and research institutions. Unfortunately, these improved services were beyond the reach of many. Also, ironically, the higher levels of consumption generally meant richer diets, more tobacco consumption, more pollution, and more accidents.

## Political Tensions

In the late 1980s, economic and political issues created tensions between rulers and ruled and also struggles within the Party. Even as prosperity bloomed, reform was growing thorny. People complained about inflation and other economic pains. The

Party, despite agreeing on the need for economic reform, was divided over what form it should take.

The pressures for political change were growing stronger. Students and intellectuals periodically raised the cry for greater participation and less corruption. In the Party, the need for honesty and competency, and even for public participation, was acknowledged, but only a few were prepared to think about relaxing the Party's monopoly on power. This muffled public unhappiness, as well as the uncertainty and division within the Party, could, under the right circumstances, become explosive.

## Tensions of 1985

These complex pressures can be seen at work in several episodes. In mid-1985 at the September Party conference mentioned previously, Chen Yun, appealing to the "socialist and communist ideal," attacked overheated, unbalanced growth, grain policy, and excessive interest in markets. With a poor harvest on the horizon, the economy overheating, and inflation rising, Zhao Ziyang and Hu Yaobang were vulnerable. Reform had weakened central management. Beijing had transferred much of its authority to the provincial and local governments before developing regulatory control through money supply and interest rates. Rampant tax evasion and large subsidy expenditures weakened state finances. Investment in energy, transportation, agriculture, and education was far from adequate. Power shortages stopped many factories several days a week.

Meanwhile, a thousand students demonstrated in Tiananmen Square, ostensibly against "Japanese economic aggression." Their real anger was about inflation, corruption, and abuse of power. The protests spread to other cities. However, with Deng's support, Zhao and Hu withstood Chen Yun's attack, and the students were soon silenced.

## The Demonstrations of 1986

In 1986, economic reforms were bogging down, especially efforts to upgrade management in state enterprises. Irritated by this "leftist" resistance, Hu Yaobang and the bold reformers reopened the debate on political reform. In June, Deng himself urged political reform. In the debate, one of Zhao Ziyang's advisers advocated socialist democracy and "scientific" decision making. A leading scientist, astrophysicist Fang Lizhi (pronounced something like "Fong Lee-jr"), began to argue for fundamental political change, in the process becoming a hero to the students. He told a Shanghai University audience that people possess inherent rights independent of government. Another eminent intellectual proposed making the National People's Congress and the Chinese People's Consultative Conference into a bicameral legislature.

Intellectuals and students could be glad that this debate even took place, though nothing came of it. Peng Zhen scoffed at those who longed for bourgeois democracy, "as if the moonlight of capitalist society were brighter than our sun." [22] A major Party document published in September 1986 failed to offer any change. In November, the National People's Congress tightened the rules restricting independent local people's congress candidates, a move that led to frustration and further protests, starting in December in the unlikely city of Hefei in Anhui Province. Hefei is the home of Science and Technology University, whose vice-president was astrophysicist Fang Lizhi, a person decidedly not in sympathy with restrictive educational policies. The trouble started when Science and Technology students protested local Party meddling in the people's congress elections. The authorities, wishing to appear reasonable, appealed for order and offered to discuss their grievances. But the students' feelings ran high, and soon the demonstration spread to 150 schools in Shanghai and sixteen other cities.

These events dramatically affected the power structure. General Secretary Hu Yaobang wanted to be conciliatory, but the hard-liners fumed at the students and got Deng Xiaoping on their side. Showing his tough side, Deng reportedly stated:

We have been too lax in curbing the tides of bourgeois liberalism. Allowing some rightist influence is essential and correct, but we have gone overboard. . . . When necessary, we must deal severely with those who defy orders. We can afford to shed some blood. Just try as much as possible not to kill anyone.[23]

Hu Yaobang, who already had strained relations with Deng Xiaoping (reportedly over Hu's moves to position himself as Deng's successor) and who was disliked by the conservatives, was held responsible for the demonstrations. He bowed to pressure and resigned as general secretary on January 16, 1987. A few of his supporters also lost their posts. The students were forced back into their bleak dormitories, and the reprisals began. A few were arrested and tried. Academic officials were dismissed. Fang Lizhi and two other prominent intellectuals were fired for inspiring the demonstrations. One remarked, "My compliments to Deng. If he continues this way he could be more and more like Mao Zedong."[24]

### Standoff After 1987

The reaction to these demonstrations strengthened the conventional reformers. As the students were silenced, the hard-liners launched one of their campaigns, this one against "bourgeois liberalization." Chen Yun now sponsored Li Peng as a second-generation leader, and Li became a key player in the power standoff.

Only two when his father was martyred by the KMT in 1930, Li Peng (rhymes with "hung") was taken in by Zhou Enlai and his wife and may have been adopted (though Li denies this). In any case, Li could not have had a more powerful patron. He studied electric power engineering in Moscow, returning in 1955 to a career in the electrical industry. During the Cultural Revolution he escaped harm. After the 1978 Third Plenum, with Chen Yun's support, Li Peng became minister of power, then deputy prime minister, and was also a member of the Party Central Committee and, in 1985, of the Politburo. State visits abroad gave him international credentials. As a person, however, he is stiff and colorless, lacking the charm of Zhou Enlai or the effervescence of Hu Yaobang. Some charge that he is not an effective administrator, but his conventional orientation and Chen Yun's backing nevertheless made him a strong candidate for senior office when Hu Yaobang resigned in January 1987. Although Premier Zhao Ziyang also became acting general Secretary, he could not hold both positions.

At the Thirteenth Party Congress in October 1987, Li Peng became a member of the five-person Politburo Standing Committee. Yao Yilin, another Chen Yun associate, joined him. Representing the bold reform, Zhao Ziyang, with Deng's support, also remained a member. Although increasingly occupied as Party general secretary, Zhao continued to influence economic policy in the State Council, through his think tanks. Hu Qili (pronounced something like "Who Chee-lee"), formerly Hu Yaobang's confederate and head of the Party Secretariat, was also on the Standing Committee. (The fifth member, Qiao Shi (pronounced something like "Chee-ow Shr"), is harder to label as a conventional or bold reformer.) The five, in Western suits, held a relaxed, jocular press conference at which they pooh-poohed reports of a rift and declared that the "reform and openness" would continue.

The political standoff also continued among the still-influential elders. They all resigned from the Politburo, but Deng remained chair of the Military Affairs Commission. He sponsored the old but vigorous General Yang Shangkun as a leading member of that commission and as president of China. As was later revealed, the Central Committee secretly agreed that Deng should remain the "helmsman" to whom important decisions would be referred.

Despite their best efforts, the conservatives could not sustain the antibourgeois liberalization campaign beyond a few months. Its impact was limited to the Party and to intellectuals. Pressure for freer expression continued in 1987 and 1988. Shanghai's *World Economic Herald* became bolder in its reporting, as did a few other papers. In June 1988, China Central Television broadcast a sensational series, "River Elegy." Using the Yel-

DENG XIAOPING

low River as a symbol of lingering, oppressive "feudal" culture, the narrator states:

> Today . . . the Chinese sigh yet another sigh . . . why is it that our feudal era never ends, why is it as endless as the ceaseless floods of the Yellow River? . . . history grinds on, slowly and heavily; in the river bed which has accumulated silt and sand of the ages. . . . It needs a great flood to wash it away. This great flood is already upon us. It is none other than industrialized civilization.[25]

Deeply offended conservatives forced the resignation of the head of Central Chinese Television, and they later blocked efforts to rebroadcast the series.

The students' dissatisfactions persisted. They endured political controls and indoctrination and in many cases had to spend their vacations working in villages or factories or in the military. Their requests for permission to demonstrate were routinely turned down. In late 1988 in Nanjing, friction between Chinese and African students briefly flared into demonstrations against the Africans. As in the anti-Japanese protests of 1985, the agitation really had more to do with the Chinese students' basic grievances.

At the same time, inflation and an overheated economy continued. In 1988, at the summer leadership retreat, Zhao Ziyang agreed to hand over much of his control over the economy to Li Peng. Having watched his fellow reformer Hu Yaobang fade from power, Zhao now found his own position weakening.

Because of crosscurrents at the top and the resulting mixed signals, people were uncertain about what was permissible, and some continued to test the limits. Then in January and February 1989, prominent intellectuals began an unprecedented petition campaign, urging the Party to pardon Wei Jingsheng and other political prisoners. Proposals circulated to institute a true rule of law or a "new authoritarianism" under Zhao Ziyang. Li Peng and the hard-liners, and possibly Deng himself, resisted these pressures. Unrest was in the air. The Party circulated instructions to expect more demonstrations, but no one imagined what was building. As one scholar who lived in Beijing at the time explained, with only slight hyperbole, "China was on the point of explosion. The economy had fallen apart. The social fabric of the country was rent. The government no longer commanded respect. Political infighting had led to multiple centers of power. Everyone, it seemed, waited for a spark." [26]

# 9

# "We Must Not Let the Next Generation Pour a Bucket of Excrement on Our Heads": The Tragedy at Tiananmen

On June 3, 1989, in the late evening, the People's Liberation Army began to assault the people of Beijing. A line of armored personnel carriers moved eastward along Changan Avenue toward Tiananmen Square. Stone-throwing crowds confronted the convoy, which then suddenly opened fire. So began China's greatest political tremor since the Cultural Revolution.

Elsewhere there had already been clashes, and by midnight they began spreading. Bullets whizzed into amazed and angry crowds. Clamor and screams filled the streets, punctuated by the crackle of AK-47s, the thud-thud of 50-caliber machine guns, tank salvos, exploding gas tanks, revving engines, vehicles crashing through barricades, and the tattoo of helicopters. Cordite smell and smoke drifted across the city as hospitals became scenes of blood and chaos.

# Seven Extraordinary Weeks

## *The Stage*

Stage center for this drama was Tiananmen Square in the heart of Beijing. It fronts the walled and moated palace complex, the Forbidden City, once home to emperors and now a tourist attraction. In front, or south, of the palace's great gate, past an area of public gardens and halls, is the grand, ocher "Heavenly Peace Gate" (Tian-an-men) with its curved double roof and balustrade from which top Party leaders review parades along Changan Avenue. Just beneath the balustrade hangs a portrait of Mao Zedong.

Changan Avenue runs east–west through Beijing's midsection. At Tiananmen, it passes the palace entrance just described and, to the south, opens onto Tiananmen Square. At the center of this vast square stands the Monument to the People's Heroes, a massive square pillar with two tiers of balustrades at its base. This monument was to be the center of demonstrations. South of this area is the Chairman Mao Memorial Hall where Mao's remains are displayed.

Two other places should be noted. Along the western edge of the square looms the Great Hall of the People, venue of state ceremonies and congresses. It became a fortress under siege from the people. Also frequently besieged was the entrance to Zhongnanhai ("Central and South Lakes") the walled, guarded compound where many Party leaders reside, on Changan Avenue, several hundred yards west of Tiananmen. All of these buildings are connected by tunnels through which leaders and security forces can move. Beijing's universities and colleges are far from Tiananmen Square, the most important ones about ten miles to the northeast.

## *The Spark*

The demonstrations began with Hu Yaobang's sudden death. Hu, the disgraced Party general secretary, considered sympathetic to intellectuals, unexpectedly suffered a heart attack on April 8 and died a week later. This touched off a student reaction on April 16 as students traveled the ten miles from their campuses to Tiananmen Square to lay wreaths at the Monument to the People's Heroes. Posters appeared on university campuses, one of them lamenting, "Those who should die still live. Those who should live have died." The campuses remained volatile, and a number of small student organizations were formed by articulate, audacious individuals who had absorbed some lessons from the Democracy Wall and from 1986/87.

As in 1986, the government hesitated to suppress the demonstrations, partly because the students had legitimate grievances and also because it could hardly forbid the people to mourn Hu Yaobang, who remained a respected leader (delegates at the 1987 Party Congress elected him to the Politburo by more votes than given to almost anyone else). In addition, representatives to the Asia Development Bank, including Taiwan's finance minister, were about to meet for the first time in Beijing on May 4. Taiwanese and other international journalists would cover this latest phase of improved relations between the PRC and Taiwan. May 4 was also the seventieth anniversary of the famous 1919 student demonstrations at Tiananmen. On the eve of this event, it would scarcely do to rough up students before a world TV audience. Finally, on May 15, a historic visit by Soviet General Secretary Mikhail Gorbachev would take place, covered by the world's press, the first such meeting in three decades.

On the night of April 17–18 the first student march took place. At Tiananmen Square the students unfurled a huge banner on the Monument to the People's Heroes, hailing Hu Yaobang as the "soul of China." Some initiated a sit-down in front of the Great Hall of the People. Others moved down Changan Avenue to demonstrate at the gate of Zhongnanhai, the restricted compound for top leaders, demanding action on corruption, education, and civil rights. In these first days the slogans generally did not attack the Party or the system but, rather, called for improvement. Much of the action was good-natured and festive.

The next night, another protest group, numbering 20,000 to 30,000 people, gathered on the square. Again, some marched to the Zhongnanhai gate and were dispersed in the early morning hours by police, who beat some of them. This abuse precipitated another protest on April 20. Although it was dampened by rain, the next day brought more action. Tens of thousands gathered into the evening. Since Hu Yaobang's funeral was scheduled for the following day, the authorities ordered the square cleared. But student leaders hatched a plan to occupy the area through the night so that the police could not cordon it off. Fifty thousand stayed, including a group of workers.

On the day of the funeral, 100,000 people massed in the square. Workers and intellectuals joined in. The students began to organize an autonomous federation of student organizations. Among the emerging leaders were Wang Dan, a history major at Beijing University and Wuer Kaixi (pronounced Woo-er Kai-see), a Beijing Normal University student of Uighur nationality. To press their demands, they announced a class boycott.

The first demonstrations ended on April 22 on a high note and with a new tactic, the boycott. For four days, there were no protests. During that time there was a shift among the Party leadership. Zhao Ziyang, the principal conciliatory voice, left the country for a scheduled visit to North Korea. In his absence Premier Li Peng now pushed for a tougher response. He met with Deng and other leaders, and they decided on a hard line which they announced through a stern editorial in the *People's Daily* on April 26. On that same day 10,000 Party cadres were assembled to be instructed in the official position. In the usual Party rhetoric, the editorial blamed "an extremely small number of people" who

were trying to destroy the democratic legal system. Their goal was to poison people's minds, to create turmoil throughout the country, to destroy political stability and unity. This was a planned conspiracy, a riot, whose real nature was to fundamentally negate the leadership of the Chinese Communist Party and to negate the socialist system. This throws down the gauntlet of serious political struggle. . . . If we take a lenient, permissive attitude toward this turmoil and just let it go, a situation of real chaos will emerge.[1]

This move deadlocked the two sides. The students would not withdraw their demands, demands that large numbers of Chinese found reasonable, and the Party stuck to its April 26 editorial.

The opposing sides lurched toward the tragic, perhaps unavoidable, culmination. Nonetheless, a major share of the onus falls on the Party dictatorship. Not only had it created this cauldron of grievances, but it also produced in its leaders, in some more than others, a contempt for the students, an inability to imagine that they deserved respect and a hearing. The leaders were obsessed with stability and order, the socialist system, and the dictatorship of the Party, though this is not to deny that they operated under severe constraints. Nor, as we shall see, should the students and other participants escape accountability.

## *Throwing Caution to the Wind*

The April 26 editorial was intended to frighten the students, and some did withdraw from the planned April 27 demonstration. Sympathetic university officials and professors begged the students to be careful, but most students were charged up by their grievances and angry about the distorted reports of "turmoil." Thousands resolved to demonstrate; some wrote their wills; and so began the sensational day of April 27. A parade set out from the university district, numbering perhaps 50,000 to 75,000 students in a column four miles long, with possibly an equal number of unorganized workers and students alongside. They marched for fourteen hours in a great thirty-mile circuit through the city, repeatedly encountering lines of police and soldiers. Each time the sea of people burst through the dike more irrepressibly than before. Hundreds of thousands of onlookers cheered and gave the students food, drink, and popsicles. Wuer Kaixi later remarked that this high point was the one moment when he truly believed the movement would succeed.

The authorities now declared a willingness to talk, and the media were permitted to report more openly. These tactical moves, however, did not constitute a change of heart. Officials met with the student leaders of only sanctioned school organizations; Wuer Kaixi and the other autonomous student leaders were not allowed to participate fully. In the first meeting, on April 29, the officials took a patronizing tone and remained unresponsive to the students' main demands. There were a few more informal meetings on succeeding days. The situation was stalemated. Although the students were demanding genuine dialogue, it was unclear just what they wanted and who would speak for them. The authorities were also divided. Deng and other top leaders probably had no intention of ever renouncing the April 26 editorial. The more conciliatory officials, sympathetic to Zhao Ziyang and bold reform, tried to broker a dialogue, but they wanted the students to stop demonstrating. For their part, wary students remembered earlier dissidents who were punished once their demonstrations were over.

On May 2 and 3 the student federation demanded talks with high officials to be broadcast live. If not, they vowed to demonstrate on May 4, the anniversary of the famous 1919 protests. Meanwhile Zhao Ziyang returned from North Korea. He had telegraphed his approval of the April 26 editorial, but now he urged his colleagues to moderate. The hard-liners refused. His next option was to negotiate between the two sides: to defuse the editorial by ignoring it while signaling the students that there could be dialogue. If he could bring this off, his political fortunes would revive, and Li Peng, Chen Yun, and the others would have to retreat. It depended on whether the students could be persuaded to clear the square.

Zhao addressed a meeting on May 3 in the Great Hall of the People. To 3,000 selected young men and women, accompanied by other high Party leaders, he advocated toleration and also called for stability and unity. On May 4, he addressed the Asian

Development Bank delegates in words really intended for the demonstrators:

> Though demonstrations are still under way in Beijing and some other big cities in the country, I still believe there will be no big riots and the demonstrations will gradually calm down. . . . The students are satisfied with the achievements of China's 10-year reform. . . . What they are most dissatisfied with are errors and mistakes in the government's work. . . . The students' demands for correcting errors so as to march forward coincide with those of the party and the government.[2]

But on that symbolic day, the students were making good on their promise to demonstrate. One hundred thousand were again in the square. Hundreds of Chinese journalists also organized a protest, demanding press freedom. The movement spread to Tianjin, Shanghai, and other major cities. The hard-liners were appalled by this disorder and considered Zhao's speech a disgraceful breach of Party discipline. Accordingly, the split in the leadership widened. Just when hope was growing in the square, nourished by Zhao's remarks, Deng Xiaoping and the remaining old guard were rallying most of the junior top leaders to support a crackdown.

## Hunger

The success of the May 4 demonstrations was bittersweet because the authorities continued to dodge a televised dialogue. Some students, reading the situation and Zhao's signals, decided to return to classes, but others doggedly pressed on, seeking new ways to exert pressure. One gambit was a bicycle demonstration during which thousands of students, singing and ringing their bells, rode to the offices of the media bureaus, carrying signs and banners calling for press freedom. But a bicycle parade proved difficult to organize and control. Then the students hit on a better tactic. On May 11, a few students started promoting a hunger strike and soon persuaded the federation leaders to join them. On May 13, a few hundred hunger strikers, accompanied by a large entourage, marched to the square and installed themselves at the Monument to the People's Heroes. New student leaders now moved to the fore, most notably Chai Ling (Chai rhymes with "my"), a twenty-three-year-old woman graduate student at Beijing Normal University, who became the leader of this risky defiance. The authorities were caught off guard again. Already morally on the defensive, they were confronted with swelling numbers of youth, soon more than 2,000, ready to die. The strikers won enormous public sympathy, especially when they began to collapse in the heat.

Just two days after the hunger strike began, the Gorbachev visit was to take place, which ruled out force to clear the square. But it also meant that if they remained, the strikers would inflict a terrible loss of face on Deng Xiaoping and the Party. Zhao Ziyang, who might regain power if the students could be persuaded to retreat, desperately appealed to them. But by now the strike had too much momentum; neither Wuer Kaixi nor Chai Ling had the power to stop it.

Beijing had never seen anything like the festival of protest that began on May 14. Demonstrators arrived by the hundreds of thousands; sometimes more than a million filled the square. May 17 was perhaps the most giddy day of all. Units of workers, teachers, journalists, doctors, nurses, police, and motorcycle groups, to name just a few, paraded with their banners. Wailing ambulances rushed away with comatose hunger strikers. Other cities saw demonstrations as well. It was a magnificent liberation. Nothing seemed too audacious. In the morning, students had rebuffed offers from the well-known journalist Dai Qing and from Zhao Ziyang himself, guaranteeing no reprisals if they would withdraw. Yan Jiaqi, a key reform adviser, joined by other intellectuals, issued a call for Deng's resignation. A student loudspeaker blared, "We demand that Deng Xiaoping, Li Peng, old people and those among the young who are incapable should immediately resign." [3] A banner read, "Come out, Deng Xiaoping! Come out, Li Peng!" [4] Students chanted,

*"Xiaoping ni hao, ni hao hutu"* (How are you, Xiaoping, how confused are you?).[5] The day even paved the way, on May 18, for a dialogue between the highest leaders and autonomous student representatives.

On May 18, as the sky darkened and it rained heavily from the afternoon into the next morning, political clouds were gathering as well. As the new lords of Tiananmen Square assured international television reporters that the state would never harm them, an autonomous workers unions formed, and as more students poured into Beijing from the provinces to join in the action, the hard-liners were laying plans to put an end to these insults.

## Martial Law

A key meeting of the Politburo Standing Committee took place on May 17 at the house of Deng Xiaoping, who was not actually a member of the committee. He fumed. Beijing was a carnival. The media had slipped completely out of control and were gaily reporting. At least twenty other cities staged demonstrations. Deng was furious at Zhao Ziyang for telling Gorbachev that major decisions were referred to Deng himself, thus pointing the finger of responsibility at him. Alone among the five Standing Committee members, Zhao urged conciliation, but the others voted for a tough response. Zhao was desperate. He resigned his Party position, but Deng refused to accept it. Next day, Zhao retracted the resignation and leaked news of the Standing Committee meeting. He sent a subordinate to Yang Shangkun, the president of China and a member of the Military Affairs Commission, urging the army to stay out of it. But Yang Shangkun was Deng's man, and Deng and others feared that Zhao and his sympathizers might attempt a coup. The commander of the Thirty-eighth Army checked into a hospital rather than order troops against the civilian population.

On May 18, the Politburo Standing Committee took the fateful step, deciding four to one to impose martial law. Zhao's

LI PENG

career was over. In the early hours of May 19, students in the square were surprised by a visit from a tired and downcast Zhao, trailed by a grim Li Peng. Li soon withdrew, but Zhao lingered, sensing that this was his last appearance, wondering perhaps how it could be that these ragged youths remained his only constituency and that their zeal had destroyed him. His remarks were televised, the media having not yet been muzzled. "We were too late coming. I'm sorry," he said. "Your criticism of us is justified. I'm not here to ask your forgiveness. I'm just saying that your bodies have become very weak. Your hunger strike is already in its seventh day. Things can't go on like this." He made a last appeal: "The channels for dialogue are wide open. . . . It could become too late if you insist on getting a satisfactory answer now."⁶ But it was already too late.

Thus it was an empty victory when on May 18, the students were finally granted a dialogue. Wuer Kaixi, Wang Dan, and other students leaders were invited to a delayed-broadcast, edited TV interview with Premier Li Peng and other top officials. The stern and defensive Li Peng displayed little sympathy for the students' complaints, and it is tempting to conclude that the dialogue was only a public relations tactic to make the government seem accommodating.

The student participants appeared confident, sometimes even interrupting the Premier. Wuer Kaixi stated that neither he nor the other leaders could control the hunger strike:

> Outside in the Square, it is not a question of the minority obeying the majority; it is a question of 99.9 percent obeying 0.1 percent. That is, as long as there is still one hunger striker who refuses to leave, then all of the other thousands won't leave either.[7]

Even if this had been a serious negotiation, there would have been little room for compromise. The dialogue thus broke off inconclusively, at which point Wuer Kaixi, who had heart problems, collapsed and was taken to the hospital, where he remained for a few days.

Shortly before midnight on May 19, Li Peng, Yang Shangkun, and the other formal Party and state leaders (with Zhao Ziyang conspicuously absent) presided over a large meeting of cadres in the Great Hall. Their speeches were telecast nationwide and broadcast into the square. Li Peng, painting the government as sincerely concerned while acknowledging the students' grievances, shook his fist stiffly as he sputtered that conspirators were at work:

> It is becoming clearer and clearer that an extremely small number of people want to achieve through turmoil their political goals, which are to negate the leadership of the Communist Party and to negate the socialist system. . . . Comrades! . . . To fulfill our responsibilities to our sacred motherland and to the entire people, we must take firm, decisive measures to put a swift end to the turmoil, protect the leadership of the Party, and protect the socialist system.[8]

This was followed by Yang Shangkun's announcement:

> [Beijing] is already in a state of anarchy. To maintain social order in the capital and restore normal routine, we have had no alternative but to move [to Beijing] some troops from the People's Liberation Army.''[9]

Later in the morning, Beijing's mayor formally declared martial law. In the dark morning hours of May 20, several columns of soldiers approached the city center.

## The People of Beijing

Events then took still another astonishing turn. As the columns entered the city, the people of Beijing poured out of their homes. Makeshift roadblocks were thrown up. Indignant citizens, old men, women, workers, and children swarmed the soldiers, admonishing, pleading, threatening, and sometimes completely immobilizing troops who were not yet primed to use deadly force. For the next two weeks, variations of this scene were repeated: It seemed that these were truly the people's soldiers, and the people demanded forbearance. The leaders were surprised again, since Chinese citizens are not inclined to defiance. Two weeks elapsed before the final repression. It may be that the authorities moved carefully in order to minimize the bloodshed, especially since many Party members and soldiers sympathized with the demonstrators. Then there was the international press, still conveying an unflattering picture of the government.

A war of attrition was called for, rather than frontal assault. During the last days in May, the hard-liners neutralized Zhao Ziyang's camp and secured the support of regional military commanders. They recovered control of the media and began to report the excesses and chaos of the demonstrations. The international TV satellite feed was cut off; Voice of America and BBC broadcasts were jammed. Loudspeaker harangues bombarded the square. Helicopters dropped leaflets. Plainclothes security men conspicuously took notes and photographs while lamppost video cameras panned the crowds. The authorities organized counterdemonstrations elsewhere in the city and festooned the major hotels, as well as the nearby Kentucky Fried Chicken restaurant, with huge banners such as "Maintain Order in the Capital!"

It looked bad for the movement. The students ended their hunger strike on the night that martial law was declared and prepared for the inevitable. Many left the square; some provincial students went home, but others stayed, as one poster despaired:

> Well, what the hell, we might as well give you our heads.
> If we keep them or lose 'em—
> it's pretty much the same.[10]

Others remained out of a sense of martyrdom, as Chai Ling noted:

> Our presence here and now at the Square is our last and only truth. If we withdraw, the only one to rejoice will be the government. . . . [W]hat we [are] waiting for [is] actually the spilling of blood, for only when the government descends to the depths of depravity and decides to deal with us by slaughtering us, only when rivers of blood flow in the Square, will the eyes of our country's people truly be opened, and only then will they unite."

On May 23, three youths from Hunan threw black paint on Mao's portrait. They were seized by the students and turned over to the authorities, and workers immediately replaced the portrait.

The army continued to be stymied in the streets whenever troops started to move. It was rumored that seven retired generals had written the leaders not to use the army. On May 23, troops withdrew to the outskirts of Beijing. Favorable media reports began to reappear; international TV coverage resumed. There was even the possibility of a constitutional solution. The National People's Congress Standing Committee had the authority to convene a special meeting and to dismiss Premier Li Peng and end martial law. The key here was Wan Li, chair of the NPC Standing Committee, currently visiting Canada and the United States. Democracy supporters scurried to line up the NPC quorum, so that Wan Li could return and call the special session. Unfortunately the PRC's constitution means little against Party power. Wan Li was intercepted as he returned via Shanghai on May 25, and two days later, he announced his support for the restoration of order.

The demonstrators had one last surprise. On May 27, students at the Central Academy of Fine Arts set to work on a statue, "The Goddess of Democracy." It was conceived as their final statement, to be unveiled on the last day of demonstrations, May 30. The statue somewhat resembled the American Statue of Liberty (an exact replica of Liberty had earlier been used in Shanghai). But she was unique: a thirty-foot white styrofoam and plaster woman grasping a torch with both hands. On May 30, she was transported in sections to the square and installed between the Monument and Tiananmen Gate. The symbolism was stunning. On the revolutionary square, facing the portrait of Chairman Mao, loomed an answer to forty years of dictatorship. It buoyed the movement briefly, as 30,000 attended the unveiling. Party leaders were livid: "The erection of a so-called statue of a goddess is an insult to our national dignity and mocks our nation's image," fumed a TV announcer.[12]

The square again grew bleak. Amid squalor and stench, the students straggled in disarray. Participation had fallen off. Even a last-minute hunger strike on June 2 by a famous pop singer failed to reignite much enthusiasm. There also were some nasty incidents, as young ruffian elements joined in.

## Crushing the "Counterrevolution"

On the evening of June 2 an incident exacerbated the situation. An army jeep struck and killed three bicyclists, which brought out large angry crowds. Then curiously, in the very early morning hours of June 3, three squads of soldiers were engulfed by citizens as they entered the city center from different directions. One column of several thousand seemed to be young, tired, poorly led troops, neither armed nor in full uniform. It disintegrated as bewildered soldiers straggled back to whence they had come. Later some buses were stopped, and the crowds found AK-47s and clubs inside. The weapons turned up later on the square, where the students tried to return them to military officials. Were these probes a deliberate tactic to create a situation in which troops were humiliated, beaten, or killed in order to justify retaliation? Many think so. The official rationale offered on June 6 cited the "shocking counterrevolutionary rebellion" of this night as the cause for PLA intervention.[13]

As the day dawned there were more incidents. Several thousand troops exited the rear of the Great Hall of the People where they were surrounded by citizens. A hostile standoff ended in mutual stone, brick, and bottle throwing and many injuries. When a student with loudspeaker announced, "The people's police loves the people; the people's police do not beat the people," a soldier ran over, kicked him in the stomach, sneering, "Who the fuck loves you?"[14]

In front of Zhongnanhai, riot police attacked a crowd with belts, truncheons, and tear gas. Lingering protesters then angrily destroyed a parked military vehicle. Near the Beijing Hotel some people were beaten by police. By the evening of June 3 the situation had turned ugly. The "Protect Tiananmen" headquarters, a recently assembled organization, issued an appeal: "History will show that this day will be a symbol of shame, a day that the people will always remember."[15] Its authors were referring to what had happened; they did not realize the aptness of their words for what was to follow.

Toward 10:00 P.M., as described at the beginning of this chapter, the first column advanced toward Tiananmen Square from the west; before long came another from the east; others marched from the south and north; and still more columns advanced from the west and south. But many still could not believe that the soldiers would fire. The events followed a crazy logic. Probably the bloodiest zone was Changan Avenue west of the square and its intersections and side streets. Sometimes the troops fired into the crowds, inflicting hundreds of casualties. Sometimes the confrontations were more restrained, involving tear gas, cattle prods, and truncheons against bricks and stones. Sometimes the troops shot above the crowds, but sometimes they fired into apartment windows, striking the inhabitants.

By midnight, clashes were occurring near and east of the square. In one reported episode, an armed personnel carrier roared into the square from the south, raced north, and turned east on Changan Avenue, careened along that boulevard for many blocks and then back, in the process crashing through barricades and even hitting a truck carrying soldiers. It arrived back at the square where crowds somehow surrounded it, took out and beat one of the soldier occupants (possibly to death) while students led the other two occupants away to safety.

By daybreak, the loudspeakers on the square were announcing a message from ''Martial Law Headquarters'':

> A serious counterrevolutionary rebellion occurred in the capital this evening. Rioters furiously attacked soldiers and robbed them of their weapons and ammunition, burned military vehicles, set up roadblocks and kidnapped officers and men in an attempt to subvert the People's Republic of China and overthrow the socialist system. The People's Liberation Army has kept an attitude of restraint for some days. However, the counterrevolutionary rebellion must now be resolutely counterattacked.[16]

Beijing was a battle zone. The square had been secured by dozens of tanks and other vehicles. Tanks and truckloads of soldiers circulated, prepared to fire into any group showing the least defiance and often firing randomly down the broad boulevards and into the small residential lanes.

News of these events produced shocked reactions across China and the world. Hundreds of thousands took to the streets in

Shanghai. Demonstrations, sometimes punctuated with violence, occurred in many other cities: Shenyang, Harbin, Changchun, Dalian, Lanzhou, Xian, Guangzhou, Nanjing, Hefei, Wuhan, Tianjin, and Changsha. The crowds and police were so violent in Chengdu that martial law was declared.

In Hong Kong, where people were already nervous about the colony's return to China in 1997, massive crowds gathered. The *Wen Wei Po,* a PRC-controlled newspaper, printed a notice that all staff ''were extremely indignant at the savage act of the Chinese Government, which massacred the patriotic students and residents in Beijing,'' and it expressed ''hatred for a handful of beasts who have betrayed the people and who should pay their blood debt.'' [17]

In every major Western city, overseas Chinese and non-Chinese demonstrated. Condemnation poured in from governments and from prominent political and cultural figures. There were calls for retaliation, boycotts, and breaking relations. But Deng Xiaoping, Li Peng, and Yang Shangkun had crossed a point of no return. They would not back down before any criticism or sanctions, domestic or international. In Chen Yun's words, ''We must not let the next generation pour a bucket of shit on our heads.'' [18]

So the dreamers of democracy woke up to repression, conformity, and continued Party dictatorship. But as the next chapter will show, the conventional reformers too discovered that their plans for a society more controlled, centralized, and socialist were not so easy to achieve.

# 10

# The Nineties

June 1989 seemed to be a great watershed. China's rulers had never faced such a challenge. Global condemnation abounded. Meanwhile the socialist block, the "East Wind" that Mao had once said was prevailing over the "West Wind," was collapsing. China seemed poised for a radical turn—before June 4, perhaps toward "democracy," then after June 4, back to heavy handed Soviet-style rule. From a later vantage point, however, Tiananmen seemed less a watershed than merely an episode. The nation continued much as it had throughout the reform period. Under a halting reform agenda, the economy was developing, although not without problems. The Party retained its grip on power.

## Regaining Control

### New Leaders and Old

Within a week of June 4, the protestors had been mostly silenced, although in Beijing and other places the scuffle of lingering resistance could be heard for weeks. On June 9 Deng Xiaoping, accompanied by Peng Zhen and other elders, appeared on TV to congratulate military and security leaders. Deng's remarks were pitiless but measured. He praised the police and military, making no mention of excesses. He accused the "handful of bad people" who had turned turmoil into "counterrevolutionary rebellion," of trying to "topple the Communist Party, and . . . overthrow the socialist system." For these "dregs" he urged "not one bit of forgiveness." He reaffirmed the authority of the center and the Four Cardinal Principles. It was fortunate, he said, that this crisis had erupted while "veteran comrades" like himself were still alive. He did not denounce Zhao Ziyang; rather, he pointed out that the events were "inevitable" given the Party's neglect of education and ideological work, and he reaffirmed "reform and opening."[1]

It remained for the leadership to regroup and hammer out policies. First was the question: Who gets power? The elders—Deng, Chen Yun, Peng Zhen, Yang Shangkun, and a few others—had reasserted their claim to ultimate authority, but they needed younger leaders to shoulder the daily burdens. They needed a new general secretary to replace Zhao Ziyang and replacements for Zhao and Hu Qili on the Politburo Standing Committee.

On June 23 the Central Committee announced the new general secretary, the dark horse Jiang Zemin (pronounced something like "Jyang Zuh-min"), who had been the mayor and Party secretary of Shanghai. He was not considered a hard-liner. But from previous assignments, he did have personal links with Li Peng and may have been connected to other conventional reformers. He had earned the enmity of intellectuals on April 26 when he dismissed the editor of the *World Economic Herald*, and he supervised the propaganda campaign following Tiananmen. But he also had a smoother side. Well groomed with his dark-rimmed glasses, he had been known as the urbane leader of Shanghai, speaker of several languages, who attracted foreign business.

The new Standing Committee was a compromise between the resurgent hard-liners and the more pragmatic Deng Xiaoping. Joining Jiang Zemin, Li Peng, and Qiao Shi were Song Ping, a conservative, and Li Ruihuan, a pragmatic administrator. Li, one of the few truly proletarian leaders, had originally been a carpenter. He drew attention in the early PRC years through his outstanding role in the construction of the Great Hall of the People (1959). More recently Li had built his reputation as mayor of Tianjin, guiding that city's rapid development by pragmatism and cutting through red tape. His political connections were with the bold reformers. Nevertheless, it was not clear whether without the backing of Deng Xiaoping and the others, Jiang Zemin and Li Peng would have staying power.

## Quelling Rebellion

The plenum issued a four-part agenda: first, quell the "counter-revolutionary rebellion"; second, work out appropriate reform and openness; third, push ideological work and patriotism; and fourth, improve the Party's image and punish corruption.

The suppression unfolded in three phases. First came the iron fist of June and July, using the well-oiled instruments of suppression. As public defiance was silenced nationwide, there was a massive roundup of students, intellectuals, workers, and other offenders. Thousands were detained and questioned, hunted down from the vast files of photographs and videos assembled by Public Security and assisted by informants and neighborhood committees. Pictures of the twenty-one students and intellectuals on the most-wanted list were shown repeatedly on TV. Detainees were shown being rudely marched along by police. Trials were held, sometimes before crowds, as a result of which about thirty-five workers were executed (but no students).

The second phase lasted about a year, during which some arrests continued quietly, with perhaps 40,000 questioned and processed. This slowdown may have been a response to world-wide shock at the first executions, and it also fit in with the Party's effort to present a kinder face. By the end of 1989 the courts had processed 200 "counterrevolutionary" cases and nearly 3,500 cases of public disturbance. Many others followed in 1990.

Finally, in January 1991 there was a flurry of trials whose verdicts were publicly announced and which involved people like Wang Dan and Wang Juntao. The thin, serious, bespectacled Beijing University history student Wang Dan was one of the principal Tiananmen leaders and headed the most-wanted list until his arrest. At his trial he refused to plead guilty, but his sentence was a moderate four years. (He was released in 1993.)

Wang Juntao (pronounced something like "Wang June-tao") represented an earlier generation. At seventeen he had joined the 1976 Tiananmen demonstrations, for which he wrote a famous poem with the line "I weep while wolves and jackals laugh" and was imprisoned.[2] After Deng Xiaoping's return to power, the Tiananmen incident was reevaluated, and Wang was exonerated and given a position in the Communist Youth League. But he would not be coopted into the power structure. In 1978 Wang Juntao joined the 1978 Democracy Wall movement and in 1980 ran unsuccessfully for a seat in a local people's congress. In 1986, with a successful entrepreneur friend, he founded a private research institute and published *Economics Weekly*. These organizations carried out public opinion surveys and promoted economic liberalization and political reform. To the old guard they represented a threat: autonomous, uncontrolled organizations, the sprouts of "civil society." In 1989 Wang was one of the older dissidents who attempted to advise the demonstrators. After June 4, he was apprehended attempting to flee the country. He and his entrepreneur friend received the heaviest sentences of all, thirteen years' imprisonment.

In all, eighteen dissidents received sentences of two to thirteen years. None was executed, and about 1,000 people were released. These moves came during the 1991 Persian Gulf crisis and the U.S.–UN military ejection of Iraq from Kuwait. The Chinese authorities had probably been waiting for such a global distraction to close the books on this episode, which they now refer to simply as "June fourth."

Because of the official secrecy, much about these procedures remains murky: the evidence against known defendants, the exact charges, the numbers tried without public notice, their names, the names of the released, the numbers sent to reeducation camps under police order without trial, the places of detention, and the treatment received. Various governments and groups such as Asia Watch and Amnesty International appealed to China to respect human rights, but all were rebuffed on grounds of interference in China's internal affairs.

During these eighteen months, the authorities punished those not subject to criminal prosecution. Zhao Ziyang remained under house confinement. A number of reformers lost their positions, including advisers in Zhao's research institutions, editors and journalists, and the heads of the Culture Ministry, United Front Work Department, Federation of Trade Unions, and the Party Propaganda Department. A campaign to discover all Party members who supported the Tiananmen demonstrations was announced for 1990. The universities moved to discipline staff and students and to restore strict control. Beijing University's president was replaced, and the incoming freshmen, along with the freshmen of Shanghai's Fudan University, were required to spend their first year in military camps. The entering classes of other schools spent shorter periods in reeducation. Some departments and faculty were punished, and stricter rules for graduate school admission and permission to go abroad were announced.

The most notorious case was that of astrophysicist Fang Lizhi and his wife Li Shuxian. Although they had had little connection with the Tiananmen demonstrations, they had long been outspoken critics of the system, and official spokespersons charged that they were behind the conspiracy to subvert the Party and the socialist system. On June 6, fearing arrest and prosecution, Fang and his wife took refuge in the United States embassy. For months their disposition remained a bone of contention between Beijing and Washington, with the Chinese declaring them to be counterrevolutionary traitors and charging the United States with meddling in China's internal affairs. In June 1990 Fang and Li were allowed to leave China.

Meanwhile, under Jiang Zemin's direction, the propagandists were at work. For days, TV and newspapers were saturated with the images of a few disemboweled, hanged, and charred remains of soldiers. The official story began by recognizing people's rightful anger over corruption and inflation. Although Zhao Ziyang deserved much of the blame for these problems, there was also a conspiracy, backed by foreign elements, to undermine socialism and destroy the Communist regime. The conspirators had seized control of the protests to further their plot. Even though the state had been patient, order had to be restored, lest China's achievements be lost. Then, as the PLA tried to restore order, the soldiers suffered savage attacks, injury, and death. Unfortunately a small number of civilians also were killed. To make sure that this was the only version heard, all publications were forced into line, and Voice of America and BBC broadcasts were jammed. From then on, the danger of "peaceful evolution" became a stock theme, such as in the 1990 *People's Daily* editorial warning of unspecified Western forces who "cannot succeed with guns and cannon, so they press a campaign of 'peaceful evolution' to infiltrate their culture and way of thinking."[3]

In this repression only a few people were executed, and ironically, in a workers' state, they included only workers. The imprisoned and "reeducated" may not have exceeded 2,000. Although this is not to minimize the suffering of those punished without legal protection, by comparison with earlier repression—like the campaigns of 1952 and 1957 (not to mention the Cultural Revolution)—the number of reprisals was limited.

Much the same could be said of other aspects of the suppression: political meetings, disciplining students, restricting publications, expelling foreign journalists, and so forth. The measures were severe and partly effective. The propaganda campaign probably convinced many rural and provincial people, who did not identify with the students or crave democracy, that the students were ungrateful and disruptive. Still, these efforts fell short of complete success. Reform, opening, inflation, corruption, consumerism, knowledge of the world, and the entire wave of change and awareness of the 1980s had blunted the traditional instruments of persuasion and coercion. The official line thus was greeted with silent sarcasm by the people of Beijing and probably by residents of those other places where such excesses had occurred.

## Economic Policy

According to the Central Committee's June communiqué, the second task was to

> continue . . . improving the economic environment and rectifying the economic order so as to better adhere to the policy of reform and opening to the outside world, and to promote economic development in a sustained, steady and coordinated way.[4]

This statement papered over a contradiction between bold and conventional reform. Was it possible to "rectify the economic order" (increase central control) and also have "reform and opening"? The goal under bold reform had become "the state regulates the market, and the market guides the enterprise." Now the conventional reformers intended to replace that with a metaphor of Chen Yun's: The market in a socialist system is like a bird, free to fly but only inside its socialist cage. The question was: Could the bird survive in a cage; could the market thrive under central planning?

### Stubborn Facts

Even in 1988, when Li Peng and the conventional reformers were beginning to wrestle the policy reins from Zhao Ziyang, they had to face some facts. China needed advanced technology, exports, and imports and so could not withdraw from the world economy. Irrational prices and shortages of transportation, energy, and raw materials persisted. Budget deficits piled up because of food subsidies and losses by state enterprises. Coastal provinces were becoming increasingly independent economically. Ten million young adults were joining the work force every year, not to mention the 100 million already-redundant peasants.

Tiananmen increased the pressure by jeopardizing China's "opening." Not only did the world condemn China, but also the blood on Changan Avenue unnerved many international businesses, which were already doubting that business in China could be profitable. They did not find the bullet holes in their office walls reassuring. The World Bank and the Asian Development Bank stopped lending money to China, and Japan suspended its large loan package.

## Austerity

To reduce inflation and cool the overheated economy, the conventional reformers imposed austerity measures. They restricted smaller enterprises (individual, private, and collective) which were said to interfere with state enterprises. Jiang Zemin, ignoring the dynamism of the small enterprises and the recent encouragement of them, now scolded the entrepreneurs for their ostentatious consumption, wasteful production, and tax evasion. They were, he said, "ruining the atmosphere of society."[5] Many small enterprises were ordered closed. Private financial organizations were outlawed. The fledgling stock and bond exchanges in Shanghai and Shenzhen were curtailed. A tax investigation campaign was launched. Banks cut back credit, the lifeblood of small enterprises, which also reduced the money supply and helped squeeze inflation.

There also was a push to increase central control over state enterprises. While calling for state factories to improve their efficiency, party committees and trade unions were once again assigned important roles. Wage inequalities were criticized, and price controls on steel and other raw materials were maintained.

The State Planning Commission, reviving a function that had been eliminated in 1987, established a "Production Commission" to oversee the allocation of materials. Tighter control also marked China's agricultural policy. Unwilling to accept the fiscal consequences of paying higher procurement prices to farmers, Beijing turned to political controls. The Party launched a revival of village branches, as stronger, closely supervised Party branches could also help control local corruption and the highly unpopular proliferation of local taxes and levies. To control abuse of the two-price system, the center reasserted its monopoly over the distribution of fertilizers and pesticides. Finally, the conventional reformers proposed reversing the parcelization of land under the "responsibility system," by promoting land consolidation and increased mechanization.

## Stabilization

These policies brought results. Inflation slowed dramatically by year's end, 1989. Both 1989 and 1990 saw excellent harvests of grain and most other crops. Li Peng could claim that retrenchment policies had succeeded in "improving the economic environment," as contrasted with the inflation, investment fever, trade deficits, and stagnant grain and cotton situation created by Zhao Ziyang's bold reformers. Efforts to reassure foreign businesses, banks, and trading partners also worked fairly well, even as the propagandists were blaming outside provocation for the "turmoil." Experience had taught the Chinese that foreigners would yammer for a while, but in the end China was too important to them to punish or ignore it for long. China could wait them out, taking refuge behind the principle of non-interference in other countries' domestic affairs. By late 1990, China's global importance became apparent at the time of the Gulf crisis, when Washington needed China's abstention on the UN Security Council vote to move militarily against Iraq.

U.S. President George Bush repeatedly resisted pressures to rescind China's "most-favored nation" trading status and impose sanctions. ("Most-favored nation" refers to the normal tariff rates that U.S. trading partners enjoy.) His administration believed that punitive policies would unnecessarily poison relations and, if imposed, would harm ordinary Chinese people, not the rulers. By early 1990, China's strict curtailment of imports and promotion of exports fended off trade deficits and actually began to produce surpluses. Entrepreneurs in Hong Kong and Taiwan, attracted to China's huge pool of cheap labor, scarcely broke stride as they launched their projects along the China coast. The World Bank resumed its loan program, as did Japan. By the summer of 1991, Japan's Prime Minister Toshiki Kaifu was visiting Beijing. Even tourism, which had plummeted, recovered moderately, as the hotel rooms left vacant by Europeans, Americans, and Japanese were filled by guests from Taiwan and Hong Kong.

## Persistent Problems

The "economic environment" was not completely rosy. The austerity set off a severe recession. The assault on local enterprises forced many out of business and led others to cut back. This action wiped out rural jobs and caused revenue shortfalls, since local governments received most of their funds from profits and taxes, which in turn adversely affected education funding and welfare. Many urban construction projects were halted, throwing the "floating" peasant laborers out of work. State enterprises, operating at a loss and with warehouses full of unsold inventories, could not clear their accounts with their creditors, thereby leaving a huge web of mutual bad debts. Indices of real GNP, industrial production, and productivity all dropped sharply. Even the "iron rice bowl" workers in state enterprises often suffered reduced wages and no bonuses.

Statistics on incomes tell the general story: In both 1988 and 1989, urban and rural incomes, adjusted for inflation, fell. Perhaps Li Peng and the conventional reformers cannot be faulted for the recession of 1989 and 1990, since all economies experience booms and busts, but they also achieved little in addressing fundamental problems.

Almost everyone now recognized that prices set at levels unreflective of scarcity and production costs would lead to inefficient resource allocation. Serious examples were energy and transportation, which had long been priced too cheaply and were therefore unable to grow as rapidly as other sectors. Nonetheless, fundamental price reform was tabled. State enterprises were notorious for their lazy work styles and inefficient use of energy and materials. The "capitalist" prescription for this is "hard budget constraints," according to which a firm has to make profits or go out of business. But the state was still not prepared to accept bankruptcies and unemployment and instead took familiar administrative steps, such as "responsibility" contracts with managers and inducements to get the workers to try harder.

Agriculture posed other dilemmas. The country needed more grain and fiber for the expanding population. Peasants would respond to prices and happily grow rice, wheat, corn, potatoes, beans, cotton, rapeseed, and peanuts if they could make money. But if the state paid more, it would have to raise retail prices or else underwrite even larger subsidies. Ironically the situation was complicated by bumper harvests in 1989 and 1990 which depressed free market prices while the state refused to buy all the tonnage that the farmers wanted to sell. Peasants complained when the underfunded state grain procurement offices paid them in IOUs. The state then resorted to coercive administrative measures to persuade the peasants to plant grain.

Another problem was the tension between the center and the provinces. During the 1980s, to foster economic development, Beijing had allowed the coastal provinces to remit set revenues to the center and to retain the surplus. Now the fiscally strapped central bureaus tried to curtail these privileges, but they met with stiff provincial resistance and by 1991 had not succeeded. A related problem was protectionism and "economic fiefdoms." As the recession constricted markets, employment, and revenues, the provincial and local cadres guarded their own backyards. Outside products were kept out. Cotton regions blocked shipments of raw fiber to the large mills in Shanghai so that new local mills could continue operations, but such local protectionism weakened market integration and economic efficiency.

In addition to these internal problems, China was being pressured from abroad by lending institutions such as the World Bank, by the General Agreement on Tariffs and Trade which it wished to join, and by the U.S. Congress which threatened to discontinue its "most-favored nation" status if China failed to address human rights and unfair trade issues.

## Bold Reform Ideas Survive

By early 1990, Li Peng and the conventional reformers were having to face up to many difficulties. Bold reform views began to resurface, and even Deng Xiaoping himself lent his voice to the call for pragmatic solutions. Actually, many enterprises had evaded the restrictive policies all along, seeking alternative financing. Coastal provinces such as Guangdong and Hainan Island strove to stimulate their export-oriented economies despite the political climate in Beijing. Policies toward the SEZs began to soften, owing to Beijing's recognition that China needed foreign capital and needed to facilitate relations with Hong Kong and Taiwan. By the spring and summer of 1990, the government was thus dabbling in price reforms.

It also became apparent that local enterprises remained the most dynamic sector of the economy. State enterprises, struggling with red ink and inefficiency, could not solve the unemployment problem. Consequently, credit restrictions and other impediments to local industry were eased, and officials stopped assailing this sector. In agriculture, the center had to reassure the peasants that the responsibility system was not about to end, having alarmed them with talk of "deepening" the reforms through land consolidation, which sounded suspiciously like recollectivization.

Deng Xiaoping pushed for the promotion of new pragmatic leaders. One of them was Zhu Rongji (pronounced something like "Joo Roong-jee"), who was named vice-premier. He had been mayor of Shanghai. Called "One-chop Zhu" by foreign business people because of his impatience with red tape, he built a no-nonsense reputation for economic development similar to Li Ruihuan's in Tianjin. Zhu also retained the respect of many students and intellectuals for his nonviolent resolution of the June 1989 demonstrations in Shanghai. By 1993 Zhu was emerging as one of the most influential leaders, alongside Jiang Zemin and Qiao Shi.

## Breaking the Logjam

Still, as late as 1990, as the Party sketched out its 1991–95 five-year plan and a ten-year plan for the 1990s, the conventional and bold reformers were at a standoff. By late 1991 Deng Xiaoping worried that as Marxist regimes around the world collapsed, socialism in China would be able to flourish only if it could create "modest prosperity" *(xiaokang)* by century's end. The Fourteenth Party Congress was scheduled for late 1992, and Deng wished to prepare for advancing a new generation of reform-minded leaders. It can also be supposed that the eighty-eight-year-old patriarch hoped to leave as his parting legacy something other than the massacre of Tiananmen. Thus Deng was anxious to pull the Party away from the logjam. In January 1992, Deng, nearly deaf and with his daughter at his arm to help him communicate, conducted a planned "inspection" tour of Shenzhen and Zhuhai, the two SEZs near Hong Kong and Macao. He also visited the nearby Pearl River delta area and then spent the lunar New Year holiday in Shanghai, where Pudong, a special economic development area, was under development.

The central media, controlled by more conventional leaders, declined at first to publicize Deng's trip and his call for more liberated thinking and courageous quick steps. But by March, his supporters had mobilized provincial, military, and other support and had made a concerted effort to encourage his policies. The pendulum now swung toward reform. The Politburo announced that it was most important to guard against the "left" (conventional reformers and ideological conservatives), declaring that a policy would be acceptable if it improved the economy, strengthened the state, and raised living standards (in a "socialist" way, of course).[6] When the Party Congress met, the Party generally supported this new direction and endorsed Deng's theory of socialism with Chinese characteristics, asserting that "a market economy under socialism must and can absolutely operate better then a market economy under capitalism."[7] The voice of conventional reform was certainly not stilled for good,

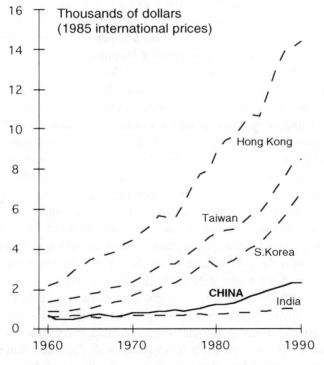

FIG. 7 Comparative growth of selected Asian economies: Real GDP per capita.

but Deng's pragmatic push for economic development, coupled with party dictatorship, was solidly in place, at least for the moment. See Figure 7 which compares China's economic growth with other Asian nations'.[8]

## Political Rigidity

### Saving the Party

The Central Committee's 1989 four-part agenda, mentioned previously, included the promotion of ideological work and patriotism, the improvement of the Party's image, and the punishment of corruption. The goal was to reduce the latent criticisms of the Party by pushing conformity and patriotism and to purify the Party in order to regain popular legitimacy.

Over the years, endless doctrinal shifts and reversals had infected ideological belief with cynicism. To counter this, the authorities dusted off the old political study meetings in schools and workplaces. They also, predictably, launched a campaign to emulate Lei Feng. To enhance the image of Party cadres as being close to the masses, they began an image campaign for the Party and army and a program of sending down middle- and junior officials to lower levels. The propagandists also warned against the international "peaceful evolution" conspiracy against China's socialist system. Even sports was enlisted for politics when Beijing hosted the summer 1990 Asian Games, in which China won the lion's share of medals. Other international athletic events were also used to build national pride.

One would think that reducing corruption would have met with immense public applause, but unfortunately, this was not so easy. The new economic system placed Party officials and cadres in the way of great temptation, with the result that corruption reached into the very highest families, who were unlikely to jail their own children. Some much-publicized corruption prosecutions were reported, but those indicted did not include many big fish. A reregistration of Party members was announced, but its purpose was mainly to discipline those who had sided with the Tiananmen students.

Still the government did restore political control. In the summer of 1991 the Party celebrated its seventieth anniversary with ample self-congratulations. In late 1992 when the Fourteenth Party Congress met, the new Central Committee, Politburo, and Standing Committee offered new leaders who seemed capable of moving forward upon the demise of Deng and the other elders. Vice-Premier Zhu Rongji, elevated to the Politburo Standing Committee, seemed likely soon to overshadow Li Peng. The rest of the leadership configuration revealed a relatively young and well-educated group, mostly men, broadly representative of the various power structures (central bureaucracy, provinces, military, etc.). Generals Yang Shangkun and his half-brother Yang Baibing, who had seemed poised to make a run for greater power, lost their leading positions. Hu Qili, a former reformist ally of Zhao Ziyang, was reelected to the Central Committee and was rumored to be in line for important duties. Zhao himself appeared in public in early 1993.

## China in a Changing World

Between 1978 and the early 1990s, the world changed dramatically. Most striking was the collapse of the Soviet Union and its satellite system, the fragmentation of Yugoslavia and Czechoslovakia, and the general refutation of socialist central planning. Meanwhile the growth of the "Pacific Rim" economies (Japan, South Korea, Taiwan, Singapore, and Hong Kong) and other Asian countries continued. As the Soviet–American competition ended, global multipolar politics set in. International business continued to leap across national boundaries and to spread technology and popular culture. With regard to the latter, it is interesting that Wuer Kaixi believed that the greatest influence on the Tiananmen students was not democratic ideals but rock music.

All of these developments have created a new situation for China's leaders. The external pressure is off, and all "three obstacles" that China held against the USSR have disappeared. American power in the Pacific is diminishing, as exemplified by the United States's abandonment of Clark Air Base and Subic Bay in the Philippines. Several regional issues have come closer to being settled, including the reintegration of Cambodia, Sino-Vietnamese and U.S.–Vietnamese tensions, Chinese relations with Indonesia and Singapore, and the approaching return of Hong Kong and Macao to China.

Ironically, these changes have put the burden on China (as on other countries) to reexamine its goals and its place in the world. Neither the socialist-versus-capitalist formula nor the rich-versus-poor formula is very convincing for a nation that trades most with capitalists and aspires to "modest prosperity." Under "reform and opening," China faces the issue of how to have economic "liveliness" without greater political and cultural pluralism. This question is complicated by growing regionalism (especially on the maritime coast) and ethnic assertiveness in Tibet (and to a lesser extent in Inner Mongolia and Xinjiang).

From outside China, it is difficult to see how the old ideology and familiar methods of control will suffice. To be sure, compared with other former Communist states, China remains orderly and is growing economically. But the world has seen how suddenly Communist regimes can collapse. As of 1993, some of China's octogenarians have left the scene, and others, even Deng, cannot be far behind. Pragmatists, including Li Ruihuan and Zhu Rongji, have entered the highest circles, and Li Peng is widely disliked. How well can the new leadership sustain the system and address China's many problems?

China's global role also must be redefined. The PRC is no longer a model revolution, and little curiosity remains about the secret of Marxist–Leninist development. If China is a model, it is of rapid development through the partial abandonment of central planning. In some ways it is a world power only by virtue of its size. Although it is moving rapidly in its coastal areas toward the status of a semideveloped economy, China's claim to leadership among Third World nations is weak. Finally, its "neomercantilist" policies of aggressive exports and restricted imports threatens to alienate the United States and other trading partners.

## A Medley of Problems

Can China's economy grow fast enough to give hundreds of millions of people better living standards? In the countryside, even after tens of millions of peasants have found nonfarm jobs or moved to towns and cities, the total farm population is still larger than ever. The amount of arable land shrinks yearly, while other resources—natural, environmental, and human—are coming under increasing pressure as living standards improve. The environment has not fared well; the air in many cities is sometimes scarcely fit to breathe. A worried United States has even undertaken to give China technical assistance to produce refrigerators that do not use ozone-destroying chlorofluorocarbons, and Japan is seeking ways to limit the spread of acid rain from China's coal combustion.

Economic justice also presents challenges. While the coastal provinces expand rapidly and account for most of China's foreign investment and trade, the inland provinces are struggling to shake off poverty. Local disparities persist. Another major issue, differing from region to region, is China's ethnic minorities. Some cope very well, as for example, the Koreans in the northeast; others live in greater or lesser tension with the Han majority and the government. The Tibetans in the Tibetan Autonomous Region are the best known (though actually more Tibetans live in other provinces). Beijing has sought unsuccessfully a policy that would persuade the Tibetans to stop seeking independence, as most Han people believe strongly that all of the border provinces and peoples are an inseparable part of China.

As for the women of China, the demise of the communes and control systems that once governed behavior, and the reemergence of traditional and other arrangements, have led to complex results. Although for many women there are new economic opportunities, many others remain on the land while their husbands and brothers seek industrial employment. Bride price, forced abortions, female infanticide, the kidnapping of women for sale, and other abuses are still frequently reported.

In regard to ideology and culture, the reform period has stirred the once-quiescent pot into a roiling soup of contradiction and confusion. Marxism and socialism are hard pressed to retain any integrity, as official ideologies attempt to refashion some of the fundamental building blocks. What, after all, does socialism mean when it must find a place for all kinds of "capitalistic" elements? Calling it "socialism with Chinese characteristics" helps a little, but not much. Furthermore, Marxism's decline has left a cultural vacuum. Consumption, money-making, and Hong Kong fashions cannot define a fully meaningful existence. Traditional practices and folk religion have reappeared in the villages but may also be unable to shape life in a modern context of mobility, gender demands, and international economics.

Western ideas like freedom, democracy, and individualism flourish among the educated, but not necessarily among ordinary people; because Western societies, the United States in particular, present ambiguous models, the "streets of gold" myths clashing with news reports of drugs, crime, and chaos. Hence the intellectual and cultural challenge: how to fashion on the rubble of Marxism (and while the rulers stubbornly chant their Marxist mantras) a reasonably coherent set of values and social principles.

In 1959 Mao proclaimed, "The achievements are tremendous, the problems are numerous, the experience is rich, and the future is bright." [9] As he spoke, much had indeed been done to pull the country up, but the Great Leap Forward was propelling China into calamity. His optimism would have been more appropriate for Deng Xiaoping's era, during which the achievements, especially economic, have indeed been remarkable. However one should not overlook the tragedy nor forget the formidable persistent problems. Every nation confronts political, economic, cultural, environmental, and social challenges, but each faces a unique set of them. In China those challenges that particularly stand out are the country's great size, which magnifies everything, and the legacy of Marxism. The future may well be bright, but there will likely be some dark passages along the way.

# Notes

## Introduction

1. Author's translation. For the Chinese text and another translation, see Mao Tse-tung, *The Poems of Mao Tse-tung,* trans. Willis Barstone (New York: Bantam Books, 1972), 92–93.

## Chapter 1

1. G. William Skinner, "Regional Urbanization in Nineteenth-Century China," in *The City in Late Imperial China,* ed. G. William Skinner (Stanford, Calif.: Stanford University Press, 1977), 211–49; Central Intelligence Agency, *People's Republic of China Atlas* (Washington, D.C.: U.S. Government Printing Office, 1971), 39, 59.

2. Skinner, "Regional Urbanization," 223.

3. R. H. Tawney, *Land and Labor in China* (Boston: Beacon Press, 1966), 42. Compare Lucian W. Pye, *China, an Introduction* (Boston: Little, Brown, 1978), 89–90.

4. Ramon H. Meyers, *The Chinese Economy Past and Present* (Belmont, Calif.: Wadsworth, 1980), 16. The subject of land tenure and distribution is very complex, as regional and local variations are many. For discussions on land distribution and peasant "immiseration," see Joseph Esherick, "Number Games: A Note on Land Distribution in Pre-Revolutionary China," *Modern China,* 7 (October 1981): 387–411; and Lloyd E. Eastman, *Family, Fields, and Ancestors: Constancy and Changes in China's Social and Economic History, 1550–1949* (New York: Oxford University Press, 1988), 80–100. See also Cheryl Payer, "Was the Chinese Peasant Exploited?" *Journal of Peasant Studies,* 2 (January 1975): 229–36; and Lilian Li, Book Review, *Pacific Affairs,* 64 (Spring 1991): 96–97. On Mao's 1930 examination of Xunwu County in Jiangxi Province, where clan ownership of land was high, see Jonathan D. Spence, *The Search for Modern China* (New York: Norton, 1990), 373.

5. Edgar Snow, *Red Star Over China* (New York: Grove Press, 1961), 16.

6. For Mao's classic statement on mass line, see Mao Tse-tung, *Selected Works of Mao Tse-tung* (Peking: Foreign Languages Press, 1965), vol. 3: 226.

7. Helen Foster Snow, who visited Yanan, used this term. See Helen Foster Snow, *The Chinese Communists: Sketches and Autobiographies of the Old Guard* (Westport, Conn.: Greenwood, 1972), xiv.

8. James Pinkney Harrison, *The Long March to Power: A History of the Chinese Communist Party, 1921–1972* (New York: Praeger, 1972). Later figures are from *Beijing Review,* September 6, 1982: 20–24; and *China Quarterly,* 127 (September 1991): 660.

9. Ibid., 294, 396.

10. Congressional Quarterly, *China: U.S. Policy Since 1945* (Washington, D.C.: Congressional Quarterly, 1980), 84.

11. Tang Tsou, *America's Failure in China* (Chicago: University of Chicago Press, 1963), 495.

12. Donald W. Klein and Anne B. Clark, *Biographic Dictionary of Chinese Communism, 1921–1965,* 2 vols. (New York: Columbia University Press, 1981), 626.

13. Mao Tse-tung, *Selected Works of Mao Tse-tung,* vol. 2 (Peking: Foreign Languages Press, 1953), 272.

14. Raymond F. Wylie, *The Emergence of Maoism: Mao Tse-tung, Ch'en Po-ta and the Search for Chinese Theory, 1935–1945* (Stanford, Calif.: Stanford University, 1980), 13.

15. Helen Snow, *The Chinese Communists,* 164.

16. Klein and Clark, *Biographic Dictionary of Chinese Communism,* 109.

17. Ibid., 821.

18. Edgar Snow, *Red Star over China,* 294.

19. Chung Hua-min and Arthur C. Miller, *Madame Mao: A Profile of Chiang Ch'ing* (Hong Kong: Union Research Institute, 1968), 53–54, cited in Parris Chang, *Radicals and Radical Ideology in China's Cultural Revolution* (New York: Research Institute on Communist Affairs, 1973), 72.

20. Quoted in Robert C. Tucker, *The Marxian Revolutionary Idea* (New York: Norton, 1969), 16.

21. Meyers, *The Chinese Economy,* 36. The author of this passage is not a Marxist himself.

22. Ibid., 180–82.

23. Prasenjit Duara, *Culture, Power, and the State: Rural North China, 1900–1942* (Stanford, Calif.: Stanford University Press, 1988), 252.

## Chapter 2

1. Mao Tse-tung, *Selected Works of Mao Tse-tung* (Peking: Foreign Languages Press, 1977), vol. 5: 17.

2. Yu-ming Shaw, "John Leighton Stuart and U.S.-Chinese Communist Rapprochements: Was There Another 'Lost Chance in China'?" *China Quarterly,* 89 (March 1982): 82. See also John Gittings, *The World and China, 1922–1972* (New York: Harper & Row, 1974), 170.

3. Herbert Feis, *The China Tangle* (Princeton, N.J.: Princeton University, 1953), 140–41.

4. Stuart R. Schram (ed.), *Chairman Mao Talks to the People: Talks and Letters, 1956–1971* (New York: Pantheon, 1974), 102–3.

5. Ibid., 191.

6. Gittings, *The World and China,* 170. For a more recent treatment of the once controversial subject of America's "lost chance," see Gordon H. Chang, *Friends and Enemies: The United States, China, and the Soviet Union, 1948–1972* (Stanford, Calif.: Stanford University Press, 1990), 3–41. An official Chinese view of Sino-American relations may be found in *Beijing Review,* March 7–13, 1988. For other views, see Edwin W. Martin, *Divided Council: The Anglo-American Response to Communist Victory in China* (Lexington: University Press of Kentucky, 1986); and June M. Grasso, *Truman's Two China Policy* (Armonk, N.Y.: M. E. Sharpe, 1987).

7. James Pinkney Harrison, *Long March to Power: A History of the Chinese Communist Party, 1921–1972* (New York: Praeger, 1972), 446.

8. A. Doak Barnett, *Cadres, Bureaucracy and Political Power in Communist China* (New York: Columbia University Press, 1967), 18.

9. Mao, *Selected Works,* vol. 5: 143.

10. Ibid.

11. Ibid., vol. 5: 26–31.

12. Melvin Gurtov and Byong-Moo Hwang, *China Under Threat: The Politics of Strategy and Diplomacy* (Baltimore: Johns Hopkins University Press, 1980), 52. China's preparations for entering Korea apparently began in August. See Michael M. Sheng, "Response: Mao and Stalin: Adversaries or Comrades?" *China Quarterly,* 129 (March 1992): 182.

13. *The New York Times,* November 16, 1950.

14. Mao, *Selected Works,* vol. 5: 43.

15. Dean Acheson, *The Korean War* (New York: Norton, 1971), 66.

16. John Gardner, "The *Wu-fan* Campaign in Shanghai: A Study in the Consolidation of Urban Control," in *Chinese Communist Politics in Action,* ed. A. Doak Barnett (Seattle: University of Washington Press, 1969), 477.

17. Mao, *Selected Works,* vol. 4: 419.

18. Mao, *Selected Works,* vol. 5: 115.

19. Gurtov and Hwang, *China Under Threat,* 31.

20. Mao, *Selected Works,* vol. 5: 53; 45–56 passim.

21. Merle Goldman, *Literary Dissent in Communist China* (New York: Atheneum, 1971), 92.

22. Stuart R. Schram, *Mao Tse-tung* (New York: Simon & Schuster, 1967),

73*n*. A few years later, Mao was expressing himself in similar fashion concerning Russian flatus (see Mao, *Selected Works*, vol. 5: 317). The fact that the CCP's own dogma was a Western import only adds to the paradox.

23. Mark Selden, "The Yenan Legacy: The Mass Line," in *Chinese Communist Politics in Action*, ed. Barnett, 105.

24. Schram, *Mao Tse-tung*, 269–70.

25. Mao, *Selected Works*, vol. 5: 122.

26. Ezra Vogel, *Canton Under Communism: Programs and Politics in a Provincial Capital, 1949–1968* (New York: Harper & Row, 1971), 85.

27. Goldman, *Literary Dissent in Communist China*, 35.

28. Vogel, *Canton Under Communism*, 87.

29. Gardner, "The *Wu-fan* Campaign in Shanghai," 524.

30. Mao, *Selected Works*, vol. 4: 438.

31. Derk Bodde, *Peking Diary: 1948–1949, A Year of Revolution* (Greenwich, Conn.: Fawcett, 1967), 117.

# Chapter 3

1. John G. Gurley, *China's Economy and the Maoist Strategy* (New York: Monthly Review Press, 1976), 238–40.

2. Mao Tse-tung, *Selected Works of Mao Tse-tung* (Peking: Foreign Languages Press, 1977), vol. 5: 192.

3. Christopher Howe, *China's Economy: A Basic Guide* (New York: Basic Books, 1978), xxvii. See also Alexander Eckstein, *China's Economic Development: The Interplay of Scarcity and Ideology* (Ann Arbor: University of Michigan Press, 1975), 308–10.

4. Parris Chang, *Policy and Power in China* (University Park: Pennsylvania State University Press, 1975), 10.

5. Mao, *Selected Works*, vol. 5: 201.

6. Ibid., vol. 5: 172.

7. Ibid., vol. 5: 185.

8. Ibid., vol. 5: 196.

9. Donald J. Munro, "Egalitarian Ideal and Educational Fact in Communist China," in *China: Management of a Revolutionary Society*, ed. John M. Lindbeck (Seattle: University of Washington Press, 1971), 296.

10. Stuart R. Schram (ed.), *Chairman Mao Talks to the People: Talks and Letters, 1956–1971* (New York: Pantheon, 1974), 138.

11. Ibid., vol. 5: 26–31. On the recently uncovered telegrams from Mao to Stalin and to Zhou Enlai regarding the entry of Chinese troups, see *New York Times*, February 26, 1992; and Sheng, "Response: Mao and Stalin," 180–83.

12. Chang, *Policy and Power in China*, 225.

13. Mark Selden, *The People's Republic of China: A Documentary History of Revolutionary Change* (New York: Monthly Review Press, 1979), 351.

14. Merle Goldman, *Literary Dissent in Communist China* (New York: Atheneum, 1971), 150–51.

15. Schram (ed.), *Chairman Mao Talks to the People*, 70.

16. Wilson, *The People's Emperor, Mao*, 317.

17. Mao, *Selected Works*, vol. 5: 244.

18. Schram (ed.), *Chairman Mao Talks to the People*, 72.

19. Ibid., 75.

20. Mao, *Selected Works*, vol. 5: 443–44.

21. Roderick MacFarquhar, *The Origins of the Cultural Revolution, 1: Contradictions Among the People, 1956–1957* (New York: Columbia University Press, 1974), 87–88; also Chang, *Policy and Power in China*, 26–27. For the view that the "reckless advance" criticism was an affront that Mao never forgave, see Stuart R. Schram, "The Limits of Cataclismic Change: Reflections on the Place of the 'Great Proletarian Cultural Revolution' in the Political Development of the People's Republic of China," *China Quarterly*, 108 (December 1986): 615.

22. Quoted in Wilson, *The People's Emperor, Mao*, 327.

23. Mao, *Selected Works*, vol. 5: 243–44.

24. Chang, *Policy and Power in China*, 226.

25. Wilson, *The People's Emperor, Mao*, 345.

26. Ibid., 347.

27. Ibid.

## Chapter 4

1. State Statistical Bureau, *Zhongguo Tongji Nianjian: 1991* (Beijing: Zhongguo Tongji Chubanshe, 1991), 33, 79. The statistics behind Figure 5 must be used cautiously. Official Chinese estimates are believed to exaggerate economic growth, and there are weaknesses in the basic data and the price deflators. Also national income growth might not correlate directly with improved living standards or assure equitable distribution of income. Nonetheless Figure 5 probably gives a good rough idea of the direction and magnitude of changes in per capita national income adjusted for inflation, a significant measure of economic performance.

2. Harvard University Center for International Affairs and the East Asian Research Center, *Communist China, 1955–1959: Policy Documents with Analysis* (Cambridge, Mass.: Harvard University Press, 1965), 329.

3. Dick Wilson, *The People's Emperor, Mao: A Biography of Mao Tsetung* (New York: Lee Publishers Group, 1979), 348. See also Roderick

MacFarquhar, *The Origins of the Cultural Revolution, 1: Contradictions Among the People, 1956–1957* (New York: Columbia University Press, 1974), 289ff.

4. Harvard Center, *Communist China, 1955–1959*, 179.

5. MacFarquhar, *Origins of the Cultural Revolution: 1*, 287.

6. Mao, *Selected Works*, vol. 5: 482.

7. Harold C. Hinton (ed.), *The People's Republic of China, 1949–1979: A Documentary Survey* (Wilmington, Del.: Scholarly Resources, 1980), vol. 2: 605.

8. James Pinkney Harrison, *The Long March to Power: A History of the Chinese Communist Party, 1921–1972* (New York: Praeger, 1972), 474. See also Frederick C. Teiwes, *Politics and Purges in China* (White Plains, N.Y.: M. E. Sharpe, 1979), 349.

9. Harvard Center, *Communist China, 1955–1959*, 16.

10. The following discussion and quotations are taken from Stuart R. Schram, ed., *Chairman Mao Talks to the People: Talks and Letters: 1956–1971* (New York: Pantheon, 1974), 91–124.

11. Hinton (ed.), *The People's Republic of China, 1949–1979*, vol. 2: 639–40.

12. Harvard Center, *Communist China, 1955–1959*, 167.

13. Ibid., 424; also Hinton (ed.), *The People's Republic of China, 1949–1979*, vol. 2: 638.

14. Hinton (ed.), *The People's Republic of China, 1949–1979*, vol. 2: 638.

15. Parris Chang, *Policy and Power in China* (University Park, Pa.: Pennsylvania State University Press, 1975), 83.

16. Richard H. Solomon, *Mao's Revolution and the Chinese Political Culture* (Berkeley: University of California, 1971), 344. Translation altered.

17. Mark Selden, *The People's Republic of China: A Documentary History of Revolutionary Change* (New York: Monthly Review Press, 1979), 413.

18. Chang, *Policy and Power in China*, 114.

19. Han Suyin, *Wind in the Tower* (Boston: Little-Brown, 1976), 128–29.

20. Hinton, *The People's Republic of China*, vol. 2: 685.

21. Kenneth Lieberthal, *A Research Guide to Central Party and Government Meetings in China, 1949–1975* (White Plains, N.Y.: International Arts and Sciences Press, 1976), 133–34.

22. Schram (ed.), *Chairman Mao Talks to the People*, 129.

23. Ellis Joffe, *Between Two Plenums: China's Interleadership Conflict* (Ann Arbor, Mich.: University of Michigan, 1975), 17.

24. Seldon, *The People's Republic of China*, 480.

25. Chang, *Politics and Power in China*, 120.

26. David A. Charles, "The Dismissal of Marshal Peng Te-huai," *China Quarterly*, 8 (1961): 32.

## Chapter 5

1. Shigeru Ishikawa, "China's Economic Growth Since 1949—An Assessment," *China Quarterly,* 94 (June 1983): 247. On the famine and population decline, see Carl Riskin, *China's Political Economy: The Quest for Development Since 1949* (New York: Oxford University Press, 1987), 136.

2. Harold C. Hinton (ed.), *The People's Republic of China, 1949–1979: A Documentary Survey* (Wilmington, Del.: Scholarly Resources, 1980), vol. 2: 862–69 (translation slightly altered).

3. Ibid., vol. 2: 881. The earlier editorial may be found on pp. 874–76 of vol. 2.

4. Sven Lindqvist, *China in Crisis* (New York: Crowell, 1965), 77.

5. Hinton, *The People's Republic of China,* vol. 2: 909f.

6. Stuart R. Schram (ed.), *Chairman Mao Talks to the People: Talks and Letters: 1956–1971* (New York: Pantheon, 1974), 187.

7. Ibid., 167.

8. Nicholas R. Lardy and Kenneth Lieberthal, *Chen Yun's Strategy for China's Development: A Non-Maoist Alternative* (White Plains, N.Y.: M. E. Sharpe, 1983), 194.

9. Richard Baum, *Prelude to Revolution: Mao, the Party, and the Peasant Question, 1962–1966* (New York: Columbia University Press, 1975), 17.

10. Schram, *Chairman Mao Talks to the People,* 190.

11. Frederick C. Teiwes, *Politics and Purges in China* (White Plains, N.Y.: M. E. Sharpe, 1979), 511.

12. Stuart R. Schram, "Introduction: the Cultural Revolution in Historical Perspective," in *Authority, Participation, and Cultural Change in China* (Cambridge: Cambridge University Press, 1973), 84.

13. Ellis Joffe, *Between Two Plenums: China's Intraleadership Conflict, 1959–1962* (Ann Arbor: University of Michigan Center for Chinese Studies, 1975), 54.

14. Hinton (ed.), *The People's Republic of China,* 912.

15. Thomas P. Bernstein, *Up to the Mountains and Down to the Villages: The Transfer of Youth from Urban to Rural China* (New Haven, Conn.: Yale University Press, 1977), 56.

16. Ibid., 96–98.

17. Merle Goldman, *China's Intellectuals: Advise and Dissent* (Cambridge, Mass.: Harvard University Press, 1981), 108.

18. Ibid., 77.

19. Teiwes, *Politics and Purges in China,* 579.

20. K. H. Fan (ed.), *Mao Tse-tung and Lin Piao: Post Revolutionary Writings,* (Garden City, N.Y.: Anchor-Doubleday, 1972), xv.

21, Goldman, *China's Intellectuals,* 93. For a summary of Maoist and Liuist approaches to education in this period, see Suzanne Ogden, *China's Unresolved Issues: Politics, Development, and Culture,* 2d ed. (Englewood Cliffs, N.J.: Prentice-Hall, 1992), 300–7.

22. A. Doak Barnett, *China After Mao* (Princeton, N.J.: Princeton University Press, 1967), 128–29, 149.

23. Roxanne Witke, *Comrade Chiang Ch'ing* (Boston: Little Brown, 1977), 310.

24. Ellis Joffe, "The Chinese Army Under Lin Piao: Prelude to Political Intervention," in *China: Management of a Revolutionary Society,* ed. John M. Lindbeck (Seattle: University of Washington Press, 1971), 359–60.

25. Barnett, *China After Mao,* 123.

26. Byung-joon Ahn, *Chinese Politics and the Cultural Revolution: Dynamics of Policy Processes* (Seattle: University of Washington Press, 1976), 184.

27. Martin Ebon, *Lin Biao: The Life and Writings of China's New Ruler* (New York: Stein & Day, 1970), 224–25.

28. Quoted in Frank E. Rogers, "Sino-American Relations and the Vietnam War, 1964–66," *China Quarterly,* 66 (June 1976): 303.

29. Baum, *Prelude to Revolution,* 143.

30. Ahn, *Chinese Politics and the Cultural Revolution,* 196–97.

## Chapter 6

1. Richard Baum, "China: Year of the Mangoes," in *China in Ferment: Perspectives on the Cultural Revolution,* ed. Richard Baum (Englewood Cliffs, N.J.: Prentice-Hall, 1971), 156n.

2. K. H. Fan, *The Chinese Cultural Revolution: Selected Documents* (New York: Grove Press, 1968), 132.

3. David Milton, Nancy Milton and Franz Schurmann (eds.), *People's China: Social Experimentation, Politics, Entry onto the World Scene, 1966 Through 1972* (New York: Vintage Press, 1974), 284.

4. Harold C. Hinton (ed.), *The People's Republic of China, 1949–1979: A Documentary Survey* (Wilmington, Del.: Scholarly Resources, 1980), vol. 3: 1318–19.

5. Ibid., vol. 3: 1521.

6. Byung-Joon Ahn, *Chinese Politics and the Cultural Revolution: Dynamics of Policy Processes* (Seattle: University of Washington Press, 1976), 223. Regarding the earlier "dog" saying, the original saying, "[Don't] beat a dog that has already fallen in the water," was adapted by noted writer Lu Xun in the title of his 1925 essay, "Severely Beat a Dog Which Has Fallen into the

Water,'' sometimes translated as '' 'Fair Play' Should Be Put Off for the Time Being.''

7. Hinton (ed.), *The People's Republic of China,* vol. 3: 1553.

8. Fan, *The Chinese Cultural Revolution,* 169.

9. Hinton (ed.), *The People's Republic of China,* vol. 3: 1577.

10. Fan, *The Chinese Cultural Revolution,* 163.

11. Mao Tse-tung, *Selected Works of Mao Tse-tung* (Peking: Foreign Languages Press, 1965), vol. 1: 28.

12. Stuart R. Schram, *Chairman Mao Talks to the People: Talks and Letters: 1956–1971* (New York: Pantheon, 1974), 265.

13. Ibid., 273.

14. Ibid., 277.

15. David Milton and Nancy Dall Milton, *The Wind Will Not Subside: Years in Revolutionary China—1964–1969* (New York: Random House, 1976), 291.

16. Edward E. Rice, *Mao's Way* (Berkeley and Los Angeles: University of California Press, 1972), 424 (translation altered).

17. Milton and Milton, *The Wind Will Not Subside,* 321.

18. Ibid., 335.

19. Rice, *Mao's Way,* 454–55.

20. Ross Terrill, *The White-boned Demon: A Biography of Madame Mao Zedong* (New York: Morrow, 1984), 298.

20. Anne F. Thurston, ''Victims of China's Cultural Revolution: The Invisible Wounds,'' *Pacific Affairs,* 58 (Spring 1985): 20. Articles discussing some Chinese analysis are by Stuart R. Schram, ''The Limits of Cataclysmic Change: Reflections on the Place of the 'Great Proletarian Cultural Revolution' in the Political Development of the People's Republic of China,'' *China Quarterly,* 108 (December 1986): 613–24; and Bill Brugger, ''From 'Revisionism' to 'Alienation,' from Great Leaps to 'Third Wave','' *China Quarterly,* 108 (December 1986): 643–51.

21. Lynn T. White, III, *Policies of Chaos: The Organizational Causes of Violence in China's Cultural Revolution* (Princeton, N.J.: Princeton University Press, 1989), 7.

22. For a full treatment of these themes, see ibid.

23. Tang Tsou, ''The Cultural Revolution and the Chinese Political System,'' in Baum (ed.), *China in Ferment,* 192.

24. Hinton, *The People's Republic of China,* vol. 4: 2224.

25. Milton et al., *People's China,* 218.

26. *Beijing Review,* July 6, 1981: 20.

27. Jonathan D. Spence, *The Search for Modern China* (New York: Norton, 1990), 440.

28. Robert Michael Field, "The Performance of Industry During the Cultural Revolution: Second Thoughts," *China Quarterly*, 108 (December 1986): 639. For a similar view, see Lucian W. Pye, "Reassessing the Cultural Revolution," *China Quarterly*, 108 (December 1986): 610.

## Chapter 7

1. Harold C. Hinton (ed.), *The People's Republic of China, 1949–1979: A Documentary Survey* (Wilmington, Del.: Scholarly Resources, 1980), vol. 4: 2239 (romanization changed).

2. Ross Terrill, *Mao: A Biography* (New York: Harper & Row, 1980), 342.

3. Mao Tse-tung, *Selected Works of Mao Tse-tung* (Peking: Foreign Languages Press, 1965), vol. 2: 224.

4. Quoted in Philip Bridgham, "Mao's Cultural Revolution: The Struggle to Consolidate Power," *China Quarterly*, 41 (January–March 1970): 22.

5. Thomas Fingar, "Introduction: The Quest for Independence," in *China's Quest for Independence: Policy Evolution in the 1970s*, ed. Thomas Fingar (Boulder, Colo.: Westview Press, 1980), 43.

6. However, Zhou's writ did not reach everywhere. In 1968 he was unable to prevent the torture and death of his own adopted daughter. And in 1972 all he could do for the relatives of Peng Dehuai, who had long been held incommunicado in solitary confinement, was to express his concern and report on Peng's health. See Fox Butterfield, *China: Alive in the Bitter Sea* (New York: New York Times Books, 1982), 355; and Foreign Broadcast Information Service, *Daily Report—People's Republic of China* (U.S. Department of Commerce, National Technical Information Service), January 24, 1979, E5–E8.

7. Ross Terrill, *Flowers on an Iron Tree: Five Cities of China* (Boston: Little Brown, 1975), 201.

8. Hinton (ed.), *The People's Republic of China*, vol. 4: 2477.

9. Ibid., vol. 4: 2468.

10. Ibid., vol. 4: 2484.

11. Ibid., vol. 4: 2497.

12. Ibid., vol. 4: 2504.

13. Ibid., vol. 4: 2529.

14. Ibid., vol. 4: 2534 (translation altered).

15. Jurgen Domes, *Socialism in the Chinese Countryside: Rural Societal Policies in the People's Republic of China, 1949–1979* (Montreal: McGill-Queen's University Press, 1980), 90 (romanizations have been changed).

16. Ibid., 93.

17. Tang Tsou, Marc Blecher, and Mitch Meisner, "National Agricultural Policy: the Dazhai Model and Local Change in the Post-Mao Era," in Mark

Selden and Victor Lippit, *The Transition to Socialism in China* (Armonk, N.Y.: M. E. Sharpe, 1982), 274.

18. Terrill, *Mao,* 406.

19. Ibid., 413.

20. Philip Short, *The Dragon and the Bear: China and Russia in the Eighties* (New York: William Morrow, 1982), 201.

21. Terrill, *Mao,* 409.


## Chapter 8

1. "Quarterly Chronicle and Documentation," *China Quarterly,* 72 (December 1977): 858.

2. Harold C. Hinton (ed.), *The People's Republic of China, 1949–1979: A Documentary Survey* (Wilmington, Del.: Scholarly Resources, 1980), vol. 4: 2655–56. Emphasis added.

3. Ibid., vol. 4: 2826–27.

4. Ibid., vol. 4: 2719.

5. Quoted in Philip Short, *The Dragon and the Bear: China and Russia in the Eighties* (New York: Morrow, 1982), 243.

6. Ibid., 386.

7. *China Quarterly,* 95 (September 1983): 585.

8. Harry Harding, *China's Second Revolution: Reform After Mao* (Washington, D.C.: Brookings Institution, 1987), 168.

9. Fox Butterfield, *China: Alive in the Bitter Sea* (New York: New York Times Books, 1982), 300.

10. John Fraser, *The Chinese: Portrait of a People* (New York: Summit Books, 1980), 209.

11. James D. Seymour, *China: The Fifth Modernization: China's Human Rights Movement, 1978–1979* (Stanfordville, N.Y.: Human Rights Publishing Group, 1980), 63.

12. Ibid., 50.

13. The 1982 Constitution of the People's Republic of China declared the state to be a "people's democratic dictatorship" rather than a "dictatorship of the proletariat." Deng's first Cardinal Principle was altered accordingly.

14. Barrett L. McCormick, "Leninist Implementation: The Election Campaign," in *Policy Implementation in Post-Mao China,* ed. David M. Lampton (Berkeley and Los Angeles: University of California Press, 1987), 390.

15. Hinton (ed.), *The People's Republic of China,* vol. 4: 2985. Formal expression was later given to this appraisal of Mao at the Sixth Plenum, in the "Resolution on Certain Questions in the History of Our Party." See *Beijing Review,* July 6, 1981; also David S. Goodman, "The Sixth Plenum of the

11th Central Committee of the CCP: Look Back in Anger?'' *China Quarterly,* 87 (September 1981): 518–27.

16. *New York Times,* August 31, 1980 (spelling changed).

17. Bill Brugger, *Chinese Marxism in Flux, 1978–84* (Armonk, N.Y.: M. E. Sharpe, 1985), 10–11.

18. *New York Times,* December 17, 1984.

19. Alvin Rabushka, *The New China* (Boulder, Colo.: Westview Press, 1987), 71.

20. *China Quarterly,* 97 (March 1984): 161.

21. Stuart R. Schram, '' 'Economics in Command?' Ideology & Policy Since the Third Plenum, 1978–84,'' *China Quarterly,* 99 (September 1984): 452.

22. Tony Saich, ''Reforming the Political Structure,'' in *Reforming the Revolution: China in Transition,* ed. Robert Benewick and Paul Wingrove (Boulder, Colo.: Westview Press, 1988), 31.

23. *Christian Science Monitor,* January 14, 1987. See also *New York Times,* March 8, 1987.

24. *New York Times Book Review,* August 9, 1987. The speaker was Wang Ruowang, a Marxist theoretician. The other intellectual was Liu Binyan, a famous investigative reporter.

25. Han Minzhu (ed.), *Cries for Democracy: Writings and Speeches from the 1989 Chinese Democracy Movement* (Princeton, N.J.: Princeton University Press, 1990), 21, 22 (text rearranged).

26. Lee Feigon, *China Rising: The Meaning of Tiananmen* (Chicago: Ivan R. Dee, 1990), 122–23.

## Chapter 9

1. Han Minzhu (ed.), *Cries for Democracy: Writings and Speeches from the 1989 Chinese Democracy Movement* (Princeton, N.J.: Princeton University Press, 1990), 84–85.

2. *Los Angeles Times,* June 25, 1989.

3. Ibid.

4. *New York Times,* May 18, 1989.

5. Lawrence R. Sullivan, ''The Emergence of Civil Society in China, Spring 1989,'' in *The Chinese People's Movement: Perspectives on Spring 1989,* ed. Tony Saich (Armonk, New York: M. E. Sharpe, 1991), 132.

6. Scott Simmie and Bob Nixon, *Tiananmen Square* (Seattle: University of Washington Press, 1989), 125.

7. ''Dialogue Between Li Peng and Students on the Hunger Strike (May 18, 1989),'' *Chinese Law and Government,* 23 (Spring 1990): 47.

8. Han Minzhu (ed.), *Cries for Democracy,* 257.

9. Ibid.

10. Ibid., 320.

11. Ibid., 327.

12. *Los Angeles Times,* June 25, 1989.

13. Amnesty International, *People's Republic of China: Preliminary Findings on Killings of Unarmed Civilians, Arbitrary Arrests and Summary Executions Since June 3, 1989* (New York: Amnesty International USA, August 1989), 3.

14. Lee Feigon, *China Rising: The Meaning of Tiananmen* (Chicago: Ivan R. Dee, 1990), 234.

15. Han Minzhu (ed.), *Cries for Democracy,* 359.

16. *Los Angeles Times,* June 25, 1989.

17. Michel Oksenberg et al. (eds.), *Beijing Spring, 1989: Confrontation and Conflict: The Basic Documents* (Armonk, N.Y.: M. E. Sharpe, 1990), 396.

18. *Guardian Weekly,* June 3, 1990.

## Chapter 10

1. Michel Oksenberg et al. (eds.), *Beijing Spring, 1989: Confrontation and Conflict: The Basic Documents* (Armonk, N.Y.: M. E. Sharpe, 1990), 376–82.

2. *New York Times,* February 13, 1991.

3. Ibid., December 28, 1990.

4. *Foreign Broadcast Information Service, Daily Report: People's Republic of China,* June 26, 1989, 15–16.

5. *New York Times,* July 16, 1989.

6. *China News Analysis,* April 15, 1992, 3.

7. *China News Analysis,* November 1, 1992, 2.

8. National Bureau of Economic Research and Harvard University, "The Penn World Table (Mark 5.5)," Cambridge: National Bureau of Economic Research, 1993 (electronically obtained). See Robert Summers and Alan Heston, "The Penn World Table (Mark 5): An Expanded Set of International Comparisons, 1950–1988," *Quarterly Journal of Economics,* 106 (May 1991): 327–68. These estimaes represent an attempt to solve the difficult problem of cross-national comparison and should be interpreted cautiously.

9. Mark Seldon, *The People's Republic of China: A Documentary History of Revolutionary Change* (New York: Monthly Review Press, 1979), 480.

# Suggested Readings

The enormous literature on China cannot be adequately represented by a brief list. The student who wishes to get a sense of the breadth of scholarship in this field is invited to examine the book review sections of publications such as *The China Quarterly* or *The Journal of Asian Studies*. What follows here is a sampling of some of the more important and interesting writing accessible to the serious general reader.

## General History

Associated Press Writers and Photographers. *China: From the Long March to Tiananmen Square*. New York: Henry Holt & Co., 1990. A useful general summary of the Chinese Communist movement accompanied by photographs, with particular emphasis on explaining the genesis of the 1989 Tiananmen events.

Eastman, Lloyd E. *Family, Fields, and Ancestors: Constancy and Changes in China's Social and Economic History, 1550–1949*. New York: Oxford University Press, 1988. A collection of essays by a historian of the Republican period, synthesizing recent scholarship on the social and economic background to the People's Republic.

Hinton, Harold C. (ed.). *The People's Republic of China, 1949–1979: A Documentary Survey*. 5 vols. Wilmington, Del.: Scholarly Resources, 1980. A comprehensive collection of previously translated materials covering every aspect of domestic and foreign policy.

——— (ed.). *The People's Republic of China, 1979–1984: A Documentary Survey*. 2 vols. Wilmington, Del.: Scholarly Resources, 1986. The continuation of the earlier five-volume collection. Coverage includes domestic and foreign policy.

MacFarquhar, Roderick, and John K. Fairbank (eds.). *The Cambridge History of China, Volume 14: The People's Republic, Part 1: The Emergence of Revolutionary China, 1949–1965*. New York: Cambridge University Press, 1987. Part of a multivolume history of China, this first volume on the PRC includes essays by major scholars on politics, economics, culture, education, foreign affairs, and a bibliography. Despite its stubborn loyalty to an obsolescent spelling system, it is an outstanding resource.

——— (eds.). *The Cambridge History of China, Volume 15: The People's Republic, Part 2: Revolutions Within the Chinese Revolution, 1966–1982*. New York: Cambridge University Press, 1991. This second volume on the PRC contains essays by major scholars on politics, economics, rural and urban life, education, culture, relations with the U.S. and the USSR, Taiwan, plus a bibliography.

Mao, Tse-tung [Mao Zedong]. *Chairman Mao Talks to the People: Talks and Letters: 1956–1971*. Edited by Stuart R. Schram. New York: Pantheon Books, 1974. A collection of Mao's utterances revealing the colorful and contradictory character of the revolutionary leader.

———. *Selected Works*. 5 vols. Peking: Foreign Languages Press, 1961–77. Edited speeches and writings from 1927 to 1957.

Meisner, Maurice. *Mao's China and After: A History of the People's Republic*. New York: The Free Press, 1985. A revision of the author's *Mao's China* and a general history of the People's Republic with a pronounced political science orientation.

Salisbury, Harrison E. *The New Emperors: China in the Era of Mao and Deng*. Boston: Little, Brown, 1992. Although criticized as journalistic and sensationalist, this sweeping account of China's leaders makes lively reading. Based on extensive interviews and other (sometimes dubious) sources.

Selden, Mark (ed.). *The People's Republic of China: A Documentary History of Revolutionary Change*. New York: Monthly Review Press, 1979. Documents and commentary from the civil war years to Mao's death.

Spence, Jonathan D. *The Search for Modern China*. New York: W. W. Norton, 1990. An outstanding historian's broad narrative of China from 1600 to the present, richly detailed and well illustrated.

Terrill, Ross. *China in Our Time: The Epic Saga of the People's Republic, from the Communist Victory to Tiananmen Square and Beyond*. New York: Simon & Schuster, 1992. Highly readable account of PRC history and of the author's changing personal reactions to events. By an Australian-born author who visited China many times, beginning in 1964.

## History of Specific Periods

*Pre-1949*

Brandt, Conrad, Benjamin Schwartz, and John K. Fairbank. *A Documentary Survey of Chinese Communism*. Cambridge: Harvard University Press, 1959. Important documents from the early days of the CCP until liberation.

Pepper, Suzanne. *Civil War in China: The Political Struggle, 1945–1949*. Berkeley: University of California Press, 1978. A study of the civil war years that brings out the weaknesses of the Nationalist regime.

Snow, Edgar. *Red Star Over China*. Revised and enlarged ed. New York: Grove Press, 1968. Influential reportage of the Chinese Communists on the eve of the anti-Japanese war; first published in 1938. Contains unique autobiographical material on Mao.

*The 1950s*

Barnett, A. Doak. *Communist China: The Early Years, 1949–1955*. New York: Praeger, 1964. An account of the consolidation period by one of the most eminent American experts.

Center of International Affairs and the East Asian Research Center. *Communist China 1955–1959: Policy Documents with Analysis*. Cambridge: Harvard University Press, 1965. Documents relating to the First Five-Year Plan and the Great Leap Forward.

Hinton, William. *Fanshen: A Documentary of Revolution in a Chinese Village*. New York: Random House, 1966. A famous firsthand account of revolutionary transformation in north China during the years leading up to and immediately after liberation.

Kau, Michael Y. M., and John K. Leung (eds.). *The Writings of Mao Zedong, 1949–1976: Vol. 1, September 1949–December 1955*. Armonk, N.Y.: M. E. Sharpe, 1986. Part of an ongoing effort to translate all newly available writings of Mao.

MacFarquhar, Roderick. *The Origins of the Cultural Revolution, 1: Contradictions Among the People 1956–1957*. New York: Columbia University Press, 1974. A detailed study of pre-Great Leap Forward period politics, particularly the Hundred Flowers movement.

*The Great Leap and the Early 1960s*

Baum, Richard. *Prelude to Revolution: Mao, the Party, and the Peasant Question, 1962–1966*. New York: Columbia University Press, 1975. A study of the Socialist Education movement (1962–66) providing insights into the nature of mobilization campaigns.

Lindqvist, Sven. *China in Crisis*. New York: Crowell, 1965. Observations of a Swedish student in China during the post-Great Leap Forward crisis of the early 1960s.

MacFarquhar, Roderick. *The Origins of the Cultural Revolution, 2: The Great Leap Forward*. New York: Columbia University Press, 1983. The continuation of the author's three-volume study, focusing on the politics of the Great Leap Forward. Rich in detail.

————, Timothy Cheek, and Eugene Wu (eds.). *The Secret Speeches of Chairman Mao: From the Hundred Flowers to the Great Leap Forward*. Cambridge: Harvard University Press, 1989. A collection of Mao's speeches and communications from more than twenty unofficial collections.

### From the Cultural Revolution to Mao's Death

Cheng, Nien. *Life and Death in Shanghai*. New York: Grove Press, 1987. An autobiographical account, by a woman of privilege, of seven years of imprisonment during the Cultural Revolution.

Fan, K. H. *The Cultural Revolution: Selected Documents*. New York: Grove Press, 1968. Translations of important pronouncements and documents.

Goldman, Merle. *China's Intellectuals: Advise and Dissent*. Cambridge: Harvard University Press, 1981. A study of establishment and dissenting intellectuals and how they played a role in the political events before and during the Cultural Revolution.

Liang, Heng, and Judith Shapiro. *Son of the Revolution*. New York: Knopf, 1983. Autobiographical account of a young man who grew up during the Cultural Revolution ferment and, after many vicissitudes, met and married an American.

Hunter, Neal. *Shanghai Journal: An Eyewitness Account of the Cultural Revolution*. Boston: Beacon Press, 1971. Describes the early years of the Cultural Revolution as experienced firsthand in Shanghai.

Lee, Hong Yung. *Politics of the Chinese Cultural Revolution: A Case Study*. Berkeley: University of California Press, 1978. A many-faceted survey and analysis, which emphasizes cleavages and factionalism within the Party, the Red Guards, and the worker rebels and between the Party and the people.

Milton, David, and Nancy Dall Milton. *The Wind Will Not Subside*. New York: Pantheon, 1976. A sympathetic first-hand account of the Cultural Revolution by American language teachers in Beijing.

Robinson, Thomas W. (ed.). *The Cultural Revolution in China*. Berkeley: University of California Press, 1971. Analyses of the Cultural Revolution by several specialists.

Thurston, Anne. *Enemies of the People: The Ordeal of the Intellectuals in*

*China's Great Cultural Revolution*. Cambridge: Harvard University Press, 1988. One of the best accounts of the ordeal of the intellectuals in the Cultural Revolution. It is based on interviews conducted by the author in 1980 and 1981.

Yuan, Gao. *Born Red: A Chronicle of the Cultural Revolution*. Stanford: Stanford University Press, 1987. A moving account of the tragedy of the Cultural Revolution, by a man who participated as a high school student.

## The Reform Era

Bernstein, Richard. *From the Center of the Earth: A Search for the Truth About China*. Boston: Little Brown, 1982. Wide-ranging reportage of China during the early years of reform.

Bonavia, David. *The Chinese*. New York: Lippincott and Crowell, 1980. A description of rural and urban social life in the post-Mao era with comparisons drawn to the Soviet Union.

Butterfield, Fox. *China: Alive in the Bitter Sea*. New York: New York Times Books, 1982. A highly critical description of post-Mao China by a *New York Times* correspondent, treating topics ranging from bureaucratic structure to love and sex. The Chinese government denounced this book when it was published.

Fraser, John. *The Chinese: Portrait of a People*. New York: Summit Books, 1980. A rather personal account of a Canadian journalist's experiences in Beijing during the time of the Democracy Wall movement (1979).

Liang, Heng, and Judith Shapiro. *After the Nightmare*. New York: Knopf, 1986. Description by an emigré intellectual and his wife (see above) of a 1985 visit to places he knew during the Cultural Revolution. Finds many warts on Deng's China.

Mosher, Steven W. *Broken Earth: The Rural Chinese*. New York: The Free Press, 1983. A very unfavorable picture of rural China in the early 1980s, written by an anthropologist who studied in a southern village. The book and its author were controversial.

Yim, Kwan Ha (ed.). *China Under Deng*. New York: Facts on File, 1991. Materials previously published by Facts on File from 1979 to 1989, organized chronologically.

## Tiananmen

Amnesty International. *China: The Massacre of June 1989 and Its Aftermath*. New York: Amnesty International Publications, 1990. A detailed although sometimes nonanalytic collection of eyewitness accounts and

Chinese articles relating to the suppression of the demonstrations in Beijing and Chengdu, and the subsequent crackdown.

DesForges, Roger V., Ning Luo, and Yenbo Wu (eds.). *China: The Crisis of 1989, Origins and Implications*. Buffalo: Council on International Studies and Programs, State University of New York, 1990. An excellent two-volume anthology of essays from a conference of specialists analyzing Tiananmen events from historical, economic, political, social, international, and other perspectives.

Duke, Michael S. *The Iron House: A Memoir of the Chinese Democracy Movement and the Tiananmen Massacre*. Layton, Utah: Gibbs Smith, 1990. The personal account of a professor, fluent in Chinese, who describes events leading up to the massacre and the confusing emotions and misconceptions experienced by the participants.

Feigon, Lee. *China Rising: The Meaning of Tiananmen*. Chicago: Ivan R. Dee, 1990. An early attempt to put the 1989 events in historical perspective and to bring out some of the complexities and weaknesses in the democracy movement.

Han, Minzhu (ed.). *Cries for Democracy: Writings and Speeches from the 1989 Chinese Democracy Movement*. Princeton: Princeton University Press, 1990. An extensive collection of speeches, posters, and other materials from the various participants in the protest movement.

Jiang, Zhifeng. *Countdown to Tiananmen: The View from the Top*. San Francisco: Democratic China Books, Inc., Pacific News Service Inc., 1990. A partial translation of the Chinese "The Zhongnanhai Bridge Club That Has Cast Its Last Trump," this is a memoir by a man who claims to have been a staff aide to top Party officials. He offers his critical examination of policy decisions during the crisis.

Lord, Bette Bao. *Legacies: A Chinese Mosaic*. New York: Knopf, 1990. An account of ordinary Chinese, based on interviews conducted during the 1989 Tiananmen events by noted Chinese-American author and wife of a former U.S. ambassador to China.

Oksenberg, Michel, Lawrence R. Sullivan, and Marc Lambert (eds.). *Beijing Spring 1989: Confrontation and Conflict, The Basic Documents*. Armonk, N.Y.: M. E. Sharpe, 1990. Translated documents relating to the events at Tiananmen and the background from a central and official perspective, as distinguished from voices of the street.

Porter, Edgar A., and Mardy Fones (eds.). *Journalism from Tiananmen: Anthology by Gannett Foundation Fellows University of Hawaii*. Honolulu: University of Hawaii, 1990. Essays by six authors describing the life and mood in Beijing and other cities in the aftermath of the suppression at Tiananmen.

Saich, Tony (ed.). *The Chinese People's Movement: Perspectives on Spring 1989*. Armonk, N.Y.: M. E. Sharpe, 1991. An outstanding anthology which includes an account of events, together with essays on the larger background and context, plus an extensive bibliography.

Simmie, Scott, and Bob Nixon. *Tiananmen Square: An Eyewitness Account of the Chinese People's Passionate Quest for Democracy*. Seattle: University of Washington Press, 1989. A journalistic account of the condition of intellectuals and the student demonstrations, but somewhat simplistic in its larger explanations.

Tong, Shen, with Marianne Yeh. *Almost A Revolution: The Story of a Chinese Student's Journey From Boyhood to Leadership in Tiananmen Square*. Boston: Houghton Mifflin, 1990. This book by an important participant in the Tiananmen events provides insight into the events and cultural forces, domestic and foreign, that influenced the students, and also describes the divisions among the Tiananmen demonstrators.

Unger, Jonathan (ed.). *The Pro-Democracy Protests in China: Reports from the Provinces*. Armonk, N.Y.: M. E. Sharpe, 1991. A collection of reports on the pro-democracy demonstrations that took place around the country in 1989, showing considerable regional variations in intensity.

Yang, Winston L. Y., and Marsha L. Wagner (eds.). *Tiananmen: China's Struggle for Democracy, Its Prelude, Aftermath and Impact*. Baltimore: University of Maryland School of Law, 1990. A collection of essays, some excellent, but undermined by the editors' inability to control their outrage.

Yu, Mok Chiu, and J. Frank Harrison (eds.). *Voices from Tiananmen Square: Beijing Spring and the Democracy Movement*. Montreal and New York: Black Rose Books, 1990. Despite the editors' strongly negative bias, this is an excellent collection of statements from participants in the Tiananmen demonstrations, many unavailable elsewhere.

## Politics and Foreign Relations

Barnett, A. Doak. *The Making of Foreign Policy in China: Structure and Process*. Boulder: Westview Press, 1985. Based on 1984 interviews with top Chinese leaders, including Zhao Ziyang, this book provides a focused examination of policy formulation and implementation.

Barmé, Geremie, and John Minford (eds.). *Seeds of Fire: Chinese Voices of Conscience*. New York: Hill and Wang, 1988. A collection of writings by political dissidents and of political pieces by creative writers.

Burns, John P., and Stanley Rosen. *Policy Conflicts in Post-Mao China: A Documentary Survey with Analysis*. Armonk, N.Y.: M. E. Sharpe, 1986. A diverse selection of 86 Chinese radio and press reports from 1979 to 1985, with introductions.

Camilleri, Joseph. *Chinese Foreign Policy: The Maoist Era and Its Aftermath*. Seattle: University of Washington Press, 1980. An excellent survey of foreign policy up to the late 1970s.

Chang, Gordon H. *Friends and Enemies: The United States, China, and the Soviet Union, 1948–1972*. Stanford: Stanford University Press, 1990. A history of official American analyses of Sino-Soviet relations, based on newly opened archives. This book underscores the stresses between Moscow and Beijing.

Chang, Parris. *Policy and Power in China*. University Park: Pennsylvania State University Press, 1975. A study of the policy-making process prior to the Cultural Revolution, examining whether the earlier monolithic structure had been replaced by a "struggle between two lines."

Gittings, John. *The World and China, 1922–1972*. New York: Harper & Row, 1974. An overview of China's foreign affairs that explores connections between the pre-Communist and PRC policies. Based on careful analysis of Chinese sources.

Goldman, Merle, Timothy Cheek, and Carol Lee Hamrin (eds.). *China's Intellectuals and the State: In Search of a New Relationship*. Cambridge: Harvard University Press, 1987. Essays on the relationship of intellectuals and the state in the Deng Xiaoping era.

Gurtov, Melvin, and Byong-Moo Hwant. *China Under Threat: The Politics of Strategy and Diplomacy*. Baltimore: Johns Hopkins University Press, 1980. An excellent examination of five case studies in foreign policy-making (from 1950 to 1965), arguing that domestic issues were the primary determinants.

Hamrin, Carol Lee. *China and the Challenge of the Future: Changing Political Patterns*. Boulder: Westview Press, 1989. An outstanding account of the reform period and of the policy process, based on interviews with decision makers.

———, and Timothy Cheek (eds.). *China's Establishment Intellectuals*. Armonk, N.Y.: M. E. Sharpe, 1986. Essays exploring the relationship between leading intellectuals and China's political leadership.

Harding, Harry. *Organizing China: The Problem of Bureaucracy, 1949–1976*. Stanford: Stanford University Press, 1981. Excellent study of the development of organizational policy affecting the Party and the state administration.

——— (ed.). *China's Foreign Relations in the 1980s*. New Haven: Yale University Press, 1984. A collection of essays examining the relationship between domestic reforms and the new "open door" toward the industrialized west.

———. *China's Second Revolution: Reform After Mao*. Washington, D.C.: The Brookings Institution, 1987. A comprehensive discussion of economic and political reform under Deng Xiaoping, particularly strong on economics.

Kim, Samuel S. (ed.). *China and the World: New Directions in Chinese Foreign Relations*. 2d rev. ed. Boulder: Westview Press, 1989. A dozen essays on aspects of China's foreign relations in the reform period by experts in the field.

———. *China In and Out of the Changing World Order*. Princeton: Princeton University Center of International Studies, 1991. A brief essay attempting to analyze China's recent foreign policy in terms of its contribution to creating a new world order. He finds China's approach to be state-centered, neo-mercantilist, and essentially unprincipled.

Kraus, Richard Curt. *Class Conflict in Chinese Socialism*. New York: Columbia University Press, 1981. A study of the policies toward class designations after 1949 showing how the bases for class attribution changed from economic background, to political behavior, to entrenched interests.

Lieberthal, Kenneth, and Michel Oksenberg. *Policy Making in China: Leaders, Structures, and Processes*. Princeton: Princeton University Press, 1988. Using three case studies, the authors analyze the decision-making process within Chinese bureaucracies. A highly regarded study.

Nathan, Andrew. *Chinese Democracy*. New York: Knopf, 1985. Berkeley: University of California Press, 1986. An analysis of the concept of democracy in Chinese political culture.

Nee, Victor, and David Mozingo (eds.). *State and Society in Contemporary China*. Ithaca, N.Y.: Cornell University Press, 1983. Essays by prominent American political scientists on the nature and exercise of state power before and after Mao.

Pye, Lucian. *The Dynamics of Chinese Politics*. Cambridge: Oelgeschlager, Gunn, and Hain, 1981. A psychocultural analysis of factional behavior in Chinese politics.

Solomon, Richard. *Mao's Revolution and the Chinese Political Culture*. Berkeley: University of California Press, 1971. A provocative analysis of Chinese politics from the perspective of political culture, socialization, and Mao's personality.

Sutter, Robert G. *Chinese Foreign Policy: Developments After Mao*. New York: Praeger, 1986. An account of the complexities of major foreign policy decisions from the death of Mao to the mid-1980s.

Teiwes, Frederick C. *Politics and Purges in China*. White Plains, N.Y.: M. E. Sharpe, 1979. An analysis of organizational norms governing political activity within the Party elite and the degree to which Mao respected them.

White, Lynn. *Policies of Chaos: The Organizational Causes of Violence in China's Cultural Revolution*. Princeton: Princeton University Press, 1989. From a close study of Shanghai, the author develops the theme that the chaotic violence of the Cultural Revolution can be traced back to long-standing policies of class labeling, clientelism, and policy implementation through campaigns.

Whyte, Martin King. *Small Groups and Political Rituals in China*. Berkeley: University of California Press, 1974. Systematic study of the "small group," a key institution for organizing criticism and self-criticism. The study is based on interviews with Hong Kong refugees.

Yahuda, Michael. *Towards the End of Isolationism*. New York: St. Martin's Press, 1984. A broad study of the geopolitical basis for the continuity in foreign policy after the death of Mao.

## Economic Development

Ash, Robert F., and Y. Y. Kueh. "The Chinese Economy in the 1990s." Special Issue of *The China Quarterly*, No. 131 (September 1992). Eight essays on various aspects of China's economic performance and prospects.

Banister, Judith. *China's Changing Population*. Stanford: Stanford University Press, 1987. A thorough discussion of fertility, mortality, and other population topics for the entire Communist period.

Barnett, A. Doak. *China's Economy in Global Perspective*. Washington, D.C.: The Brookings Institution, 1981. An encyclopedic survey of all facets of the Chinese economic system.

Byrd, William A. *The Market Mechanism and Economic Reforms in China*. Armonk, N.Y.: M. E. Sharpe, 1991. A rather technical study of China's economy in the 1980s, arguing that a two-tier policy, incorporating both plan and market, has helped negotiate the difficult transition to a more productive economy.

He, Bochuan. *China on the Edge: The Crisis of Ecology and Development*. Berkeley: Pacific View Press, 1991. Originally published and then suppressed in the People's Republic, this work attacks both Mao and Deng's environmental and economic policies. The discussions of water, air, land, and forest degradation are alarming.

Howe, Christopher. *China's Economy: A Basic Guide*. New York: Basic Books, 1978. A good introduction to the economic system prior to the recent reforms.

Lardy, Nicholas R. *Foreign Trade and Economic Reform in China, 1978–1990*. Cambridge and New York: Cambridge University Press, 1992. A study of the role that rapidly expanding foreign trade has played in China's economic growth under the reforms.

Nee, Victor, and David Stark (eds.). *Remaking the Economic Institutions of Socialism: China and Eastern Europe*. Stanford: Stanford University Press, 1989. A collection of articles comparing the process of economic transformation in China and in former Soviet satellites.

Nolan, Peter, and Dong Furen. *Market Forces in China: Competition and Small Business—the Wenzhou Debate*. London: ZED Books, 1989. Essays by Chinese and Western economists on the dynamic local enterprise sector, in particular the rapid development of the Wenzhou area.

Rabushka, Alvin. *The New China: Comparative Economic Development in Mainland China, Taiwan, and Hong Kong*. Boulder: Westview Press, 1987. A brief, accessible comparative examination of economic change in three different Chinese settings.

Riskin, Carl. *China's Political Economy, the Quest for Development since 1949*. New York: Oxford University Press, 1987. A thorough analysis of economic development from 1949 to 1985.

Ross, Lester. *Environmental Policy in China*. Bloomington: Indiana University Press, 1988. A study comparing the relative efficacy for environmental control of three approaches: bureaucratic-authoritative, campaign-exhortation, and market-exchange.

Smil, Vaclav. *The Bad Earth: Environmental Degradation in China*. Armonk, N.Y.: M. E. Sharpe, 1984. An important survey of revelations made in the late 1970s concerning China's deteriorating environment.

## Social Conditions and Human Rights

Amnesty International. *China: Punishment Without Crime: Administrative Detention*. New York: Amnesty International Publications, 1991. Describes "administrative detention," the practices under which individuals are held without charges or judicial procedures. The Chinese government denies violations, but since 1989 has suppressed discussions of these issues. AI offers evidence that large numbers of people are involved.

———. *People's Republic of China: Repression in Tibet, 1987–1992*. New York: Amnesty International Publications, 1992. Concludes that there are many prisoners of conscience in Tibet and much abuse of legal procedures and penal conditions.

Andors, Phyllis. *The Unfinished Liberation of Chinese Women, 1949–1980*. Bloomington: Indiana University Press, 1983. The most cogently argued and persuasive explanation to date of why socialism has failed to realize the avowed feminist goals of the CCP.

Bao, Ruo-wang. *Prisoner of Mao*. London: Andre Deutsch, 1975. A rare account of China's prisons in the early 1960s by a Franco-Chinese.

Chan, Anita. *Children of Mao: Personality Development and Political Activism in the Red Guard Generation*. Seattle: University of Washington Press, 1985. A study of personality development in fourteen young Chinese, based on interviews.

———, Richard Madsen, and Jonathan Unger. *Chen Village: The Recent History of a Peasant Community in Mao's China*. Berkeley: University of California Press, 1984. A study of the effects of changing policies on the people of a single south China village, based on systematic interviews of exiles in Hong Kong.

Chu, Godwin C., and Francis L. K. Hsu. *Moving a Mountain: Cultural Change in China*. Honolulu: University Press of Hawaii, 1979. A collection of studies on how different segments of Chinese society reacted and adapted to the government's efforts at political and social transformation.

Cohen, Jerome A. *The Criminal Process in the People's Republic of China, 1949–63: An Introduction*. Cambridge: Harvard University Press, 1968. A pioneering study of the judicial system as it existed prior to the Cultural Revolution.

Croll, Elisabeth. *Chinese Women Since Mao*. Armonk, N.Y.: M. E. Sharpe, 1983. A brief assessment of the achievements and shortcomings of gender-related policies, especially after 1976, showing how other objectives, such as general economic development, frequently conflicted with full equality for women.

Davin, Delia. *Woman-Work: Women and the Party in Revolutionary China*. Oxford: Clarendon Press, 1976. A study of official policies toward women from the time of the Soviets in the 1930s, with particular emphasis on the 1950s. A painstakingly researched work.

Davis-Friedman, Deborah. *Long Lives: Chinese Elderly and the Communist Revolution*. Cambridge: Harvard University Press, 1983. A study of policies toward China's growing population of the elderly.

Dixon, John. *The Chinese Welfare System*. New York: Praeger, 1981. A broad examination of social welfare policies and their effects.

Frolic, B. Michael. *Mao's People: Sixteen Portraits of Life in Revolutionary China*. Cambridge: Harvard University Press, 1980. Revealing individual and composite depictions of individuals and their adaptation to the revolution.

Grunfeld, A. Tom. *The Making of Modern Tibet*. Armonk, N.Y.: M. E. Sharpe, 1987. A detailed account of Tibet's history, one half covering earliest times until 1950, the other half dealing with the period since 1950. The author attempts an even-handed approach and is less critical of Chinese policies than other observers.

Heberer, Thomas. *China and Its National Minorities, Autonomy or Assimilation*. Armonk, N.Y.: M. E. Sharpe, 1989. A broad discussion of issues relating to China's minorities.;

Henderson, Gail, and Myron Cohen. *The Chinese Hospital: A Socialist Work Unit*. New Haven: Yale University Press, 1984. A close description of a "danwei" or work unit, based on first-hand observation.

Honig, Emily, and Hershatter, Gail. *Personal Voices: Chinese Women in the 1980s*. Stanford: Stanford University Press, 1988. A study of socialization, adornment, love, marriage, family, divorce, work, violence, and inequality, based on interviews and printed sources. Shows the difficult road women have yet to travel in China.

Huang, Shu-min. *The Spiral Road: Change in a Chinese Village Through the Eyes of a Communist Party Leader*. Boulder: Westview Press, 1989. The biography of a village Party leader in coastal Fujian Province, revealing in microcosm the stages of the revolution and the changes under reform.

Johnson, Kay Ann. *Women, the Family and Peasant Revolution in China*. Chicago: University of Chicago Press, 1983. A study of policies affecting rural women from 1920 to 1979.

Kraus, Richard Curt. *Pianos and Politics in China: Middle Class Ambitions and the Struggle over Western Music*. New York: Oxford University Press, 1989. A study of how the piano, symbol of middle-class gentility, modernity, and westernization, figured in China's political vicissitudes. The author focuses particularly on the careers of four important musicians.

Link, Perry, Richard Madsen, and Paul Pickowicz (eds.). *Unofficial China: Popular Culture and Thought in the People's Republic*. Boulder: Westview Press, 1989. A collection of articles on diverse topics such as wedding and funeral rituals, youth attitudes, popular cinema, and domestic interiors.

Liu, Binyan. *China's Crisis, China's Hope*. Translated by Howard Goldblatt. Cambridge: Harvard University Press, 1990. A somewhat optimistic prognosis for China by its most renowned journalist-writer, now living in exile, who sees himself as a loyal opposition.

Pepper, Suzanne. *China's Education Reform in the 1980s: Policies, Issues and Historical Perspectives*. Berkeley: University of California Press, 1990. An excellent brief discussion of education policy in the reform period, viewed in the context of historical difficulties and dilemmas and with international comparisons.

Schell, Orville. *To Get Rich is Glorious*. New York: Pantheon Books, 1984.
A journalistic description of Chinese society under the influence of
reforms and Western influence, based on travels in 1983 and 1984.

————. *Discos and Democracy: China in the Throes of Reform*. New York:
1988. A reportorial account of China in 1986 and 1987, particularly
interesting for its description of three major intellectuals, Fang Lizhi,
Liu Binyan, and Wang Ruo-wang, all since exiled.

Seymour, James D. (ed.). *China: The Fifth Modernization: China's Human
Rights Movement, 1977–1979*. Stanfordville, N.Y.: Human Rights
Publishing Group, 1980. This collection contains materials written
by dissidents, some of whom were subsequently imprisoned.

Shirk, Susan. *Competitive Comrades: Career Incentives and Student Strategies in China*. Berkeley: University of California Press, 1982. A
revealing study, based partly on interviews, of the effect that revolutionary educational policies had on the behavior of urban students
in the period prior to the Cultural Revolution.

Unger, Jonathan. *Education under Mao: Class and Competition in Canton
Schools, 1960–1980*. New York: Columbia University Press, 1982.
Examines the effect of changing class policies on the educational
opportunities facing various social groups.

Whyte, Martin King, and William L. Parish. *Urban Life in Contemporary
China*. Chicago: University of Chicago Press, 1984. A study of the
economic and social life of people in Chinese cities, especially in
the mid-1970s.

Wolf, Margery. *Revolution Postponed: Women in Contemporary China*. Stanford: Stanford University Press, 1985. As the title implies, this study
argues that, despite some progress, the revolution in the status of
Chinese women has been continually postponed, both under Mao
and in the subsequent reform period.

————, and Roxane Witke. *Women in Chinese Society*. Stanford: Stanford
University Press, 1975. A collection of ten essays on the status of
women in Chinese society both before and after liberation and also
in Taiwan. Authored from a variety of perspectives: historical, an-
thropological, sociological, and literary.

Yue, Daiyun. *To the Storm: The Odyssey of a Revolutionary Chinese Woman*.
Berkeley: University of California Press, 1985. An intellectual
woman's account of dedication to, and victimization by, the Chinese
revolution.

Zhang, Xinxin, and Sang Ye. *Chinese Lives: An Oral History of Contemporary China*. Edited by W. J. F. Jenner and Delia Davin. New York:
Pantheon Books, 1987. A look at China in the mid-1980s from the
perspective of the person on the street. From interviews conducted
in 1984 by a Chinese writer and a Chinese journalist.

## Biographies

Bachman, David M. *Chen Yun and the Chinese Political System*. Berkeley: Institute of East Asian Studies, Center for Chinese Studies, University of California, 1985. A chronicle of Chen's career up to 1984 and a discussion of his economic thought and his role in the post-Mao reforms.

Dittmer, Lowell. *Liu Shao-ch'i and the Chinese Cultural Revolution*. Berkeley: University of California Press, 1975. A political biography of Mao's second-in-command and a study of the Mao-Liu rupture from the perspective of their personalities, styles, and policies.

Domes, Jürgen. *P'eng Te-huai: The Man and the Image*. Stanford: Stanford University Press, 1985. As the title implies, this is not only a biography of Peng Dehuai but also a study of the political uses of his image after his downfall.

Ebon, Martin. *Lin Biao: The Life and Writings of China's New Leader*. New York: Stein and Day, 1970. Biographical information and documents on Lin and other radicals, compiled just prior to Lin's fall.

Klein, Donald W., and Anne B. Clark. *Biographic Dictionary of Chinese Communism, 1921–1965*. Cambridge: Harvard University Press, 1971. A two-volume biographical dictionary of all major figures during the early years and up to the Cultural Revolution.

Pye, Lucian. *Mao Tse-tung: The Man in the Leader*. New York: Basic Books, 1976. A stimulating and exploratory psychobiography that attempts to explain Mao's personality primarily by his relationship to his mother.

Robinson, Thomas W. "Chou En-lai and the Cultural Revolution in China." In *The Cultural Revolution in China*, edited by Thomas W. Robinson. Berkeley: University of California Press, 1971. An illuminating comparison of the political styles of Zhou Enlai, Mao Zedong, and Lin Biao.

Schram, Stuart R. *Mao Tse-tung*. New York: Simon & Schuster, 1967. An authoritative account of Mao's life not including the last decade.

———. *Mao Zedong: A Preliminary Reassessment*. New York: St. Martin's Press, 1984. An examination of Mao's development as a political thinker, starting with his early contributions and ending with the Cultural Revolution years when Maoism itself became a major problem.

Shambaugh, David L. *The Making of a Premier: Zhao Ziyang's Provincial Career*. Boulder: Westview Press, 1984. A political biography, showing what qualities and credentials enabled Zhao to rise to the top.

Spence, Jonathan D. *The Gate of Heavenly Peace: The Chinese and Their*

*Revolution, 1895–1980.* New York: Viking Press, 1981. An absorbing account of the lives of major leftist intellectuals from the turn of the century through the 1970s.

Terrill, Ross. *The White-boned Demon: A Biography of Madame Mao Zedong.* New York: Morrow, 1984. A popular biography of Jiang Qing that uses many unorthodox sources.

Wilson, Dick. *Zhou Enlai: A Biography.* New York: Viking Press, 1984. A carefully crafted and much needed survey of the public life of China's most admired revolutionary leader.

Witke, Roxane. *Comrade Chiang Ch'ing.* Boston: Little Brown, 1977. A biography of Mao's wife built around interviews granted to Professor Witke in 1972. Publication of this book helped poison the relationship between Mao and Jiang Qing.

Yang, Zhongmei. *Hu Haobang: A Chinese Biography.* Translated by William A. Wycoff. Armonk, N.Y.: M. E. Sharpe, 1988. A highly favorable account of Hu's career, ideas, and character.

## Literature, Arts, and Criticism

Ansley, Clive. *The Heresy of Wu Han: His Play "Hai Jui's Dismissal" and Its Role in China's Cultural Revolution.* Toronto: University of Toronto Press, 1971. This is the famous historical play that triggered the Cultural Revolution.

Bei, Dao. *The August Sleepwalker.* Translated by Bonnie S. McDougall. New York: New Directions, 1990. A collection of the work of one of China's most highly regarded young poets.

Chen, Ruoxi. *The Old Man and Other Stories.* Hong Kong: Renditions Paperback, 1986. Simple, beautiful, painful tales about life in China. (See also Ch'en Jo-hsi.)

Ch'en Jo-hsi, *The Execution of Mayor Yin, and Other Stories from the Great Proletarian Cultural Revolution.* Bloomington: University of Indiana Press, 1978. A collection of powerful short stories about the waning years of the Cultural Revolution, written by an overseas Chinese who returned to the motherland and then left in disillusionment.

Chen, Yuan-tsung. *The Dragon's Village.* New York: Penguin Books, 1980. A novel about the land reform period, portraying the experiences of idealistic young Party workers who come from Shanghai and must cope with the complexity and violence of a miserable northern village.

Duke, Michael S. (ed.). *Contemporary Chinese Literature: An Anthology of Post-Mao fiction and Poetry.* Armonk, N.Y.: M. E. Sharpe, 1985. A collection from the early-1980s.

────── (ed.). *Modern Chinese Women Writers: Critical Appraisals*. Armonk,
N.Y.: M. E. Sharpe, 1989. A collection of articles about the work
of Chinese women writers from the mainland, Taiwan, and elsewhere in the world.

Goldblatt, Howard, *Worlds Apart: Recent Chinese Writing and Its Audiences*.
Armonk, N.Y.: M. E. Sharpe, 1990. A collection of critical essays,
by major scholars in the field, on contemporary writers from the
mainland and Taiwan.

Goodman, David S. G. (ed.). *Beijing Street Voices: The Poetry and Politics
of China's Democracy Movement*. London: Marion Boyars, 1981.
Translations and analyses of poems written during the Democracy
Wall period.

Hung, Eva (ed.). *Contemporary Women Writers, Hong Kong and Taiwan*.
Hong Kong: Hong Kong University Press, 1990. Stories by seven
contemporary women writers on China's periphery.

Jia, Pingwa. *Turbulence*. Translated by Howard Goldblatt. Baton Rouge: Lou-
isiana State University Press, 1991. Less a literary milestone than a
depiction of society in a northwest village during the post-Mao reforms.

Laing, Ellen Johnston. *The Winking Owl: Art in the People's Republic of
China*. Berkeley: University of California Press, 1988. A survey of
visual arts in the PRC up to 1976, examining how they were shaped
by politics.

Link, Perry (ed.). *Stubborn Weeds: Popular and Controversial Chinese Literature after the Cultural Revolution*. Bloomington: Indiana University Press, 1983. Poems, stories, humor, and drama, including the
controversial play *What If I Really Were?*

────── (ed.). *"People or Monsters" and Other Stories and Reportage from
China After Mao*. Bloomington: Indiana University Press, 1983. A
collection featuring Liu Binyan's famous exposé of a notoriously
corrupt local Party leader.

Liu, Shaotang. *Catkin Willow Flats*. Beijing: Panda Books, 1984. Short stories with a regional flavor.

Pai, Hsien-yung. *Crystal Boys*. San Francisco: Gay Sunshine Press, 1990.
Written by a Taiwanese, this is the first novel whose subject is ho-
mosexuality in the highly disapproving context of Chinese culture.

Shen, Rong. *At Middle Age*. Beijing: Panda Books, 1982. A novel about a
woman doctor who almost kills herself with unselfish overwork. The
book explores the frustrations and the practical and financial problems faced by middle-level intellectuals in the years since the Cultural Revolution.

Siu, Helen F., and Zelda Stern (eds.). *Mao's Harvest: Voices from China's*

*New Generation*. New York: Oxford University Press, 1983. A collection of post-Mao writings selected and arranged around sociological and political themes.

Yang, Jiang. *Six Chapters from My Life "Downunder"*. Hong Kong: The Chinese University Press, 1984. An intellectual woman's sensitive and understated account of her rustication during the Cultural Revolution.

Zhang, Jie. *Love Must Not Be Forgotten*. Beijing: Panda Books, 1987. Stories portraying women's unhappiness in contemporary China.

## Taiwan and Hong Kong

Hicks, George L. *Hong Kong Countdown*. Hong Kong: Writers' & Publishers' Cooperative, 1989. A readable, passionate discussion of Hong Kong's reversion to the Mainland. Critical of Great Britain and China; pessimistic for Hong Kong's future.

Myers, Ramon H. (ed.). *Two Societies in Opposition: The Republic of China and the People's Republic of China after Forty Years*. Stanford: Hoover Institution Press, 1991. A thoughtful symposium comparing the development experience of Taiwan and the Mainland.

Senese, Donald J., and Diane D. Pikcunas. *Can the Two Chinas Become One?* Washington, D.C.: The Council for Social and Economic Studies, 1989. A well-organized, concise, and informative presentation of social and political information on the PRC and Taiwan in the 1980s.

Vogel, Ezra. *The Four Little Dragons: The Spread of Industrialization in East Asia*. Cambridge: Harvard University Press, 1991. A brief overview of the industrial transformation of Taiwan, Hong Kong, Singapore, and South Korea.

Winckler, Edwin A., and Susan Greenhalgh (eds.). *Contending Approaches to the Political Economy of Taiwan*. Armonk, N.Y.: M. E. Sharpe, 1988. A collection of essays on Taiwan's prewar and postwar development from different theoretical perspectives.

# Index